CHRONICLES
of a
FASHION BUYER

The Mostly True Adventures of an
International Fashion Buyer

MERCEDES GONZALEZ

Chronicles of a Fashion Buyer

MERCEDES GONZALEZ

The Mostly True Adventures of an
International Fashion Buyer

SCHIFFER FASHION PRESS

Developmental Edit by Jesse J. Marth
Production Edit by Helena Neufeld
Copyedit / Proofread by Kim Hufford / Tod Benedict
Designed by Danielle D. Farmer
Cover design by Adrianna Kinal
Pink lace fabric textile texture to background © Ragnarocks. Courtesy of www.bigstockphoto.com.
Type set in Century Schoolbook Std

ISBN: 978-0-7643-5623-0
Printed in the United States of America

Published by Schiffer Fashion Press
An Imprint of Schiffer Publishing, Ltd.
4880 Lower Valley Road
Atglen, PA 19310
Phone: (610) 593-1777; Fax: (610) 593-2002
E-mail: Info@schifferbooks.com
Web: www.schifferbooks.com

For our complete selection of fine books on this and related subjects, please visit our website at www.schifferbooks.com. You may also write for a free catalog.

Schiffer Publishing's titles are available at special discounts for bulk purchases for sales promotions or premiums. Special editions, including personalized covers, corporate imprints, and excerpts, can be created in large quantities for special needs. For more information, contact the publisher.

We are always looking for people to write books on new and related subjects. If you have an idea for a book, please contact us at proposals@schifferbooks.com.

Other Schiffer Books on Related Subjects:
Made for Walking: A Modest History of the Fashion Boot by Andy Peake, ISBN: 978-0-7643-5499-1
Pleating: Fundamentals for Fashion Design by Leon Kalajian, George Kalajian; Foreword by Jack Sauma, ISBN: 978-0-7643-5296-6

Dedicated to the most interesting man in the world, my dear and loving husband. The fun is just beginning.

CONTENTS

INTRODUCTION

$\mathcal{T}$his started as a basic how-to book: how to open and run a successful retail store and how to start a fashion line on a shoestring budget. The stories I tell and the examples I use grew too large to fit in a simple how-to book. Some of these stories come from very real personal experiences, some of them are inspired by others, and some are not true at all. The purpose they serve is to teach a credible lesson about real life in the global fashion industry.

The Long and Short of My Story

I grew up on the Upper West Side of New York City, and it irks me to no end when people glamorize the 1970s as "edgy" and "raw." Trust me when I tell you that there is nothing glamorous about heroin junkies and cat-sized rats in the park. It wasn't until I was a teenager and my parents bought a house (the typical American dream) in New Jersey that I realized all that time we had been poor. My parents were the masters of spin, and they never spoke about money in front of my brother and sisters. We had everything we needed, and I had a happy home with little family drama, unlike many others in my neighborhood. However, I still refer to those high school years as the dark years. I was miserable.

On a good day, the drive into New York was only fifteen minutes, but none of my classmates went "over there." I was the "city kid" who wore Diana Vreeland Kabuki-style makeup to school. In response to their weak efforts to bully me, I'd scoff, "What? No, I didn't put my makeup on in the dark. You just don't get it." All those years of fighting the hoodrat girls on my block to get to school gave me a confidence and a look that said "don't fuck with me." All I wanted was to go back to New York. Crackheads (the heroin junkies were now crackheads) and daily muggings were better than the small-minded people I went to school with. There was only one way out: get outstanding grades so I could go to New York University. Until then, I could spy on Uncle Manolo for my mom.

Uncle Manolo was a *garmento*. He was my mother's brother, and he never married. He was a big, fat guy and the polar opposite of my parents. I adored and worshipped him. He gambled, womanized, drank too much, spoke like a truck driver, and made the Sopranos look like kindergarten teachers. My mom, on the other hand, *was* a kindergarten teacher and a real church lady. My father was a barber and a Master Mason. They were both very strict with us kids, never even letting us go to our friends' houses to play. "They can come here," Mom would say. Meanwhile, my uncle would send me over to the OTB (off-track betting), where I would place bets for him twice a day. For those of you who have never heard of the OTB storefronts, this is where you could find the underbelly of the city. The dregs of society, winos, and the homeless would go to place their dollar bets and wait for their horses to win. Thinking back, it might have been a combination of my mother's prayers and the cockiness I picked up from my uncle that kept me alive.

Uncle Manolo made old-lady, polyester print dresses with a button-down front, self-belt, and two patch pockets. This was his claim to fame. Everybody's granny wore one. Later on, he devised a snap that looked like a button so the old ladies with arthritic fingers could just snap the dress closed and not feel bad. Genius! My mother encouraged me to go work with him each summer so I could report all scandals back to her. Even though Uncle Manolo didn't like children much, he welcomed me as long as I stayed out of his way and "made myself useful." He never spoke down to me. On the contrary, he treated me like one of the boys. He allowed me to do whatever I wanted. I'm not so sure he understood that I was still a child at thirteen, but his greatest gift to me was allowing me to learn from my own mistakes. Every valuable business lesson I failed to learn in school, I learned from him. To this day, I can still hear his random words of wisdom in my head— "You need to know the price of rice in China to understand this business."

His influence is still apparent in me today. The reason I even drink Jack and Coke is because of Uncle Manolo.

I worked hard. I packed boxes. I looked for new ways to make money for the company. One summer, he bought all this Malibu trim to put on the dresses with the idea of making them look more sophisticated. That idea was a total failure. Instead of looking sophisticated, they looked like dresses made for a cheap gypsy whore. So, to impress him, I took it upon myself to offer the trim as a gift to every retailer who bought a dozen dresses. They could wrap the trim around their mannequin necks and dress up the displays. That idea was a hit.

A few years later I did get into NYU on a scholarship, and, like many first-generation Cuban immigrants, my parents had high expectations and offered me a few choices: I could be a doctor, or I could be a doctor. As someone who is severely dyslexic, that was never going be an easy task. Nonetheless, during my first year of school, I volunteered at St. Vincent's Hospital and realized the life of a doctor was not for me. I noticed it was a business like any other business, but how could you charge someone who was sick? I had to tell my father that being a doctor was not going to happen. We had the typical Clash of the Titans fight, but there was no winning this argument. Finally, I said, "Fine, I'll be a doctor, and I'll work for the Peace Corps." That got his attention. Like many Cubans of his era, my father believed President Kennedy had sold out the Cuban people, so anything having to do with the Kennedys was cursed and forbidden, including the Peace Corps.

"OK," my father relented. "You can study anything you want—as long as you don't end up a garmento like your uncle."

And that was fine with me. I had no intention of working in fashion. It was the mid-'80s, and I was in my Gordon Gekko phase. I wanted to work on Wall Street and be Michael Milken. As it would happen, just as I was graduating, Wall Street crashed and Michael Milken was arrested for insider trading. My fancy degree in economics didn't seem to even be worth the price of toilet paper. The only job offers I received were for around $10,000 a year. I was facing working two jobs and eighty hours a week just to survive.

Uncle Manolo came to my rescue. He was the only one who would pay me a decent salary. I told myself this was only going to be temporary. So, my stint as a garmento began. I did every job, from sweeping the factory floor to sales, from production to filing papers until my fingerprints wore off. Working on Wall Street now seemed like a distant dream. I wanted to be a buyer: saving the world one dress at a time, running ethical, sustainable, organic factories that ran on solar-powered fairy dust and unicorn tears. I was going to live the glamorous life, flying on the Concorde and going to all the fashion shows. I was in for a big surprise.

Warning: I am an advocate of child labor, I love GMO cotton, and there is no such thing as anything genuinely organic. I loathe "Small Business" anything. A fair wage isn't a living wage. Bamboo is as sustainable as eating Drano on toast for breakfast. This is an industry of spin masters. It's all smoke and mirrors.

I should also mention that I hate higher education. In fact, I have a distrust of the overly educated. School alone is not enough to prepare anyone for this business. It's all about real life, boots-on-the-ground, roll-up-your-sleeves experiences. Education has a way of crushing the entrepreneurial free will. I was often sent to the principal's office and my report card was full of comments like "she doesn't work well with others," "doesn't like to share," "is bossy," "is too chatty," and "is defiant in class." I was, and I am. In my professional life, these attributes have all worked to my advantage. All the great visionaries, not that I'm comparing myself to them, have dropped out of school. The richest man in fashion, Amancio Ortega of Zara, is worth $82 billion, yet dropped out of school at the age of fourteen.

$\mathcal{L}$ooked like I wasn't going to work that day. I had spent the night watching the Hong Kong market crash; the economic tidal wave wrapped itself around the world, crushing every market in its way, ending the next day in Australia. Black Monday became black Tuesday, then became black rest-of-the-year.

I had landed a job right after college with Midland Bank as an analyst doing the due diligence on companies that were positioning themselves for an IPO (initial public offering). I had been on the job a month, but I was not doing what I wanted to do. I wanted to buy and sell foreign currencies, and Midland wasn't even an international bank. The market crash wasn't too heartbreaking for me, since I wasn't happy doing what I was doing, but it was a job.

After the dust settled, it became apparent that Wall Street didn't need any rookie analyst, as seasoned professionals were now working on commission-based salaries. I went to my uncle Manolo for a job. It would be temporary, just until the bear became a bull.

"I told you Wall Street was full of shit. You can't buy and sell paper; that's fake bullshit." He talked in a tone that was more like yelling than speaking, but that was his everyday inside voice. "Find something to do and make yourself useful." That was Manolo talk for *you've been hired*.

Short Sleeves Long Sleeves

One of the lessons I learned in school was the importance of diversification. My uncle made only one type of dress. It was a printed polyester shirtdress with patch pockets and a self-belt. His idea of diversification was to make them in long and short sleeves. I suggested that we add new styles, like something that can be worn in the winter months. That way we could have a wider reach of retailers in the north and have a product that could be sold twelve months a year. I was thinking a full collection of five deliveries, but his idea was to make a pant. (Yes sir, a pant.) I had talked him out of a skirt, which was a battle on its own since he hadn't needed to make a pattern. Well, at least this wasn't your ordinary pant. This was double-knit polyester with an elastic waistband that came in nineteen fashion colors. I use the word "fashion" loosely, since he didn't follow any trends or use Pantone colors. That polyester was so stiff that I swear the pant could stand up on its own. I used to tell buyers that the pants were not only durable, but bulletproof. They might have been. They were an immediate hit. In fact, it was in the Sunday pullout circular of many national newspapers. Two for $19, of course, in your choice of nineteen fashion colors.

I had earned the respect of my uncle, which I figured out only when he was bragging to a friend who just made handkerchiefs. I shouldn't say "just made handkerchiefs," because they weren't your ordinary, everyday white handkerchiefs. He made them in every style humanly possible, at every price point, for every type of store. He asked me to explain the concept of diversification, which I did with much academic rhetoric. Uncle's friend took my advice to heart, because soon after he was also making scarves. Scarves, you might note, are just handkerchiefs made larger. So much for diversification.

My uncle lived in the moment, and while the pant idea was OK, in his words, he "needed the next big thing." Sitting in Ben's Kosher Deli (they still make the best matzo ball soup in the city), I overheard a couple of garmentos talking about the shitload of money they were making selling to Walmart. I didn't know what Walmart was at the time, but by the sound of it, Walmart was the next big Kmart. Let me take you back in time.

No one wanted to sell to Walmart because it was so lowbrow and tiny compared to Kmart. In fact, Kmart, in one year, had opened more stores than Walmart had in ten years. But this was what made selling to Walmart so appealing. They had steady growth and were desperate for product, but there was a catch. The guys went on and on about how they had to go to China for production, since Walmart's pricing was so low. They argued that it wasn't about making a percent in sales, it was about making a clean quarter on every item.

So, what did I do? I came back from lunch and did a little homework. I was glad I had kept my Wall Street connections so I could do my research. It seemed like Walmart was on the cusp of a massive growth spurt. They were acquiring businesses and growing in twenty-seven states!

"Tío Manolo, we have to sell to a chain in the South called Walmart, but to do so, I have to go to China and source a cheaper factory," I said all in one breath, and as fast as I could, hoping he wouldn't pay too much attention and just say yes.

"Who the fuck is Walmart and what the hell is in China that you don't have here?" That also came out in one loud breath.

"Walmart is a chain of . . . of . . . of . . . "—I didn't have the right words to describe it, but I thought I'd better come up with something good and fast, or I was going to lose this conversation—". . . of SUPER stores. I mean, they have everything and they sell it at bulk pricing."

"We can't discount, that's not our business. Plus, we'll hurt the other retailers that sell our goods."

"No, that's why we have to go to China. We can make it there cheaper and we don't have to discount, we can just change the brand name."

He was looking interested, and then he hit hard. "What the fuck do you know about China except for eating Chinese food?"

"Remember that I went to school for international business, and China was the main focus?" I snapped back. Hmm, I am actually using some of my education, I thought to myself. My uncle and just about all of his friends didn't go to college and were all self-made businessmen.

"Well, you better put that diploma to good use, because right now you can use it for toilet paper." I agreed.

Four days, three meetings with the travel agent, two books on doing business with China, a stack of traveler's checks, and I was off to China. Twenty slow-motion hours later and I was in Hong Kong. Then it sunk in. Holy shit, I was in fucking China. What the fuck was I doing in fucking China? I spent the first three days/nights, who the hell knows, crying in bed. I didn't even know what time of day it was and I needed to find a factory. All with no Google, no cell phones, and no help desk.

I was trying hard to relax. Deep breaths. My heart was racing. I had a pain in my chest like I'd never felt before. I raised my left hand up, stretched it to the left and then to the right. Were these the symptoms of a heart attack? What were the symptoms of a heart attack? Was I having a heart attack? I made myself sit down, had a drink, and went to my happy place.

What the fuck! Sitting there wasn't going to work. I couldn't afford to be stressed and paralyzed in fear, since I didn't have a trust fund or a sugar daddy. My motivation came from having an uncle who was going to kill me. I had to shake it off and put my big-girl panties on!

The next morning, I asked the doorman if he could direct me to the Garment District. I was sure that every place in the world had a Garment District. He spoke perfect English, as Hong Kong at the time was still ruled by the English. He mentioned that his aunt was a patternmaker, and she would know where the Garment District was. Eureka, there was a Garment District!

I was staying at the Shangri-La, the most beautiful hotel I had ever been to, even to this day. Service at the Shangri-La was beyond impeccable. After my third day of ordering the same room service, the chef called my room and asked if he could send me up something different, while keeping the flavors that I seemed to like. Incredible! He didn't want me to be bored with the same food every day, and he was proud of his culture's cuisine. Everything he sent up was new to me and I loved it all. Chinese food in China is not the same as New York Chinese. There is no MSG and there are some interesting choices of protein. Pigeon, anyone? His hearty, satisfying cooking gave me courage and comfort. Trying something new wasn't so scary.

The following morning, there was a knock on my door. "Madam, it's the bellman. I am here to take you to the center." I opened the door and the young bellman, who I had met when I first arrived, informed me that it was his aunt who was the patternmaker. He had been given the day off to take me to the agent building. I asked him how much it would cost. He said $100. I thought it was a bargain. It wasn't until later that I understood what he meant. It turned out that he was taking me as a courtesy of the hotel, and he had informed me that he was well paid, making $100 a month. Oy vey. Well, it was still money very well spent.

We arrived at the agent building, which was a short walk from the hotel. That was a good sign. It was a magnificent building with a central atrium that let in the natural sunlight. I could see the rays of light reflecting off the clear glass office walls that filled the space like honeycombs. It felt like the clouds had parted and the angels were playing "Ode to Joy" on the trumpets in the sky!

I noticed that the directory was written in Chinese and English. Another good sign. The building was very well organized. Each floor was dedicated to one thing. One was toys with wheels: roller skates, skateboards, bicycles, and such. There was a housewares floor with just kitchen items, but not electronics. Home electronics, such as vacuums, were on another level. Then there was the old-lady floor! I had never been so freaking happy to see a rainbow of pastel polyesters that would have rivaled any float at a gay pride parade! It was all very organized by tops, bottoms, and dresses. There were many tiny glass box offices with agents sitting in solitary confinement, reading yesterday's paper over and over again. Their dress samples were crammed into every nook. One had a sample hanging that could have been the twin to the dress my uncle had been making for more than twenty years. Jackpot! He opened the door, and a burst of cigarette smoke slapped me in the face.

Mr. Charlie Chan, a tiny Yoda-looking man, missing one side molar where, I later found out, he permanently held a cigarette. He would eat, speak, and I'm pretty sure sleep with it stuck in there. He checked me out with a doubtful expression. He had a weathered, aged look despite never having worked outdoors, and managed to wrinkle it a bit more trying to figure out what I was doing there. It was only then that I realized that besides the woman rolling a food cart down the hall and another sweeping the downstairs, I was the only other woman in the building.

I pulled out my samples and pointed to the one that was hanging in his room.

"How much?" I asked. A rookie mistake — you never start by asking the price. In fact, when the time is right, you tell them the price you want and start from there. "Let me see," he said in clear English while taking the sample from my hand. He turned it inside out, looked at the seams, and pulled them.

"Crooked seams," he said. So what, I thought to myself, they were $28 retail dresses. I grabbed his sample from the wall, looking for production mistakes. I must say it was very well made, but I was there for price, not for production perfection. It had to be sellable, not perfect.

"How much?" I asked again.

"How many?" he said.

"Depends on price," I said. This ping-pong match went on for about twenty minutes when finally we agreed on $3.25 FOB mainland for a twenty-foot-high cube container. I just want to let you know that the only thing I understood about that whole conversation was the $3.25 US! I didn't know that 3,500 dresses fit in a twenty-foot-high cube. I also didn't know what a twenty-foot-high cube was, nor did I know where mainland was, or the term FOB (Free on Board). But I didn't care. It was $3.25 and in the United States that same dress was costing us $12.

Courage in a Bowl of Soup

I decided that night I would celebrate by eating outside the hotel. So, I promptly crossed the street and went into the first restaurant I found. It was early, so the restaurant was empty. The waiter sat me down at an enormous round table with a red tablecloth and plastic flowers. He gave me the International Menu that had photos of all the food they served. There were plenty of familiar looking foods, some not so familiar, and some that I didn't want to become familiar with at all. There was an excellent selection of soups. I picked one that looked to be shredded beef with noodles, a boiled egg, and maybe some parsley leaves. Perfect! "I'll take this one," I said to the waiter, pointing to the soup.

"No, no, no, not for you," said the waiter.

Maybe I was missing something in his broken English. "Yes for me, soup please."

"No, no, no, not for woman soup."

What? What the hell had he just said? Not for woman soup? What kind of crap was this?

"Yes, for women soup, bring now." Why was it that I always started speaking in broken English when speaking to someone who didn't understand English? Wouldn't it be smarter to just speak slower and clearer? "Bring soup now," I demanded. As he scurried off, I yelled, "And bring me a Coke!" Damn, I thought, I got this. It was all going to be all right. I was the boss now, and I was going to be the man in my uncle's eyes.

While I was daydreaming my delusional thoughts of grandeur, or maybe I had nodded off (I had no idea what a drag jet lag was), the soup was placed in front of me. But the waiter didn't leave. He just hovered over me, a little too close to my space, and stared. It was almost like he was daring me to eat it. I gave him my best stink eye, telepathically telling him to fuck off, but he just moved behind me, out of my line of sight. I could feel him right on top of me. Was the soup deadly spicy? I had forgotten Asian food could have a significant kick to it. Was it just bitter and you needed to acquire a taste for it? Was it made from some raw microbial-infested delicacy that would keep me in the bathroom for days? Well, it was too late to chicken out now. I went for it. Yum, it tasted like a beef stew. It was tasty and delicate with nothing overwhelming. Very familiar, nothing scary here. As I was finishing it, I looked around. All of the waiters were staring at me! Would there be a delayed reaction? Was my head going to explode? What was the problem with these guys?

You know what? Who cares? The soup hit the spot, it was 6 p.m., and I was ready for bed.

I found out the hard way that I needed to get a visa to go to the factory to finalize the negotiations. This set me back a day, so I took the day off and jumped on the ferry to go shopping in Kowloon. I spent the day shopping the local market, which included a tour of the more than 200-year-old jade market with its $1,000 hand-carved rings. Since of course, I couldn't afford anything, I made my way back to the hotel, hopping back on the local ferry, and decided to go back to the soup restaurant. That night, I walked into the same restaurant. Why mess around when you've found a good place and a good meal? I was early for dinner once again. The place was empty, but this time the waiters were peeking behind the curtain or being called to come out from the kitchen, and the ones setting up the bar were all pointing and giggling at me. Who cares? I was seated and a different waiter than the one from the night before handed me the menu. Before he could turn away, I grabbed him, opened the menu, and pointed to the same soup. He looked at me and shook his head. "No good."

"No, it's very good," I said.

He did a kind of vulgar gesture. He made a fist, slapped the top of his arm moving in an upward direction, and said "Not woman soup, man soup. Makes blood strong."

I was thinking to myself, was this guy kidding me? I had just flown halfway around the world, didn't know my ass from elbow, but found what I came for, just to be spoken down to by some chauvinistic pig giving me the international sign for "go fuck yourself"? I didn't think so. "Bring the soup," I yelled at him. This time I didn't hesitate and drank it. The waiters were super amused and watched me from the far corners of the restaurant, trying not to be obvious while being very obvious. But really, who the fuck cares? Not me! I was the one paying the bill. I tried to hurt them in some way by not leaving a tip. But the joke was on me, since it's not customary to tip in China. Once again, the soup hit the spot and put me in a happy food coma. I felt mentally and physically ready for the first time since I had been in China.

I spent the next couple of days on the mainland. I had a crash course on harmonized codes, duties, and quotas. I found a telex machine at the factory that I could use to send a message to my uncle's friend. He was a button salesman named Joe whose company had been exporting buttons from China for years. He was also one of the alarmists about doing business in China. He would be able to tell my uncle I was alive and was coming home in two days with good news and samples.

A telex was a strange type of typewriter. You would ring a bell until someone on the other side would pick up. It wasn't easy, since someone would have to be at the New York City office pretty early in the morning. Since telex machines charged you by the letter, that message ended up looking like this: "cmng hme n 2 dys wth gd nws smpls." The trick was to use a minimal amount of words and take out all the vowels.

I got back to Hong Kong, and guess what I did next? That's right, I went back to the same restaurant. For any of you who have traveled to unfamiliar places on business, you know there is no time to be adventurous with food. You find a good place and you eat there every day. But I had already made up my mind that day that I was going to try something else. I walked into the restaurant and was greeted a little more warmly. Weird. Well, maybe I had earned their respect. Hey boys, get used to modern women, we're here, we mean business, we . . . darn, women, we need a cool war cry. Why do gay people get all the cool cheers? We're here, we're queer, and we like to say hello! I'll have to work on something catchy for next time.

The place was jam-packed. It was loud and chaotic. There was an army of waiters; one walked me to the far back room, which I hadn't even known existed, and sat me at a large table with other Chinese businessmen who were all dressed in the same navy suit. Anticipating what I wanted, he pointed to the menu, but I took it from him. "I am going to try something new tonight," I said, at which he let out a sigh of relief. While carefully reviewing the menu, in the distance I heard English being spoken. It wasn't just American English, it was New York City English! I picked up my chair, bag, and menu and made my way through the tangle of people and tables to the gentlemen I heard talking.

"Hi, there! Can I join you?" It wasn't like they had much of a choice; I had already wedged in my chair. "I'm from New York, too! What brings you to Hong Kong?"

"Funny," said the guy wearing a dark suit and yarmulke on his head. "I was going to ask you the same thing."

I can't tell you how happy I was to be speaking in full English sentences. "It's a long story, but I am here to source some manufacturing for my uncle who is a dress manufacturer in New York."

"No kidding," said the other guy, who was wearing a white shirt and slacks without a suit jacket. "We're in the business, too."

"Really, what type?"

"Children's."

"Is it your first time?"

"No, we have been coming for about three years."

"Great, so I can milk you for some information." I needed so much help with the shipping lingo. Just then, the waiter came to take our order. I smugly pointed to the beef stew and said, "This is delicious; I highly recommend it." They both looked at each other. They knew something about this soup.

"Ok, so what is the story with this soup? The waiter gives me a hard time every time I try to order it."

"You had it a couple of times?" they asked, laughing.

I went from big-shot to a little don't-know-shit-shot in a second. "Yes," I said in a low voice. "What is the stupid story with the soup?"

"Do you know what kind of meat it is?"

"Oh dear God, please don't tell me dog!" I said, freaking out.

"Oh no, no, no, not dog. It's rattlesnake."

I was taken aback a little bit, but I asked, "So what is the big deal about rattlesnake?"

"Well," he started to explain, blushing a little. "You know how the Chinese have a medicinal purpose for most soups?" I nodded, pretending I knew. "Well, this one is called the strength soup."

"Yeah?" It was still not sounding like a big deal.

"Well," he hesitated. "It's the traditional soup that men drink before they have sex with prostitutes."

"Oh. Oh, ohhhh, I get it . . . ha, ha, ha." I tried to downplay the whole thing and move on to another subject.

I wanted to ask how they knew about the soup, but the man with the yarmulke was eating in a non-kosher restaurant and the guy without a suit jacket looked hungover. I learned that not all the things you see and do in China should ever be spoken about. Ever! The jacketless guy took out his yarmulke and ate with it on before stuffing it back in his pant pocket after the bill was paid. We ate from little hand push carts that offered different items. This is where I had to use my senses of smell and sight to pick my food. It was a bit primitive, but effective.

It's Not an Order

Back at the New York office, no one was impressed with my success, because it wasn't a sale until it was an order. Not even Martha was impressed. Martha was the bookkeeper. She was also the only woman my uncle never questioned. While she had the title of bookkeeper, Martha was the one who ran both the office and factory operations, hired and fired people, dealt with the inspectors, ordered all the fabrics and trims, and set the production timetables for the orders. To top it off, she was kind to me. Martha was very underappreciated, even by me. She made everything seem so simple and straightforward. She was a single woman who lived in the apartment where she was born, on the Lower East Side. She was of Cuban and Spanish descent and had many friends to vacation and play Canasta with. She had come to work for my uncle when she was in her late twenties and was with the company until the day my uncle died. She was secretly in love with my uncle, but it was a secret only to him. The bickering between Martha and Manolo was comical to the point of entertainment, and on occasion, I knew which buttons to push for my enjoyment.

Until someone called Walmart, there was no order. The whole time I was so preoccupied with the supply chain, sourcing, sampling, and costing that the most critical part, the sale itself, hadn't been thought through. I had no idea how to get this done. I had no idea whom to call. I had no understanding of how the process even worked. So, in what became my typical plan of action, I flew to meet the situation head-on. In this case, it meant flying down to Bentonville, Arkansas, the corporate headquarters of Walmart.

My flight to China was less eventful than trying to get to Bentonville. The travel agent advised me not to fly into Drake Field. Drake was a small airport and it would have taken a total of three flights and a layover in Dallas to get there. So, I flew into Little Rock, Arkansas, and from there it would be a three-hour drive into Bentonville. Not such an easy feat for someone who had a driver's license but no practical driving experience. I am a city girl after all. I didn't take driver's ed. in high school. I was never moving out of the city, and if I did, I would undoubtedly have a driver.

So there I was in Small Town USA, in the shadow of what was becoming the most powerful mega-retailer in the history of all retail. Yet I was sitting on a webbed outdoor lounge chair in a sparsely decorated waiting room in the Walmart headquarters. The room was gray and black but everyone walking in seemed ridiculously happy and upbeat. It was part of the Walmart Kool-Aid they must have been drinking. The receptionist, who looked older than I think she was, with her slightly blue-tinted, perfectly teased hair and frumpy dress, greeted me cheerfully enough to scare me a bit. I was not used to people being nice for the sake of being nice. Who did that?

"Do you have an appointment, sweetheart?"

"No."

"Do you know who you would like to see?"

"No."

"Do you know what department?"

"Yes ma'am, women's dresses." I perked up because I actually had an answer.

"Honey, we have twelve buyers who do women's dresses."

"Oh, right. Well, the person who buys old-lady dresses."

"We don't have a department called old ladies. Do you mean Missy?" She said this genuinely trying to be helpful.

"Not really, I think they might all be married. So maybe a Mrs. Department." Faking it was not going to work today. I had never heard that term before.

"Dear, you have a seat right there. I'll find someone to talk to you."

Day One

Sitting in the lobby waiting room was quite the experience, watching salesmen from all corners of the earth selling everything you could imagine, from farm animal feed to pots and pans. They had samples, and cardboard cutouts of stands, and different packaging, and catalogs, and order forms, and advertising options—I had samples. Guess something was better than nothing. As the staff walked past me, I made sure I kept one of my samples visible just to catch someone's attention, but like drone worker bees they all seemed to have an urgent mission to attend. Boredom and sleepiness set in. I had done the two crossword puzzles in the dated paper. I hate crossword puzzles. There were no smartphones, so checking emails (a thing of the future) or playing Candy Crush (yet to be imagined) wasn't an option. I sat and sat and sat and smiled at the staff, hoping someone would rescue me. By 4 p.m., the receptionist walked over and informed me that the person I needed to see was Mr. Wilson, but that he was working the floor that day and would be in tomorrow. I thanked her for the update and asked if I could make an appointment. "Oh dear," she said, "I have no way of getting in touch with him. Just come back at 8 a.m."

I stood up to leave, but the chair was stuck to the back of my legs. I lifted the whole lounger up, tripping over it and exposing the deep track marks on the back of my legs from the chair's webbing, as well as my underwear to the receptionist.

"Tomorrow—pants," I said to her, trying hard to keep it cool.

Day Two

I was there at 7:45 a.m.—*The first man in, the last man out*—but there were already a dozen vendors standing around waiting. I didn't want to be the only one sitting, so I found a spot in the corner. Mr. Wilson promptly walked in. He reminded me of the doctor in that Norman Rockwell painting of the boy with his dog. He shook a few hands. Then the receptionist stopped him and pointed to me. "I'll be with you as soon as I can, Hun," he said with a reassuring smile. I made sure not to sit in the lounge chair. I didn't want to trip myself up again, and it's tough to look city cool when you are lounging in an old-lady dress and reading comic books. That's right, comic books. Last night I'd gone for a walk around town and found the original five-and-Dime that Mr. Walton had opened. The layout was boring and practical. Nothing about it stood out or hinted at the monster Walmart was about to become. I was not impressed, and even started to doubt all the Walmart talk I had heard in New York. I mean, half the crap they said about China wasn't true, so why would Walmart stories be any different? They had a small section of books, but most were about raising children and bible stories. The only genre that I was remotely interested in was the comic books. They were kind of nostalgic and calming at the same time. The hours came and went, the vendors came and went, the staff came and went, but what never came and went was the receptionist. I don't even remember her once going to the bathroom.

By the end of the day, Mr. Wilson was walking out the door when he saw me standing there. "Sorry honey, the day was just jam-packed. Come back tomorrow and I'll see ya'll in the morning."

Day Three

Without even taking off his hat, but giving everyone a warm good morning, Mr. Wilson put his hand on my lower back and led me right into his office. Eww, why was he touching me? Must be a southern thing, I thought.

"Honey, thank you so much for waiting yesterday."

I guess he didn't know I had been waiting for two days, and what was up with this "honey" thing? I should have read a book about southern culture, because this place was becoming a bigger shock than being in China. At least I knew enough to call people sir and ma'am.

"That's fine, sir, I would have waited three more days to see you. I am looking forward to doing business with you," I said, as I started to pull out the dresses from my bag.

"Now hold on. We haven't been properly introduced."

Oh dear, so this was why he'd taken all day to see a few vendors. "So sorry sir, I wanted to get straight to business; I know you are a busy man."

"Not too busy to get to know a pretty young lady."

What the fuck? This wasn't southern charm. This guy was just a creep. Dang it! If there had only been Twitter back then, I could have hashtagged the moment with a #metoo, but a hashtag was still a pound sign on a push-button telephone.

"Why, thank you, sir." The internal pep talk was starting. Just take one for the team, Mercedes. You got this.

I still talk a lot to myself, and I answer. Some of the best conversations I've had, I've had alone.

"Well sir, I work for my uncle in New York City. He has been making these super-comfortable, easy-to-wash-and-wear dresses for over twenty years."

"You're selling to me again. Tell me about yourself."

Ugh. "Well, sir, there isn't much to say. Why don't you tell me about how you became a buyer? That seems like such an interesting job." I hoped my dry sarcasm wasn't obvious. He smiled. This was going to take a while. All I wanted was a yes or no to the dresses. This waiting and talking was giving me heartburn, or was it the fried pickles I had eaten last night? I don't even like pickles.

I was back to paying attention. I hoped he didn't say anything I would be quizzed on. His story was pretty interesting and typical of many of the people who started with the company. He was one of the first employees at Walmart. He had already been with the company for more than twenty years, starting as a stock boy and working himself to store manager. Then he worked in corporate purchasing for different departments. The buyers often got rotated from department to department, preventing them from getting kickbacks from the vendors, something I knew very well from all the years of stuffing Christmas cards with Benjamins for my uncle's buyers. "The cost of doing business," he would say.

Wilson mentioned that he had just been assigned to the Women's Missy Dress department for the spring season, which by the way, I now knew wasn't a marital indication, but a product category. And guess what? I was an expert on those old-lady polyester dresses.

I took advantage of his naivety and shared some consumer behaviors. "Did you know that this consumer loves patch pockets? They love to put their hankies and keys in them."

"Ah, that's a good point."

"They like clothing that is machine washable and dryable. They see value in that. Ours is!" I threw in.

Nodding his head, he said, "Good, good, go on."

I told him that our prints hid cooking stains. Now I was just making shit up. There wasn't much more to say about these dresses. It was a dress. Nothing more, nothing less. There were a few minutes of awkward stares. I didn't know precisely how this dance went. In the showroom, the buyers came to buy. I didn't have to sell them anything; they just bought. Now, I wasn't sure how to end a presentation that I hadn't given, or was that the presentation and sales pitch? When did we talk about price and deliveries?

I launched in, "How about we write up an order so you can see for yourself that these are going to be your best sellers?" I put it out there. Without much hesitation, he picked up the line sheet I had put on his desk when I first walked in. He circled the price and mentioned that it had to be FOB to his warehouse. Wait a second! I knew what that meant! I said, "Of course." I felt so proud of myself. He checked off the prints and colors he wanted and asked about the sizing. "It's true to size," I said. This was an industry bullshit answer that is meant to mean it might fit. But it was an acceptable answer. He then wrote me a test order for just over a million dollars. I didn't realize it at the time because it was written on a spreadsheet and it was hard to read, but oh boy, once I added it up I almost tested the stain claim of my old-lady dress. Yet it wasn't an order until you had the order confirmation and met the requirements in the vendor compliance manual.

Bankers and Booze

"Who is going to watch production?" asked my uncle. Not a "job well done," or "great job," or even a fancy lunch at Arno's. I could see that Manolo was concerned, but I was not sure why. He was pouring a glass of whiskey straight. I'll tell you something about my uncle: I never, until just then, had ever seen him drink alone.

"I guess I will. I can just go back to China and sit on the factory and make sure everything is ok."

"What do you know about production?"

"Please, Manolo, let's just do this, it's a Spring order and we have to get started right away."

He owned two factories, one on 38th Street and another in Hialeah, Florida. The seamstresses and patternmakers were mostly Cuban. The only man was the cutter, a Puerto Rican ex-con from the barrio. He was a scary-looking guy who would totally freak out if anyone even thought about touching his scissors. I once heard him tell a messenger who picked up his scissors to cut open a box, "You can mess with my wife before you can mess with my scissors." I asked Manolo why he had such a rough guy working for him.

"First," he said, "he's the best. Second, take in a stray dog and he is your most loyal companion. Third, it's none of your fucking business. When you pay him you can ask me the fuck why."

Both of his New York factories ran on fear and good wages. That's what he told me. What motivates workers is fear that they are going to be fired, but you also have to pay them more than everyone else, so they don't leave. I asked, "Didn't I better the production and IRs in Florida?"

"Yeah, after you started crying like a girl."

Let me tell you how that was wrong on so many levels. First, "crying like a girl" is rude and discriminating. Yeah right, who am I kidding? That's not even a point to be made with him.

THE *most important thing was that my uncle paid piece work in Florida. That means the workers got x number of dollar(s) on each garment. They worked on a piece from start to finish. The faster they sewed, the more they would make, but it was still very little pay. He had a QC person (quality control) who would take a garment off the count if any mistakes were found. My bright idea was to pay the seamstresses a fair living wage for a day's work. Ha! Production capacities dropped and damages increased. Not a winning combination. I had unwittingly taken away their incentive to work. I flew down to Florida to get my head out of my ass and see what I could do. I had worked up this whole big speech about how I was trying to be fair and help the working class by sharing in the profits for a job well done. But all that came out of my mouth was "How—" before I started not crying, but sobbing. How could they have taken advantage of a situation that was for their benefit? How could they not have seen that this would lessen stressful working conditions? How could they not have seen that this was a better system for all? They sat me down, offered me a Cafecito, and we came to an understanding, or I should say I had a new understanding. They were happy with the old system, and they even had side bets on who would sew the fastest with the best quality control. The winner of the week would take home the pot.*

"Walk me down to the bank. We need to talk to them." I get it now; my uncle had been a cash man his whole life. He had all of his bookkeeping in the pocket of his custom-made G George shirt, which was always a little too transparent. All the garmentos got their shirts made at G George. The Gambinos, the Gottis, the Genovese—all of them. On the front of an envelope were the people who owed Manolo money, and on the back of the envelope were the people he owed money. I asked him once what was inside the envelope and he answered that it was none of my fucking business.

The dress building in NYC's Garment District was 1400 Broadway. It had an Israeli bank that Manolo used and had a very friendly bank manager. They would have drinks at Arno's and then walk back to the bank after a liquid lunch, so Manolo could pick up cash taken right from the bank vault to pay the sewers in the factory. The idea was to be introduced to the bank president, since now we were doing serious business. My uncle greeted him in perfect Hebrew. Besides picking up Yiddish and Hebrew from people in the Garment District, we all found out when I was thirteen that Grandma, his mother, was a Moroccan Jew. But that's another story.

Selling to Walmart and manufacturing in Asia was not a cash business. There were letters of credit to be written, wire transfers to be made, and industry credit terms to be given. Thankfully, my uncle's reputation for being a straight-up man enabled him to have the full support of the bank. Notice that I said reputation, and not credit scores or collaterals. Things were done differently in those days.

Running a Sweatshop

Plane rides to China were long and tedious. There is only so much reading a person can do. I have developed a trick over the years to put myself in a Dramamine, Tylenol PM, and whiskey coma that can last a good twelve hours. This being just my second trip, I was lucky enough to sit next to a man who in the industry was known as the Umbrella King. He made umbrellas for everyone at every price, including Walmart. He spent hours talking to me about strategies and tips so I wouldn't get "screwed." All we needed was a campfire and s'mores and it would be the perfect setting for the Walmart horror stories that he was sharing. We were staying in the same hotel in Guangzhou. At the time, there weren't many hotels in that area to stay in. This made me happy and gave me a bit of confidence that I had some type of lifeline. He did seem genuine, and I was trying hard not to hate the fact that everything I said to him was met with "cute," "that's cute, kid," and "very cute." I even got a double "cute-cute." I thought to myself, well, I'm glad my million-dollar-order story is amusing to you, but as he went on I started imagining that I was yelling at him with my arms in a Wonder Woman pose. Too many comic books in Bentonville.

It was my first . . . ok, lots of firsts, so I am going to stop saying that, and you can assume that everything you are going to read is my first. My first meltdown, my first panic attack, my first shady handshake, my first bar fight. Joking! I was a teen when that happened.

It was my first time inspecting a factory in China. I knew from working in my uncle's factory what to sort of expect, but here I found it to be very different. The ladies who worked for my uncle took Cafecito breaks twice a day while indulging in gossip. They also dressed up to go to work. Here, there was one break for lunch, and they all wore uniforms. I was on the watch for child labor, sweatshops, and all the dreadful stories that just about everyone who knew anyone who worked in China had told me. "You are going to find workers chained to the machines." "You can tell the color of the season by the color of the stream running in the back of the factory." "You are going to find little girls who can't reach the machines sitting on stacks of books to work." I was ready to walk out if there were any unethical situations.

I got picked up pretty early, which was good because it was early evening in New York time, and I hadn't slept since we landed at 9 p.m. China time. My driver was the tiniest man I had ever seen. He could barely look over the steering wheel. Was he sitting on books? Was he actually a child? No, he was just a tiny man. Was I secretly wishing to witness one of these atrocities? It was about a forty-minute drive, and there was a big problem —the hotel didn't serve coffee, and it was way too early or way too late not to have a cup of coffee. I was really struggling with staying coherent and was getting a slight caffeine-withdrawal headache. But the car was air-conditioned. This, I understood, was a super-luxury. It helped a little to sit back and watch mainland China unfold. Outside, masses of people were going to work, going to school, and going to market. I tried to recontextualize it as more-familiar situations. This was a middle-class neighborhood, and these kids were going to public schools. It was crowded, but not as crowded as trying to cross the street at 42nd and 8th Avenue to get to the bus station in New York

City. I loved the matching headscarves and A-line skirts. Then, at one of the intersections, on the side of the dirt-covered road, there was a frail, old man sitting alone. He had an oversized sack-like garment over his bare legs, no shoes, and a long wooden walking stick that he was clutching with both hands. He wasn't well.

At the factory, a man I was told was the floor manager greeted me. He was a young man in a crisp white shirt, with shiny black matching belt and shoes. He spoke English very well and definitely kept to the script. He answered all of my predictable questions with predictable answers. He was eager to take me to where all the printed fabrics were. There was even sample yardage of each print. The patternmaker was a young girl, which was surprising to me, since all the patternmakers I knew from the United States were in their fifties with thirty years of experience. It's like when you meet young doctors. You don't really trust them, but you know they have to be good, or they wouldn't be in practice. She was showing me how she was going to place the prints, how the printed pockets were going to look, the matching trims (something we never used), and the plastic buttons dyed to match the fabric (something we also never did). I couldn't understand a thing they were saying. It wasn't because of their English, but because I had become lightheaded and I suddenly realized how hot the factory was. OH MY GOD, this factory was as hot as a glass greenhouse in July! OH MY GOD, this was a sweatshop! OH MY GOD, there were children running the factory. With my blood rushing from my face, I dropped like a hot potato.

I had never passed out before. It's not as graceful as the daytime soap operas make it look on TV. There was no back of the hand to the forehead while I gently melted to the floor. I hit my head on the corner of the table and bounced off it. The word they used to describe my fall was "crumble." I found myself pretty much where I had fallen. No one did anything to help me, and once I woke up I was directed to the bathroom, where I found a unicorn lump growing from the center of my head. Upon my return to the sample room, they began the conversation precisely where it left off. I guessed this was a typical thing. I was scrambling to remember what had bothered me. The prints were fine, the placements were fine, the fabric felt good. Ay! The heat. The sweatshop. As I started to go back into panic mode, I realized I was the only one that was sweating. How spoiled of me to assume that the entire world embraced air conditioners like they did in the US. In some countries they are still regarded as health hazards.

On the drive back to the factory that evening, I saw a stack of rags and the walking stick where the old man had been. I wondered if someone had picked him up and left behind the dirty clothing.

While I was telling my story that evening to the Umbrella King, he started to laugh, saying, "That's cute, kid." It seemed pretty normal for someone to either pass out or throw up on their first day of a factory visit. How fun. They never warned me about that in business school. I decided to try to stay on New York time and visit the factory late in the afternoon, when it was cooler. Maybe I wouldn't feel the jet lag as much. He told me about his day, and how an American had gotten arrested because he was so happy with the speed of his production that he gave all the factory workers a $20 bill as a bonus. Apparently, that was against the law in China. The government had very rigid rules for employee compensation. This did worry me, because I didn't know the things I didn't know.

Back at the factory, production was in full swing. More than 150,000 dresses were being cut. They worked like an assembly line. It was much more efficient than piece work. Everyone was an expert in just one area: collars, pockets, hems, belts, buttons. It was a fantastic whirlwind of activity, all done in silence. There was no gossiping going on here. The workers seemed indifferent, impassive, and intense.

I stayed at the factory late enough to see the second shift arrive. They were very young. I would guess they were around thirteen to sixteen years old. It didn't bother me as much as I thought it would, because they seemed happy. I was given the stock answer, which was that the girls went to school in the daytime, went home and cooked food for their parents, and then took a short night shift in the factory. Worked for me. After all, you are talking to someone who at age fourteen was packing boxes. Now that I think about it, one of the most valuable business lessons I learned wasn't from school, but from packing boxes.

I was on summer vacation, packing boxes at the warehouse, which was one floor under my uncle's office. The company's policy was that when you ran out of a style (keep in mind they were all the same dress, except for the length of the sleeve and the print) you were to substitute a similarly colored dress, or as my uncle would say, "Just throw another goddamn dress in there." I called my uncle to let him know we were out of a style. He asked me if I had my head shoved up my ass again, because I knew what to do.

Two minutes later, he was standing in front of me with an invoice in his hand, shaking it around like he was looking to do that to someone's neck. "Are you packing Tammy from Tampa's order?"

"Yes."

"Jesus! That woman is a crazy psycho bitch! Unpack someone else's box and make sure Tammy's is perfect. I don't want that bitch to call me!"

Huh? What had just happened here? He was afraid of a tiny, anorexic seventy-year-old bleached blonde with leather skin? That was new to me. Do you know how labor intensive it is to unpack and repack a box? Lesson learned: it was better to be respected and feared than loved.

My time and production were almost done. I had one last trip to the factory and a fancy dinner planned with the Umbrella King. I left early in the morning, since there was a lot to get done in a day. It's interesting that no matter how little or much time you have to check on your production, everything gets done on the last day. At the factory, I was going to meet the shipping agent and a customs broker. I also had to negotiate my quotas for bringing in polyester dresses. There was a time when a set number of items could be brought in under a harmonized code. If someone wasn't using all the quotas they had set aside, they could sell it to you.

I wanted to take it all in while driving to the factory that morning. Would I ever be back here again? Was this scheme going to be successful? Then panic. Was everything legal? Was I complicit? I remember my uncle saying I needed to know the price of rice in China to understand how business was doing. What was the price of rice? Where could one find out? I was losing focus when we stopped at the intersection. I looked a little more closely this time, and the pile of rags wasn't just thrown there. The old man had died where he had sat, and for the past ten days, he had been disintegrating back into the earth. The dust and dirt and rags had all become one.

I wished the Umbrella King had been with me. I was one hundred percent clueless about what was right, but not as cheap; or what was cheaper, but maybe not one hundred percent legit. I went with the legit and costly, because I didn't want the goods to get stuck in customs or for me to end up in jail. No joke, transshipment is a serious offense.

While the Umbrella King and I were waiting in the lobby of the hotel for our ride to this fancy dinner, I told him about the whole shipping situation.

"Cute, you went in without knowing the quotas or the duties. How do you know they didn't cheat you?"

When I told him who was doing the shipment, he said they were the right ones to call, and all that conversation they had with me was just a formality. They would get the job done. He told me to let it go. Formality for whom? Me? I didn't understand.

"What do you mean get the job done? It sounds like they are going to do a hit on someone."

"Not quite, but there are palms to get greased. You don't want your goods to get lost, do you?" Get lost, I thought? That was when I started channeling my mother's good grace with God. Please God, don't let anything bad happen to my shipment. Trying to *Let go and let God*, I asked, "So where are we eating, and what is this all about?"

Monkey See, Monkey Do

It seemed a rival factory wanted his business. He was going to give it to them, since they had better speed to market and pricing and had developed a new technology that offered a comfort grip on the handles of oversized golf umbrellas. He wasn't ready to let on that they had his business until he got all his gifts. The Chinese are notorious gift-givers, from Rolex watches to Johnny Walker limited-edition whiskey. The grand finale was this dinner. He had warned me several times to eat everything they gave us. It would be insulting for us not to accept and eat the food, but he warned me not to clean my plate. That would have been a sign that I was hungry and poor. Culturally, I knew I had a lot to learn, so I took his advice to heart, but he was talking to someone who ate rattlesnake soup. Tone it down buddy, I had this. A perfect technique I had devised was to wash down mystery foods with a Jack and Coke—it's all good.

They picked us up in a stretch Mercedes. I didn't even know this type of car existed. My uncle had a very generic black car, and a driver named Matthew who was a religious southern man and didn't judge us. "Jesus walked with thieves and prostitutes," he would remind me.

I could tell that they weren't pleased to see a woman in the group. It's my understanding that a lot of these dinners end with massages and happy endings. Maybe Umbrella King brought me just for that reason. He was a happily married man with small children. He had met his wife in high school. While he went to work in his father's mattress business, he put her through medical school. She worked in a research laboratory and they had two small girls.

I lost track of how long it took us to get to the restaurant, but it sat atop a steep mountain off a long, narrow, dirt-covered, curvy road. There were security checkpoints at two of the different pass areas where the road widened a bit to let other cars pass. I thought it was weird, but the man who seemed to be the boss indicated that only the very wealthy ate here, and to have so many wealthy people in one place made it a target. The sun was setting and the fog was on the move. Bela Lugosi would have approved of the location.

The restaurant hung over the side of the mountain. It was held up by a massive labyrinth of beams made entirely of dark wood. You knew it was an ancient edifice because of all the artistry in the woodwork. During this time in China, they were building enormous skyscrapers that were boring eyesores. This was something of great beauty and grace and kept in immaculate condition. In the entrance was a cross-beam ceiling with flickering gas lamps, flames and all. After a few steps in, I found myself standing on a long fish tank embedded in the floor with exotic fish swimming around. I was so enthralled looking down at the fish tank that it took a nudge from the King to make me look to the right. There was a wall of feral-looking cats in perfectly symmetrical bamboo cages. I knew why they were there. I told myself to take a deep breath and compartmentalize . . . it was just like lobsters in a fish tank at the local seafood place in New York. Walking fast, I passed them and held my breath. I am deathly allergic to cats, but there wasn't a hint of an itchy eye or cat stink.

We sat in the back room. Boss was greeted by everyone, including the chef, who was then introduced to the King. I was completely ignored. The large, round wood table, matching the wood that the restaurant was made from, did not have a tablecloth. The waiter (not sure what the cat executioner is called) was showing off a cat that had been chosen for dinner. The cat was being held by long bamboo tongs. It was wildly scratching the air and screeching. Then they disappeared into what I think was the kitchen. The chef left, and another person brought bottles, not glasses, of whiskey. Yet another person came and was nodding and bowing to all the men. At this point there were six men, plus the King and myself. Some of the other people had been waiting in the restaurant for us. They all seemed like clones of each other— same build, same suit, and same stupid yes-man grin.

The nodding man stood on the far side of the table across from me and started turning the table. A metal plate then rose up, and inside of it was a live little monkey. I was thinking it was the entertainment. You know, like the old-timey shows where the peanut vendor is playing his music box and the fully dressed monkey dances around collecting coins in his tin can. His hands were tied in front of him. He had the biggest, saddest eyes. He was staring right at me. I suddenly put together the cat and the monkey. I held on to the bottom of my chair, bracing myself.

It all happened so fast. The man got a head nod from Boss, like he was approving a bottle of fine wine. He lowered the box just to the top of the monkey's head, and with a snap of the guillotine blade, sliced off the top of his head so cleanly that it stayed on. I wasn't even sure of what had happened until the waiter removed the top of its skull, giving us access to the brains with extra-long chopsticks. Just then, the King shot up like a bullet out of his seat and declared that he was a kosher Jew, and God forbid him from eating monkey brains. I immediately jumped on that bandwagon. "I'm a Jew, too," I said, choking back tears.

They quickly put the top of the monkey's head on and lowered it out of sight, but it was there. I knew it was there, and we had to have dinner on the grave of the monkey. We ended up having one of the fishes we had so casually walked all over. Fried! I took one bite of fish, two shots of whiskey, and was finished with my meal. I had no way to justify, quantify, or solidify deep down in my subconscious what had just happened. I knew I wasn't alone in my despair. The King's hands hadn't stopped shaking.

On the flight back, the King and I were on the same plane. Back then, and even now, it wasn't so farfetched to see the same people in the same planes going to the same events or doing the same thing. We didn't say much to each other on that flight back, since I was pretty angry that he had been adamant that I was the one who needed to be culturally correct. I would have eaten the fucking monkey brain and been a team player. I was the only woman at the table—I didn't want to be the only pussy, too.

Hurry Up and Wait

I had just gotten home when the phone rang.

"Aren't you coming to work today?"

"Manolo, I just landed." I felt I was grown enough, even if just for today, to call him Manolo, and not Tío or Tío Manolo. That decision went without recognition.

"And . . . ?"

I was soon in his office telling him all the details about the shipment, the next steps, and how I negotiated the quotas. These were things he didn't really understand, but he seemed relieved that at least I did. I didn't.

I made sure to leave the monkey story untold. I just couldn't bear the fact that this was a thing. Years later, I saw what I think was a *Vice Magazine* story about how these rich assholes get a kick out of showing off who can pay an enormous amount of money for the rarest endangered animal. They invite friends and business associates to share in the meal. These are the assholes that encourage the near extinction of the rhino (their horns are said to be a cure-all, but it's really just to show off wealth), the elephant for their ivory tusks, the shark for shark fin soup, the ocelot for coats, the jaguar for home décor, the gharial for wallets, and wildcats for stews. I am not saying that all the world's endangered animals are the fault of the Chinese, but I am not saying they're not.

"A lot of things are changing fast here, and this is going to be a good step into the future." Manolo was always so vague about everything. After all these years that I knew him, I realized that no one knew him. My mother had no idea, his friends didn't know him, and his lovers came and went before they knew him. We never had an in-depth conversation about life, its meaning, the process, goals, wants, desires, or feelings. He had two emotional levels: angry and not angry.

The pressure was on. *Hurry up and wait.* It wasn't like I could punch in a tracking number and the information would pop up on a computer screen. I didn't even have a computer! Once a week you would get a paper called the *Shipping Journal* that you could find in an "industry" newspaper stand in the Garment District, right next to the *Women's Wear Daily*.

You would look up the name of the vessel, but don't you dare call it a boat. I was laughed at by our shipping agent, a man, for that. I reminded him that I was the one signing his checks, so if I wanted to call it a fucking yacht, I could, but I never again did call it a boat. The shipping journal would give you an update on where the vessel was stopped or the ETA. It took thirty days to get to the port of Los Angeles, ten days to unload it and clear customs, and five days to truck it to Arkansas.

For those forty-five days, I suffered from the most horrible recurring dream; Walmart canceled the order, and I had to keep all the goods in my tiny studio apartment. In my dream, my apartment was a rack-filled jungle. I knew my bed was somewhere in this massive tangle of old-lady polyester dresses, but they stuck to me and drowned me, suffocating me like quicksand. Then I would suddenly wake up a sweaty mess, trapped in my sheets.

It's an Order When It's Paid

Walmart received the goods with proper vendor compliance. When they sent out the sales report after the first week, our dresses had a sell-through rate of sixty-eight percent—a new record in the Women's Missy Dress department. You go, Mr. Wilson!

Walmart then sent the payment in full to the bank seven days early, with a two percent anticipation discount. The bank approved it, which was fine with me, because I'd had the heads up from the Umbrella King that this would happen, so I'd built it into the price. I had charged Walmart $6.45 for the dresses, which they retailed at $11.88. They were retailing the dresses for less than what it cost us to make them in the United States. 😞

I did another collection for Walmart. You would think it would have been easier the second time around, but it wasn't. Even though we had an incredible sell-through, the second season they wanted us to add a little plastic pouch (another thing to source) with not one, but two extra buttons, along with a full inch hem on the dress. On top of that, they wanted a price reduction to $6.

This is a business of nickels and dimes. A nickel here and a dime there and you have no cash flow. Keeping in mind what those guys at Ben's Kosher Deli had said, if you could make a clean quarter on every item you sell to Walmart, you were ahead of the game. We were way ahead of the game. Walmart had increased their order, so I did have some economy of scale to negotiate with the factory and was able to keep my margins.

"Tell them," Manolo said, "Walmart made you the woman you are today, because they have busted your balls so much you don't have any left. So they don't get a discount, and they owe you dinner before they try to fuck you again."

"For Pete's sake, Manolo, I am not going to tell them that! That's not how it works. We can afford it, and I'll deal with the factory myself," I told him.

The fact was, I had already grown tired of all the traveling back and forth to China. It was not what I imagined I would be doing for a living, and surely not for the rest of my life. The stress of so many things going on and going wrong all at the same time was taking a toll on me. I had made a shitload of money for my uncle, but wasn't even getting paid the amount of money he would piss away at the horse track in a week. Wall Street wasn't recovering at the speed everyone thought it would have. The few friends I had working there had now started working for tech startups as CEOs, spending more money on drugs than development.

As the story goes, I walked into Manolo's office and told him I wanted to be a buyer.

Now that sounded like fun. I wouldn't be flying twenty hours to go work in a sweatshop. I wouldn't get yelled at in Chinese by just about everyone. I wouldn't suffer from bouts of food poisoning and get tapeworms. Gee, I miss that tapeworm; I was so skinny then. No, I wanted to go to the Paris fashion shows, visit the finest restaurants, and fly on Concorde. Glamour! Plus, no one yelled at buyers. They were spoiled and courted like queens. That was fine by me.

Spoiler alert: I hate fashion shows, I get sick on the heavy cream sauces, and the Concorde stopped flying before I was able to afford the ticket.

But I became a buyer. Manolo called Mr. Atkins, who had a buying office in NYC, a large company that provided market, vendor, and trend resources for national retail chains in the United States. My first job as a buyer—well, I should correct that, as a category researcher. I had knit tops up to $10 wholesale. There wasn't a tank top, halter top, or short- or long-sleeve crewneck tee in the market that I didn't know about. When a member store would call asking for a back-to-school promotional tee, I would spring into action!

"What exactly are you looking for? 1x1 rib? Poly/cotton blend? Tell me everything you need and I'll make it happen." I had become a knit top expert, and I took that shit really seriously.

All my years of working in production gave me a massive advantage in costing for negotiation.

"Who are you kidding, $3 for a poly/cotton 20-gram tee? I can get a dress made for that price." It earned me a lot of recognition with the department stores that were members.

Most of the girls were young (except for the GMM and DMM) and had come out of fashion schools with a degree in merchandising.

They had no real negotiating or costing skills. So I ended up doing a lot of coaching on the floor. We all worked in one giant gray space, in little cubicles that had this textured flame-retardant material that you couldn't even tape a photo to. Not that personalizing your "space" was allowed.

That was also something I had to get used to. While we were all very close in age (I think I was twenty-four at the time), I was light-years away from them. I lived on my own, had met a man I knew I was going to marry, and had more frequent-flyer miles than all of them put together. I was confident, but I could stand to lose the locker room foul mouth that seemed very situation appropriate before but now just made me look unsophisticated and uneducated.

I didn't mind starting at such an entry-level position, because it doesn't matter where you start—it matters where you end up.

BUT MY NAME IS
ON THE DOOR

I quickly grew through the ranks. It wasn't hard. I was the only one who had on-the-field combat experience. The shoeshine man once made a comment to me that's stuck with me. He went from office to office polishing shoes in the hallway, never saying much about himself, but we knew he was a Vietnam vet who had been shot in the neck and lost some of his vocal cords. He spoke with a very rough tone but was always sweet and kind. He compared the garment industry to war: how you had to be prepared for different situations, how you had to be in the trenches to understand the enemy, and how there would always be collateral damage when taking risks. How you couldn't trust anyone, since they might be a spy. Don't kid yourself; this industry is full of corporate spies! It was all excellent advice.

One day, Mr. Atkins came into the buyer's pool and asked in a slightly panicked voice, "Who can speak Spanish?" I raised my hand. "Great, come with me." He knew my reputation for being a problem-solver and a team leader. I had never been in Mr. Atkins's office. It was a cool corner office with huge floor-to-ceiling windows that showcased a holy-shit view of the Hudson River. He had decorated it with midcentury modern furniture. It had a very *Mad Men* feeling.

I took a moment to think back to all the behaviors that sent me to the principal's office. Those behaviors had become my best assets in my professional life. This cracked me up. I got decent grades in school, but the comment box on my report cards always had a note listing my bad traits: "doesn't share," "is a sore loser," "bossy," "talks too much," and my favorite, "does not play well with others." How can that be a problem, or even a statement, on a report card? Was talking in class and asking questions disrupting the class? Or was it part of the learning experience? We were lectured and tested. That was it. In study groups, someone, usually me, had to lead the team. Like in nature, the alpha always leads (wins) the team. Sometimes it happens naturally, and sometimes you have to be a little aggressive, a.k.a. bossy. I remember the teachers saying, "Mercedes, can't you let someone else have a chance?" No.

There is no reason not to be kind while being in control, but you shouldn't have to make excuses for being focused, determined, and knowing what you want. Absolutely not. Sharing is another one of those overrated, school-imposed character flaws. I was going to do all the work and share the credit? That would never happen. Let's not forget the sore loser. Why would anyone want to be a good loser? I mean, to lose your temper, throw hissy-fits, and have tantrums are things you kind of outgrow (not really). But when losing bothers you, it makes you strive to do your best and never lose again.

Mr. Atkins asked a few polite questions that weren't even related to any sort of job skills. "Where did you go to school? Where did you grow up? Have you ever been to Mexico before?" And just like that, I became the head of the South American division. The company had just landed a major department store in Mexico. I couldn't understand why the position didn't go to a senior staffer who was more qualified. I mean, really, speaking Spanish . . . that was it? If that was the case, the taco truck guy was equally qualified to land the job.

I traveled to Mexico City sixteen times that year to merchandise and plan the assortment of American brands they were introducing. Warning: after traveling to Mexico so many times, it's still not OK to drink the water. Coming back home from one of those trips, a couple of ice cubes did me in while on a flight. All I remember was the flight attendant knocking on the door of the lavatory, asking me to sit down for landing.

Shortly after that, one of the member stores of Atkins in Puerto Rico hired me directly. This company was called Gonzalez Padin (I wasn't a Gonzalez yet). They had a chain of department stores, and I was in charge of Urban and the new Boutique Area. It was a big mix of product categories. The Boutique Area carried brands like Carmen Marc Valvo and local designers like Fernando Peña. Valvo and Peña were elegant brands to buy from. You had to make an appointment at their showroom during market week, not to be confused with fashion week. Market week is the time buyers review collections for the following season. It was all very secretive. You couldn't take photos of the collection, and the line sheets were very basic. Between the glasses of champagne and catered lunches they offered, you had to write a very detailed description of each item so that you could remember what you were buying.

That was all very different from the pot-smoking off-location showrooms in the Urban Market. Even when you saw Urban at a trade show, it was a spectacle. I remember when FuBu launched at MAGIC for the first time and they wouldn't let me make an appointment before the show. Determined to buy the collection for my accounts, I made sure I was the first person at the booth on the opening day of the show. The booth was completely closed off. You couldn't peek inside to see who was there or what they were showing. I had never seen the collection in person before, but they were making such a publicity impact that the customers in Puerto Rico were screaming for the clothing. People started arriving, but I couldn't tell the buyers from the staff from the hoodrats. "We can't fit you in," said an oddly thin woman, with a large, round bottom and ridiculously long fingernails, who couldn't even hold the pen in her hand in a normal manner. Maybe that was her reason for blocking me—she couldn't write my name in the book.

"Well, I'll wait right here. I am sure you might have a cancellation," I replied. Just then, a sales rep I knew from Calvin Klein saw me waiting there.

"I can't get an appointment. Can you help me out?"

"Sure," he said, turning to the receptionist, "She's good. She's with me." And in we went. I had a flashback to Studio 54, when the red velvet rope magically opened. There was no velvet rope here, just a door, but there should have been one with all the drama.

Inside was something I had never experienced. There were so many buyers wanting to buy the collection that they had to show it in mass. That meant you sat in rows with a group of other buyers. A pretty, bored salesperson would hold up the samples then call out the style number and price. You would find them on your line sheet and circle the items. Later you would write up your order. Witnessing everyone feverishly circling items was mind-blowing. I was completely lost and couldn't understand what the hype was all about. The fabrics were basic and cheap. The styling was out there, not following any specific trend, and everything had the freaking FuBu logo on it. But I had to write something; the public was demanding it! Sitting next to me was a Japanese fellow who was completely adopting the trending New York urban look, right down to his permed hair. Certainly he must know what to buy, I thought, so I stopped looking up at the salesperson and started to copy his order notes. One item was just such a monstrosity that I couldn't write it. He must have felt my hesitation and turned to me, saying, "This is a very good seller, a very good seller." He was right. During Christmas season we reordered that number three times. Lesson learned: you can't buy what you like, you have to buy what sells.

After Gonzalez Padin, a more significant buying office stole me away. The company was opening an international division, and I would be working directly with the owner. They were snowballing by buying up smaller companies and trend forecasting mega-houses. The backstabbing and credit stealing was intense! I wasn't meant for corporate, but I had picked up a knack for predicting the consumer's behavior. The dot-com bust was just starting, and consumer confidence was down. The retailers were buying proven bodies, but I advised them that now was the time for new and wow. When the consumer is sad and depressed, they go shopping! I was right.

A short time after that, through the market grapevine, I heard that a smaller company was changing from only buying textiles for South American stores to buying RTW (ready-to-wear). It was the perfect position for me. I had become an expert in Latin American retail, and I had all the right contacts with the wholesalers. Plus, my name was already on the door: Gonzalez Partners. Mr. Gonzalez had passed away a few years earlier, leaving three of his employees as partners.

Goodbye, Uncle Manolo

I should pause here and update you on my uncle. A year after I left, his company was making $20 million a year with Walmart, plus the national discount chains he had always worked with. He was making over $100 million in sales, but my uncle was looking toward the future. Walmart kept cutting back on pricing, and soon they would start developing products themselves, thus cutting out the brands. They were also affecting many of the other retailers my uncle sold to who couldn't adapt to Walmart's aggressiveness. They were closing. Uncle's business was being cannibalized. He was one of the first to see what was to come.

He sold the company to a young man I met only at my uncle's funeral. He was enthusiastic and overly educated, with a master's degree in human studies and a trust fund. Not a winning combination for this business. If he wanted to learn about humans, he just had to ride the subway at rush hour. He would have gotten all the education he needed right there. Now I sound like Manolo.

Six months into his retirement, my uncle was found dead with his boots on. Translation: he was found dead in a Puerto Rican hotel with a prostitute. I was the one who had to fly down to claim his body. It wasn't an easy thing to do, since I didn't want to take the body back without a full investigation having been done. He had been robbed, and I wanted the prostitute jailed for stealing my uncle's watch. He never took his gold Rolex off, ever! They didn't find it in the room, and none of the staff remembered seeing it, which was pure bullshit, since he played craps and was left-handed. They had to have seen the watch! All they did was waste my time. Even with the connections I had made working with the department store, I didn't get anywhere. No one knew anything. The handling and storage fees were accumulating. I was miserable, frustrated, and overwhelmed. I cut my losses. A lesson I had learned from Manolo.

We told my mother that her brother died of a heart attack while fishing in the Caribbean. As a religious woman, it made her happy and gave her some comfort to know he died doing something he loved. Side note: my uncle never went fishing. That was his code for going on a weeklong gambling binge, usually in Las Vegas, without her calling him. During the wake, one of Manolo's friends toasted him by declaring that the man died how he lived, with his boots on. We told my mom that was a fishing term.

I miss Manolo.

His company didn't last long. The young man who replaced him never saw Walmart backing away, and kept investing in the development of a more prominent factory in Florida. His thinking was that they couldn't go direct if he owned the factories. He was part of the movement to keep manufacturing in the United States, a movement that was heartfelt, but delusional. Most consumers don't care where goods are made; they care about pricing. In the end, he filed for bankruptcy and never fully paid off the cost of Uncle's business. The deal he made with my uncle was some cash up front and a percent of sales monthly for x numbers of years. The whole deal was a little dubious, since it was written on the back of a cocktail napkin from Arno's.

My uncle was a horrible planner. He lived in the moment. He was always able to find a way to make a buck, but he didn't leave a will or inheritance for anyone. Not even me. He left the apartment on 57th

Street by default to his Russian lover (the one I liked), because the doormen testified that she was his domestic partner. She earned it. My mom gave the car to his driver, since they were both people of God.

As for myself, I'm sorry to say, I might have one photo of us somewhere in my mother's house. Probably of him at one of my birthday parties. He hated kids, but he always came to my parties.

The one thing he did give me was courage. I still hear him telling me to suck it up and shut the fuck up. He never treated me like a kid. He was why I started drinking whiskey at the age of thirteen. We were sitting at Arno's restaurant with a couple of buyers from a chain called Jamesway. Everyone ordered drinks, and I ordered a coke.

He got so mad at me and demanded, "Don't you know common business etiquette?" What you don't know is the irony in that statement. This was a man who once told a buyer who was complaining about something, "I'm listening to you. It's going in one ear, and I'm blowing it out my ass." He told me that when a buyer orders a drink, you order a drink. The only time you didn't order a drink was when you were with some pussy going to AA meetings.

"Is there some type of law that you can't drink I should know about?"

"Actually . . ." Just then the waiter came with our drinks, and he poured some of his Jack into my Coke. Cheers.

He hated when I did the math on anything. I was always looking for an ROI (return on investment) when he was looking for the OTB (off-track betting). If I were to write a book on how not to run a business, I would start with a chapter on Manolo. He never finished school, he never wrote a plan, and he never reviewed any numbers.

What he did do was manage his losses. This was different from managing risk. He had x number of dollars to invest in something, and when that money ran out, and it wasn't making him money, the project was over. He invested $10,000 for the China trip. If there hadn't been an order, there wasn't going to be a money tree to shake. How did he know how much to invest? It depended on how much money he won at the horses that day. Told you, you could write a book on what not to do. But it worked for him. I guess the lesson learned is to not overthink things. I have seen many businesses fail, or never even launch, from overthinking.

Now back to my story of Gonzalez Partners. I worked for these partners for a couple of years. From day one, the oldest partner was always talking about retiring. I started to save, hoping to buy into the partnership. I did brilliant and profitable work for them. I grew the RTW from zero to $8 million in the first year, and at ten percent commission (what they charged at the time). It wasn't chump change for the company. All of their clients' businesses grew, and I even brought in some new accounts. I was the perfect person to be one of the partners.

One of the clients I brought in was the new Sears store in Panama. The gentleman who owned it was Greek, and he told me the story of how his father worked on a shipping boat bringing goods from Greece to different parts of the world. At the age of fourteen, his father put him to work alongside him on a trip. He was seasick all the months he was on the water. He lost weight and developed scurvy. The boat's first stop was Panama, and fearing that he would die from a lack of nutrition, his father left him there. The plan was to pick him up, months later, on the way back to Greece.

Imagine being a fourteen-year-old boy who didn't speak the language, had very little money, and knew no one. Six months later, when his father was due back in Panama to pick him up, he was very well established with a modest fruit stand. He told me he did everything possible to never board a boat again. His father recognized that his son was doing well, so he set sail without him, promising to visit Panama in six months' time.

Fast forward, and the Greeks became the largest exporters of bananas to the United States. He patented a type of box that kept the bananas fresh during shipping. I had the ultimate respect for him. When you have no one to judge you and nothing to lose, you can accomplish some amazing things. He stole bananas at night from the fields and sold them on street corners by day. Today, people buy his bananas in every corner of the world.

Sears Panama was a licensing agreement between the Greeks and Sears Holding Company, based in Chicago. The two primary consultants, who were running the opening of the new Sears, had worked for Sears in the 1970s and saw the significant changes the company had gone through. They seemed to have impressive pedigrees and experience.

After my first meeting with them, I knew these consultants were clueless. I am not joking. To this day, I have no idea how these two antiquated bumbling fools were in charge of this multimillion-dollar project. Their strategies were dated and would never work in Latin America. Here is an example: they wanted to sell better price points. Sears was always known for moderate price points. Any consumer who could afford better price points could travel, usually to Miami, to go shopping.

They didn't want to have a children's toy department. That was a high-turnover area, considering that toys are a compulsion. Toys sell not only as Christmas gifts, but as birthday gifts and during report card time.

But most disturbing was that they had no system in place to verify purchase orders. I was working with the two women's department buyers. My job was to pre-shop the market to find the items that fit their price point and aesthetics. They didn't have a fashion director; the consultants didn't feel it was necessary. I should also mention that they came from hard goods. There were no fashion trends involved with car batteries and hammers, so I took it upon myself to give them some fashion forecasting. When we wrote an order, it just went to data entry and payment would be sent. No one was keeping track of the costing or the physical count at the warehouse.

Why was this important? Kickbacks! The buyers would place an order at an inflated price, not by much, and the vendors would give them a kickback for placing the order. It's a super common practice. I distinctly remember making Christmas envelopes for Manolo. He would say, "It's their Christmas," as if it were like tipping his doorman. But no, they were kickbacks.

Sears opened with much fanfare but closed within a few years due to internal situations. This means, politely, that there was no cash flow from the overcharging and the shrinkage in the warehouse. They had also made a bunch of payments for inventory to companies that didn't exist. Another mistake was that they didn't offer some of the key Sears brands, because they couldn't manage the complicated web of international licensing agreements.

There was also the incident of culture clash. One VP of sales, from an underwear brand we all grew up wearing, came to visit the store's pre-opening to validate the purchase order. I was invited to the dinner since I knew the rep from working with him in Puerto Rico, along with the owner's wife and their two children. During the dinner conversation, the owner explained his story of how he got started and why he wanted to open this Sears store. Shopping at a Sears store in Florida was his piece of the American Dream. When dinner was over, they shook hands, and the order was approved. It was a considerably sized order, since it covered basic underwear for men, women, and children.

The VP then asked the owner why he'd brought his kids to such an important business dinner, saying "Couldn't you find a babysitter?" The Greek became outraged! He had pulled his kids out of school to meet and have dinner with an important American VP. This was definitely a Latin American cultural thing. Remember, even Manolo took me to lunch meetings. The owner canceled the order and went with a Colombian underwear brand instead. You'd have thought that the Chicago consultants would've been able to help with licensing situations and the operations, but they were hired only as merchandise planners and department divisionals. How does one know what they don't know, or what they need to know?

The time had come for the oldest of the partners to announce his retirement. It would be within the year, and he wanted to make it a smooth transition. I asked during the meeting whether there would be another person to take his place as a partner, or if the two remaining partners were going to just take over his shares. It was clear that they wanted a new partner. I was determined that it would be me. One partner, whom I called Boss, was the loudest of the three, and I would say it was only by luck that he became a partner. The second one started with the company when he was very young. He kept his head down and got the job done. The one retiring was the oldest, I would say by twenty years. He was overly kind in that fake Christian way. He once called me into his office for "using the Lord's name in vain." Jesus Christ, give me a break.

They hired a guy who came from the towel industry. This person had no idea what a buyer was, and had no RTW fashion experience. They asked me to train him by taking him to the market and introducing him to the clients.

What was my naïve self thinking? I thought I was teaching him to take over some of the buying, because once I became a partner, I was going to be focused on the introduction of private labels for our clients. It would be a new project, and I'd devote a lot of my own time developing it and would introduce it as a partner. The retiring partner's role in the company had become impractical with the restructuring of the company toward RTW. I not only had increased their business, but as a partner, I would introduce this new revenue stream.

We went to MAGIC, which was the largest trade show in the country, and I daresay in the world. It was his first time attending. We walked the show together with clients. I was buying, negotiating, and training him on order writing for fashion items. "Yes, you have to write the number of pieces per size you want; these are not towels."

We stopped at the booth of a company I had been working with for a few years. I adored the owner, who was Cuban and had come to this country with just a few dollars to his name. Through hard work and a few loans from friends, he bought one of the most important men's brands in the country. I still believe in the American dream. His VP of sales, someone I was friendly with and was my salesman, came out from another appointment to say hi to me. He then congratulated Towel Boy on his new partnership, but he made sure to look straight into my eyes as he congratulated him. He was telling me what had happened. At that moment, the world stopped. At least, my world stopped. Did I understand correctly? Everything had become a little fuzzy, and I felt dizzy.

I wrote my orders, took photos for trend to update the clients that didn't attend, dined with clients, and did everything I was supposed to do, but I did it all on autopilot. I couldn't even open my mouth without my voice trembling to tell my husband what I thought was happening. So, I didn't. At the time, MAGIC was a four-day show that started on Monday and ended on Thursday. This time, it felt like I had been there for a month. On the last day of the show, I said to one of my clients that I didn't work with much, "We should throw a surprise party for Towel Boy!"

"Oh, I think they're already at the Tavern," he replied.

Just then, he realized that I didn't know. This was the final proof I needed. I was trying to make myself feel better by justifying that the Spanish Tavern was not as fancy as Arno's. Did everyone know except me? Was I the joke of the office? Of the market? The retiring partner called me at the hotel that night (you know, the kind Christian) to make sure that I was coming in that Friday. They had already left, because the cool thing for the VIPs to do at MAGIC was to fly in for a day or two and leave before the show was over, leaving the workers to do their jobs. They came only for the networking (read: insane shenanigans).

MAGIC was a very different show then. It was still primarily a men's show. The booths were massive, and they all tried to outdo each other. It wasn't unheard of to spend a million dollars on a booth back then. On the tame side, Levi's had a saloon set up. Upstairs was for viewing the collection and writing orders, and downstairs had a full bar with two bartenders serving drinks and food. On the not-so-tame side, Schott leather had a round, red rotating bed with a pinup girl you could lie down and take a photo with. And of course, there was everything in between.

"I am on the red-eye, and you have never asked me to come in on Friday after MAGIC," I told him. "So no, I am not coming in."

Ninteenth Nervous Breakdown

If I ever thought I was going to have a nervous breakdown, it would have been at the previous MAGIC show. I had spent the whole day walking the show with a new buyer. It was her first time at the show, and I guess she wanted to make an impression on her boss. She insisted on stopping at every booth to pick up catalogs, line sheets, look books, anything she could find, like she was collecting pretty seashells at the beach. Except these weighed a ton. I like to advise my clients to work the show in a see-something-and-write-it mode. They'd have time to make their final edits once they got back to the store. But that didn't apply to her, and she had collected so many catalogs and line sheets that she asked me to help her carry them.

By midnight (that would be 3 a.m. NYC time, since I always stay on NYC time), we'd finished an enormous testosterone-infused steak dinner. We said goodnight and I made my way to my hotel, which was not an easy feat, since taxis were scarce back then. Taxi lines could be an hour wait, but I got lucky. Walking into my hotel, I could no longer feel my feet from the pain. My tongue was swollen from dehydration and talking all day, repeating the same thing over and over and over. I was nauseated from the heavy, late-night steak dinner, and I was carrying fifty pounds of catalogs and line sheets for this new buyer, since she decided I now had to write her orders. She was too overwhelmed and couldn't remember a thing she liked.

All I wanted to do was snap my fingers and magically appear in my room. Hey, hadn't I just walked past this person? Was I walking around in fucking circles? I couldn't find the elevator. Tears were welling up in my eyes. I was staying at the pyramid-shaped hotel, the Luxor, which already had a beat-up, worn-out look to it. They'd made getting to the elevators a Tryon rat maze, and I was crossing and crisscrossing the casino. I started dropping catalogs, lookbooks, and line sheets in a Hansel and Gretel fashion. My shoes came off (if you know me, you know this means I am at death's door).

I saw a security guard. My savior, I thought. Smiling like the rat that won the experiment, I asked, "Sir, can you please tell me where the elevators are?"

"Oh, we don't have elevators, we have Inclinators!" he gleefully declared. I am sure he was waiting all night to say that.

"What the fuck are you talking about? Get me to the fucking ELEVATORS, or I am going to kill you."

He could sense from my tone that I was really going to fucking kill him, so he took my smelly shoes out of my hands, picked up the bag with the few catalogs I had left, put his arm around me like a wounded soldier, and walked me in a direct path to the Inclinators. "Have a good night, ma'am," he said. I think I muttered something back.

I didn't go to work on Friday.

That Monday, they were already in the conference/showroom/fabric sample room. It was a crowded, windowless room that smelled like formaldehyde, very appropriate since death hung in the air.

"Mercedes." I knew this was serious, because they all called me "Meche" which is short for Mercedes, and I hated being called that. They started with, "Lately you have had a bit of an attitude problem." I started laughing. I knew this game. I'd played it before. "You haven't been properly training Towel Boy. He is still confused about delivery seasons."

There is no such thing as a delivery season, I thought to myself.

"And your yelling on the phone, saying you weren't coming in on Friday, was another example of your bad attitude."

Oh, you want to see yelling? My blood started to boil.

"And you haven't properly been giving Towel Boy's full credentials to the clients."

"That's because he doesn't have any," I told him. He started to defend Towel Boy. "Enough," I yelled. "This is all fucking bullshit. I know you are making Towel Boy a partner, and you are making excuses to justify it. This guy isn't qualified to wipe my ass, and you are making him a partner and not me? Just be fucking honest with me one time; WHY?!"

There was a lot of yelling. Boss was reaching as hard as he could to find excuses, not to fire me, but to justify not making me a partner. He was just making shit up like someone might be recording it to cover his ass in a lawsuit.

"You are talking to someone that hasn't taken a sick day in three years! I am in the office before any of you! I grew the RTW business from nothing to everybody's paycheck!" I yelled. He wouldn't back down, and he did not hear anything I had to say.

The yelling got louder and louder. Everyone in the office was standing around the open door. No one spoke up for me: not the secretary, the assistants, or the bookkeeper, all people that I had coached and had lunch with. I threw my coffee cup at the wall. That was shocking and unexpected, even to me. I didn't know I could be so dramatic. It felt good for a second, so I went for more. I pushed all the papers, the pencil cup holder, and the order books off the table and onto the floor. I stood up, towering over them from the other side of the table. I put my hands on the edge of the table. I considered flipping it. I leaned in so close that I could feel Boss's hyperventilating breath on my face. I asked Boss one more time, "WHY NOT ME?"

And then he said it. "We would never have a woman for a partner." Well, that took balls to say to my face. I took a step back. I was crying so hard that the tears were not just running down my face but were shooting out like flames. I picked up my things. It felt like that scene in *The Jerk* with Steve Martin when he left his girlfriend, telling her that he didn't need her. "I just need this ashtray and maybe this paddleball." I was just walking around the office picking up stuff, some of it rightfully mine and some not. No one stopped me or said a word.

And Then There Were Three

My first phone call was to Ana Maria, an elegant woman who still owns a boutique in Santiago, Chile. Her family was once compared to the Kennedys, since politics was a family business and there had been some serious tragedy in their life. She was one of the clients I brought in, so I thought it was my responsibility to tell her I would no longer be working with her because I had been fired . . . or had I quit?

I started in the calmest way I could, and explained what happened without giving her too much of the drama. As if she poured cold water over me, she abruptly woke me up, saying, "Why would I stop working with you? I never even liked those guys." *Why would I stop working with you?* Those words spun around and around in my head. Why would she stop working with me? "Start your own company." She was now speaking to me in English, I guess to make sure I understood each word (Chileans speak a much different Spanish than I do).

"Yes, I could start my own business."

And then she said, "I will be your first client." My first client. My first client, I had my own client. I let it sink in. I was just three hours out of a job, and I was already building my company.

"What should I call it? Gonzalez Partners is already taken." We both laughed.

"You wouldn't want to name it that. Name it what you do. You purchase for people, and it's a global company starting in Chile." And Global Purchasing was born.

My second call was to a family department store in the Caymans. Before I could finish the story, they asked, "But you are still going to work with us, right?"

"Yes, in fact, I am starting my own company."

"Sign us up!" they said without even hesitating.

The third call was to Melissa in the Dominican Republic. This call was going to be tricky because she wasn't a client that I brought to the company, and her father, who was the owner, was very good friends with Boss, even being from the same small town in Spain. She got on the phone and told me she was going home for lunch and would call me back from there.

It seemed Boss had been calling around to all the clients, saying the most horrible, dreadful things about me—which, since they all took place that day, were correct. Even the part where I stole from them. Why *did* I take the Wite-Out?

Ana Maria had beaten me to the call, telling Melissa that we women had to stand together. Now the world made sense to me. Women! Why did Mr. Atkins choose me for that job? None of the men wanted to travel to a Third World country. Why did those consultants get the job so blindly? They were old, white men. Why didn't I get the partnership? Because I have to sit to pee. Melissa couldn't work with me directly, because of her father's influence, but she managed to find a way to meet with me during market and pay me directly, using her personal checking account.

Everyone's business grew. Ana opened two more stores, and Melissa bought her brother and father out and moved the business into a beautifully restored mansion. She turned a dusty business into the Fred Segal of the Caribbean. The sisters from the Caymans grew their business, too, but tragically lost everything after Hurricane Ivan.

I planned to work from home. The income I had from these three clients was enough to make me happy, and it was time to start a family. The family never happened, but the business kept growing by word of mouth. That became my baby.

When people tell you that there needs to be a balance between work and life, they are lying to you and probably have a job they hate. It's about integration. I am what I do. Period. Some people identify themselves by their children. I define myself by my clients. It's that simple. There is no life/work, black/white, here/there. It's all one and the same. Me.

CHEAPER ON
CANAL STREET

A friend of mine asked me for advice on a store in which she was considering becoming a partner. I should mention now that I am not a fan of partners. I find that people seek partners for three reasons: they don't have enough money, they don't have the know-how, or they are afraid of doing it alone. They may not even realize this third reason. None are valid reasons. If you don't have enough money, then you save more. If you don't know what you are doing, then you learn from doing it or you hire people who do. If you're afraid to work alone, well, then there will be two frightened people who are unable to make any decisions, instead of one.

The store wasn't doing well, despite the fact that it had an excellent location in New York's Upper East Side and a good niche. It was a boutique that sold only handbags, with a wide range of price points and styles. They had everyday fashion bags at under a hundred dollars, and then a select group of indie designers who made one-of-a-kind bags for the store. One of the owner's exclusive designers was a woman who had apprenticed with Judith Leiber. This designer was using semiprecious stones that were handset in the Leiber style. I couldn't even fathom what could be wrong with the shop. I told her I'd make a trip up to the store and see what I could find.

I went up on a Sunday morning, and the store was supposed to open at 11 a.m. It was already 11:20 a.m. and it was closed. Not knowing if I had the correct store hours, since there wasn't even a sign with the hours posted on the window, I guessed that they were closed on Sundays. Then, I spotted a young girl who couldn't have been more than twenty years old coming down the block, doing the walk of shame. She had been out all night and was just coming to work. I quickly apologized for being there *so early*, explaining that I wasn't from the neighborhood, but I had gone out to dinner the night before in the area and saw this *must-have* bag in the window.

"Where did you have dinner?" asked the girl, with a slight Spanish accent.

"Café Luxembourg," I answered.

"Oh, did you notice the bartender with the longish hair that covers one eye?"

"You mean handsome Henry?"

"Yes, that's him. That's my boyfriend."

"No joking, you must be Esmeralda."

"No, I am not," she said.

Silence. Oh, shit, I thought.

"JOKING," I exclaimed, trying to save the situation. "Ha, you should have seen your face!"

"I think we are going to get married soon."

That's a little premature, I thought to myself.

"Oh, that's wonderful! I'll have to give him an extra tip next time we are there," I said dryly.

The heavy, rusty old gate was stuck, and she was having a hard time lifting it, so I offered her a trick. "You know, if you kick it right here,"—I was kicking the chain box were the chains are collected—"when you pull up the gate, you'll scare off the rats that might be stuck in there."

Horror ran across her face.

"JOKING!" I laughed again.

Now we were both having a good laugh. We bonded over struggling with the gate. After a few heave-hos, we managed to finally get the gate up together.

She opened the door and ran inside to the back of the store, going behind a wall to shut off the alarm system. I was left standing in a dark store with an open door and $1,000 bags. I could have run out with loads. With all of my loss prevention training, I knew all of the tricks. It's never the asshole that cons grandma out of her life savings; it's that "nice guy" who is always helping out that screws you.

Hold on, side story: I took a loss prevention class out in Las Vegas at a trade show called Global Shop a few years ago. I was selected from the audience to participate in a cash-switching demonstration involving money-counting scams. The gentleman giving the demonstration was a highly renowned professional pickpocket now hired to train retailers in loss prevention. I stood next to him at a low table where he proceeded to count out single bills. He made a show of it, making sure to exaggerate the counting out of each bill. One dollar, two dollars, three dollars. He would flip each bill from one hand to the other, and then onto the table, making a loud slapping sound each time.

"How many dollars have I counted out?" he asked.

"Ten," I said. He fanned them out and counted them. There were only six. The audience started laughing and applauding at the same time, as they had been counting along with me on a monitor that showed his hands up close.

"You want to try this again?" he asked.

"Sure," I said. He reached into a cash box, shuffled a few more dollars, took them out, and started counting again, this time even more grossly exaggerated, counting them out one by one. I was paying such close attention that I didn't even blink.

"How many do I have now?"

I just took a wild guess, because I was sure he had, once again, counted to ten. "Eight," I said.

"Six," he corrected, counting them out. Gosh darn it, how was he doing this? "Thank you very much for your time; let's give this lady a round of applause for being such a good sport." He went on to talk about how most con men are just really good illusionists, like you would find right there at a Las Vegas show.

"In fact . . . excuse me, ma'am," he said just as I was reaching my seat. "Would you like your watch back?" *What the mother?* Looking down at my wrist, I noticed he had stolen my watch while I had been busy watching him count the money. Darn, when you're good, you're good.

Back to the handbags: The employee came out from the back, and we continued our conversation. We started talking about the local dive restaurants that were still around. *La Caridad 78*, anyone? We'd both grown up on the West Side (albeit she decades later), and we both agreed that the area had changed. I have very strong feelings about all of that, but I was there on a mission and had to stay focused.

"That turquoise bag in the window; can I see it? It's really the reason I came back to the East Side without having to get my visa updated." That was a dig at how the East Side is practically a different country than the West Side.

That in itself became a project, because she had to go to the back, grab the step ladder, find the keys to open the lock on the window door, climb through the window, and pull out the right bag, with me directing her from the outside of the store. She handed me the bag. It was covered in dust, but that didn't stop the bag from being drop-dead gorgeous. It had tiny turquoise stones that were handset on the gold-plated cylinder bag. It was lined in Valentino red silk and numbered and signed by the artist. It was an amazing, one-of-a-kind bag. Then I looked at the price: $1,700.

I dramatically read the price aloud: "Seventeen hundred dollars?"

She put her hand on her hip and shook a finger at me, saying, "I don't know why anyone would pay that kind of money for a stupid bag when you can go to Chinatown and buy the same thing for $25." I wasn't even shocked. We had become friends and now she was giving me "good advice."

This was the owner's fault. The missing part of the puzzle was the right team. How could the owner think it was a good idea to hire a high school dropout and pay her minimum wage to sell rich, Upper East Side ladies' bags that were worth more than she made in a month? And without the tiniest bit of training! I am not saying that everyone has to be able to afford the things they sell in the store, but the salespeople have to be able to understand the product and relate to it in some way. The owner could have hired an art student, or an emerging designer, or even a divorcée from the Upper East Side who needed a "little job" to occupy her time. Or she could have given this girl the real break she needed, like when Manolo took a chance on the talented cutter with a felony whom nobody else would employ. It's our responsibility as entrepreneurs to not only think of profit, but of people and planet.

I find that most boutique owners expect the perfect person to just walk into the shop. That doesn't happen. It takes a lot of planning and understanding to get the kind of person you want. When I first started Global Purchasing Companies, I was advised to hire people with more experience than me. It sounded like smart advice at the time, but those people turned out to be set in their ways, stuck in old-fashioned thinking. They had a hard time adapting, and they commanded very high salaries.

Now I hire only interns who work during their college years with us. I find that as long as they are nice, optimistic, and willing to learn, I can train them in anything. And, best of all, in my way of doing business.

Given the opportunity and training, I bet this girl would have been wonderful.

YOU ARE DOING
IT WRONG, SID

*Sid's Retail Lessons from
the Old World*

$\mathcal{I}$t started with a call from a very frustrated woman. She explained in a tone that implied she had told this story before, and there still hadn't been a solution. She was uttering the words like an automated customer service operator probably expecting the same type of automated response: Press 1 if you need a hug. Press 2 if you need a referee to wrangle your dad. Press 3 if you need a pyromaniac to set fire to the business. Press 4 if you need to go back to the menu.

She explained that her dad had been running a plus-size dress shop for more than forty years. She was ready to take over the business, but anytime she tried to change anything he got upset and yelled, "It's not broken, don't fix it!"

I started laughing and added, "I bet when a customer comes in, he doesn't even give you a chance to say hello before he jumps in saying he knows what she wants."

"You know my dad?" she asked.

"Yes, I do."

She was clashing with her father and causing tension within the family. She needed help from an expert, and that's why she called me. I had worked with many family-run businesses that were getting ready to be handed down, and it's never easy. Part of my job was to be that referee, and the other part was to show how new systems are more cost and time efficient. Or there's always the option of teaching them how to fill out that fire claim.

A few weeks after the phone call, I was standing in front of the store. I was literally shaking from excitement, and adrenaline was pumping through my veins. Some people jump out of airplanes to get this rush. I dress mannequins. Let me start by describing the outside of the store. It had a door in the center and two large windows on both sides of the facade. It was a plus-size store, and yet the mannequins were standard size. All the clothing was clipped in the back with those large, black clamps. The mannequins were as old as the store. Having spent more than four decades in the hot Texas sun, the hair had melted into some odd rats'-nest type of hair sculpture. In a Lower East Side boutique, it could have been passed off as edgy, and even a little avant-garde. The fabulous Einsteins came to mind, which was owned by a gender-fluid male married to a transgender artist.

However, that was the '80s East Village, and this was Southwest Texas in the late '90s. The faces had also faded, so sometime in the '80s, Sid thought it would be a good idea to paint the eyelids and lips with nail polish. As a result, the faces had a bright-blue eyeshadow with dramatic cat eye, reminding me of Elizabeth Taylor as Cleopatra, and glittery ruby-red lips like Dorothy's shoes.

Walking into the store, I seriously almost had an orgasm from all the merchandising porn I was being exposed to. I had to take a deep breath and take it all in. There were a sea of rounders that went from side to side and back to front of the whole store. Rounders are those bulky, round racks that discount stores use. Every inch of the slot walls had waterfall arms jammed in with merchandise. I felt like I was suffocating with the low drop ceiling and fluorescent lighting, where every other tube was missing (Sid later told me that it was a waste of money to have so many lights on). In the back of the store were Sid and his wife, Helen, sitting on bar stools with their arms crossed behind a clear-glass and white Formica counter. An anorexic child couldn't squeeze between the racks, let alone a plus-size customer. How could he have done *any* business in a place that looked like this? There was absolutely no sign of any retail experience. It even smelled like Grandma's house, although not of mothballs, but of old fabrics, part musty and part toxic.

If I hadn't witnessed this with my own eyes, I would tell you that you were telling me a complete lie. Customers would stand at the front of the door and greet him with a "Hey, Sid!"

He'd yell back with a smile, "What are you looking for today?" They would shout out their needs: a wedding, a job interview, graduation. He would then run around the store (well, really more like shuffle around the store), pick a few outfits, ring them up with an old metal cash box, crank out the receipt, walk over to the door, collect the payment, and be done. Whatever didn't fit, whatever didn't work, whatever they didn't like, they could return, whenever. Despite all of this, I did learn a few things from Sid, and one of them was customer service. He had a very relaxed return policy and paid attention to detail. He always remembered each customer's special occasion, no matter how small, and he always asked them how it went. He was the original in treating a customer as a guest. This was something an online retailer would never be able to do.

Sid walked over and asked if he could help me, while checking me out from head to toe. I could hear him thinking *She isn't from around these parts*. I told him who I was and introduced myself. I couldn't contain my enthusiasm! Word diarrhea came out of my mouth so quickly that even I couldn't keep up.

"Sid, oh my God, we need to change this and that. And what about—"

He cut me off right in the middle of my grandiose speech and said, "Look little lady." I towered over him but let it go. "How dare you tell me I am doing it wrong? I've been in business for forty long years. I have four daughters. I paid for their educations, paid for their weddings, helped them with the deposits for their homes. I own this building and my house, and if I wanted to retire tomorrow, I could."

How could I argue? I took another deep breath and stepped closer to him, not to intimidate him, but to whisper an answer.

"Sid," I said, pausing for dramatic effect. "How many more vacations could you have taken with your daughters? How many more stores could you have had by now? Sid, how much time are you spending with your grandchildren?" I stepped back. I could see that he was pondering my questions. Sid had survived it all: the Holocaust, being a refugee in a country where he didn't speak the language, racism, and as he put it, the trials of having four pretty daughters. At seventy-three he was still going to work every day. He came from the old school of business, where you work long hours, and you work hard. That was how you made a comfortable living.

Thinking back, I realize Sid was able to survive with such an outdated system of operation because of his great location. The store was on a beautiful main street that shut down on weekends, allowing only pedestrian traffic. It was right next door to a municipal parking lot, where the ladies could park for a quarter, stand at the front of the store, get what they needed, and get back to their car before they roasted in the Texas sun.

Working with any old-school retailer is like teaching a small child how to tie his shoelaces. You know how easy it is for you, but when you have to break it down, it becomes a significant process with questions each step of the way.

I finally persuaded Sid, at the very least, to clean up the store and give it a little bit of a facelift. But first, we needed to run a sale to get rid of the old merchandise. Sid had never run any type of sale. Not one. Ever. Instead, he would stash the clothes in storage for the next selling season. He had brands on the racks that had been out of business for at least twenty years. I cannot begin to tell you what a bad idea this is. If the customers didn't buy it the first time around, what makes you believe it would sell the next year? Think of fashion as a tomato. For a short moment in time that tomato is perfect. Not too green and not too ripe. But as it sits on the shelf, it starts to get old, mushy, and spotted. Maybe you could make soup with it, but eventually, you can't even give it away. Every day you keep a dog (the industry term for a bad style) on the floor it costs more money than just suffering the markdown and moving on. You could be using those dollars to buy styles that will sell out quickly. Five dollars in my hand will get me $10, then $20. But money stuck on a hanger gives me no cash flow and a boring store.

For this first-ever sale, I told Sid we were going to mark everything down at least fifty percent. He got very animated, of course, flailing his arms like an old Italian would do if a car racing down the street was too close to him. He yelled, "What, are you nuts?" Then he pulled a jacket dress set off the rack and said, "Look at this. What's wrong with it?" He started shaking it and showing off the details. It was such a dated style that the twenty-year cycle that trends take to come back into style was almost complete."It just hasn't met the right person yet!"

"Sid, this isn't Match.com," I said. "That suit is twenty years old. Do you know how many times you could have turned over those dollars instead of having them sit there?"

He brought up examples of other shops on the street that ran sales and still went out of business. I couldn't answer for those stores.

But I did know that sales are an essential part of retailing, and they needed to be given the proper attention to make them successful.

One of the biggest misconceptions about sales is that they cost the business money. Actually, it's the opposite. They create new money that can be invested for higher returns. And that's just one of the reasons to have a sale. Different types of sales serve different purposes. Ultimately, they're all about keeping the store fresh, building cash flow, and even bringing in a few new customers. This is something that old-school store owners hate, because sometimes those new customers come in only during a sale. But we need those bottom-feeding fish to keep the whole ecosystem alive and profitable.

Over the course of many weeks, I had somehow persuaded Sid to run the sale. Sara had taken a non-confrontational position, agreeing with me with a head nod, but never fully disagreeing with her father. This was passive-aggressive at its best. It was nothing short of a miracle that we all came to this agreement. But I had one more hurdle to overcome; I had to ask for $3,000 in advertising allowance to promote the sale. I knew he was going to go ballistic, but there was no other way around it.

There was no way to reach any of his loyal customers, because over the last forty years he had never taken a single mailing address, phone number, or email address (that's a joke, because he didn't even have a computer). Not one. I tiptoed around the situation.

"Sid, remember that woman who was in here the other day and mentioned that her sister got a job and needed new clothes? Do you have a number to call her about the sale?"

"No. She'll come in:, her sister lives out of town and comes only for the holidays." I was shaking my head.

"Sid, Maria, the lady who was looking for a dress for a shower; did she like what you picked out for her?"

"I don't know. She hasn't returned anything."

I finally asked, "Sid, don't you ever reach out or collect contact information so that you can call your customers?"

"What for? They know where to find me."

"Well, to tell them about the sale. Since we don't have their contact information, we are going to have to place ads in the paper, make some flyers, and print up some huge signs. I need around $2,000." It was more, but I wanted to break it into stages. I also wanted to do a radio ad.

"WHAT? You want me to spend money to lose money?" That was a classic Sid line.

THERE is so much bad, outdated advice in the market, like "be ready to lose money for the first three years." Who in his or her right mind would go into business to lose money? The IRS says it's okay to claim a loss for that amount of time, but that is not a business rule.

I'd been doing a retail checkup for a boutique that had been in business for just under a year. The owner was losing money every month and by the year's end would have shown a significant loss. I had pointed out a few things we could quickly correct. The biggest solutions were to drop some lines she loved and to run a big sale on the dead stock. Dead stock is merchandise that has been on the floor for more than six months.

But I didn't feel a sense of urgency from her. Actually, she seemed at peace with the fact that she was projected to lose money. When I asked, she said she wasn't worried, as she had two more years to make a profit. She wanted the store of her dreams but didn't want to start correcting things she deemed unnecessary. Those dreams quickly turn into nightmares. I have seen this same type of reaction from people who have taken out significant loans and used their life savings, to people who have trust funds.

I asked her, "What if the rule was six months to show a profit?" Her eyes opened wide. It's interesting to me how *you can change a person's perception so quickly, and with just a few words.*

Another self-defeating piece of business advice is the working-hard adage. I've seen motivational posts on Instagram like "Rise and Grind." That sounds so painful to me. My favorite quote to hate is "Entrepreneurs are willing to work 80 hours a week to avoid working 40 hours a week."

Look, starting a business is never an easy thing. But if it's painful, something is just not right. Yes, you have to dedicate the time to set the business up, but once it's running, you are the boss and not the employee. "Don't quit your day job" is my best advice. For example, I am writing this book, and because I am under a tight deadline, I write four hours a night, four nights a week, while keeping my day job and putting in thirty hours on the weekend to open a new store. Once the book is written and edited, it's done. Once the store is open, I am off the floor. As for my day job, I get to call the shots. I say whom I will work with and when I will work. I agree that it's better when you love what you do. But that other "good" advice—do what you love, and the money will follow—is a truly fucked-up piece of advice. The advice should be "do things you love that make money." It's all about perception.

Show Time

"Sid, you can run the sale, but if no one knows about it, what's the point? It's like having a party and not sending out invitations."

We placed ads in the local paper, printed up some postcards to hand out, and put signs in the window. Sara bought radio spots and coaxed Sid into doing an interview with the local morning talk shows. We spent a week red-tagging the store. Red-tagging is when you cross off the retail price and put the sales price in red. At one point while we were going through the tagging, I remember asking Sid if he was sure he didn't have any more clothing packed away downstairs or at home.

"No, no, no," he said, "Everything is on the floor." I had a hard time believing this and asked again.

"Sid," I said, stretching out his name so it sounded like it had more syllables. "Sssaaaeeeed, are you sure?"

Before I could finish, he cut me off. "I might have a few boxes in the garage, but they've been there a while, so I will just give them to charity." I was still not feeling confident in his story. Nonetheless, I let it go. We had a lot to get done, and the Sale of the Century (that's what I named it; I love dramatic sale names) was just a few days away. I had a flashback to another client who had forgotten about the clothing she had put away, get this, above the drop ceiling in the bathroom of the store. It seemed she had run out of space in her home and was now using every available inch in the shop.

It was the morning of the sale. I jumped out of bed, excited to go to battle. I had a feeling it was just going to be insane. I live for the chaotic samples sales we run in New York City, with well-heeled ladies in their panties trying on goods. I promise I'll tell you that story a little later.

Hundreds of people stood in line outside, just waiting for us to open the store. I am not joking about it being hundreds. The line stretched all the way down the street and around the corner! I was thrilled that I had been right. People had been waiting forever for this sale! This was going to be a complete sellout, I was sure. To make some extra room, we took a few of the rounders to put them outside for a sidewalk sale. We were limited to how many people we could fit in the store at a time. Sara's husband worked the door, ensuring no more than twenty Rubenesque women were in the store at a time.

The customers had all kinds of stories about Sid. One stands out specifically. A woman told me she had tried on the exact dress years ago but felt it was too expensive. Now she was going to buy it.

"How long ago was that?" I asked.

"About eight years ago." Oh dear, every dog has its day.

I noticed Sid at the other end of the room. I squinted to see what he was doing. He was cutting off the sales tags and trying to restore the original prices.

"Sid, what are you doing?" I was yelling as I pushed my way to the back through the women and the racks. "Don't worry lady, I am not trying to grab something from you; I am trying to get to the back." I'd said this more than once throughout the day. It had become a feeding frenzy! People were grabbing six or seven items at a time. They were not even looking at the size or price.

"If it doesn't fit me, it will fit someone I know," I heard someone say, justifying her aggressive grab to another woman.

"What the hell are you doing, Sid?"

"It's selling! Why are we giving it away?"

"Sid, it's selling because we are giving it away." I had to take the scissors away from him and give him a job.

"Sid, why don't you go outside and walk the line. Some of those ladies have been waiting for a couple of hours. Go talk to them and keep them entertained."

"Good idea, I'll tell them how I am going broke from this sale." I knew he was kidding. Old school would never let him say that business was terrible. It's a pride thing.

I start my fashion workshops with "Would you rather be rich or famous?" To the people who say famous, I tell them that many famous designers are broke. Instead, they should want to be the guy who sells underwear to everyone, from Walmart to Victoria's Secret. No one knows his name, but you know he lives in a huge house. In fact, that person is my mentor—excuse me—secret mentor, because he doesn't know that I idolize him. At the age of eighty-six, he still goes to work every day in his private helicopter. Ask him how business is, and he will always answer, "Could be better." Indeed.

I took a very short bathroom break, and when I got back, all the rounders that had been collapsed and put in the dressing rooms were back on the floor and fully stocked. We had been consolidating the racks to make room for more people to come inside. But now, like rabbits, the clothing was multiplying.

"What's the story?" I asked Sara. She said they had the same amount of inventory downstairs in the basement as in the store, and she wasn't counting what was in the garage at home. My blood was boiling!

If I'd had a clear understanding of how much inventory he really had, we could have planned a monthlong sale and not a four-day event. Why would Sid lie to me? I confronted him, but he wouldn't give me a straight answer. He tried to give me the "I'm an old man" routine. But this was a man who could remember every outfit and whom he'd sold it to for the past forty years! I understand now that people from his generation just don't share such business details, but you need to be honest with yourself about your business. Change is one of the hardest things for people, both in business and life. I remember reading an article in a business magazine about change. More than ninety-five percent of people who have had a heart attack do not stop smoking, change their diets, or exercise more. Even when their lives depend upon it, people find it hard to change.

Many retailers—major ones—have had to evolve over the years. The ones that don't, die. Look at what is happening today in retail. The giant pillars of the industry are crumbling like ancient Greek ruins. They all see the writing on the wall. Consumer experience, speed to market, and Omni-channel retailing are the future. Yet, they take a wait-and-see approach over analyzing market trends that are happening in the present. By the time they decide to chase it, the consumers are onto another trend.

We ended up extending the sale for a month, updating the signage and advertising with New Arrivals Every Day. This was tricky because the clothes were new to the sale, but some had been around for decades. With the money we earned, we were able to update the look of the store (including new plus-sized mannequins), buy new inventory, and add an accessories department.

Fast forward three years, and Sara has three locations and rarely works in the store, which drives Sid insane. She had implemented a POS (point of sale) system and security cameras that help her keep an eye on the stores without being there. I would get the occasional phone call from an irritated Sid complaining that Sara wasn't at any of the stores when he went for a visit.

"Oh Sid, that's the point." I'd tell him. She is working on growing her business and not working in her business. She is not the hamburger flipper. She is the boss. One of my most significant challenges is to get people to think like a boss. You can go to the best business schools in the world, and you are still taught to be upper management at best.

Just because you open a business doesn't make you an entrepreneur. Passion doesn't make you an entrepreneur. Having a plan to be a profitable, scalable business makes you an entrepreneur.

Sara did just that. She was running three profitable boutiques at a forty-eight percent maintained margin with a turnover of ten times a year. She ran one yearly Founder's Sale as an homage to her dad and had gross sales of over $4 million. None of this ever seemed to make Sid very happy, but on occasion he'd flash me a smile of pride. A national plus-size chain, which was in a very distressed situation, was looking for ways to freshen up a dusty business. They had heard of Sara's business through vendors who bragged about how much a little boutique chain would buy. The CEO and COO came to Texas to meet Sara and study her operations. Sara had significant concerns about the national chain copying what she was doing, and running her out of business. I assured her that it would never happen, since they didn't have the logistics to scale down to a boutique environment. The only thing they could do was to buy her out, and they did. Eighteen million in cash, with Sara staying on for three years as a consultant with a salary of $175,000 a year, plus a benefits package.

Sid would have been happy with that. I say would have been happy, because Sid passed away before Sara's deal was even on the table. My deepest sorrow is that Sid never saw the final deal made. I knew that Sid actually liked me only when he left his family cuckoo clock to me in his will. The note said that I understood the value of time over money.

BERGDORF BLONDE

It's Not a Hobby

It was Amber's husband who first called the office. From the start, he was very defensive toward his wife and all her business endeavors. She apparently had five different careers in the past four years. She was a stylist, an interior decorator, a party planner, a personal shopper, and an antiques dealer. Now she wanted to open a lingerie store. Her husband made it very clear that he was no longer in a position to bleed money. He came to us because this was a business that needed to be successful.

As part of our services, we offer a consultation to review concepts and the feasibility of an idea. In other words, we take a hard look at the client's concept and determine whether it's profitable or not. For our first meeting, Amber came to my office with a friend. I was taken aback. Who brings a friend with them to talk business? When it comes to business, you have no friends. They had just spent the weekend shopping in the city, and she looked like she'd just stepped out of a Ralph Lauren ad. She was a stunning Bergdorf blonde wearing a simple, giant diamond ring. She had a Cartier Love bracelet locked around her tanned wrist, a perfectly polished French manicure, and to top it all off, a Goyard tote as her catchall.

After a few minutes of forced and awkward small talk, we started with her concept. We spoke about the location—a conservative suburb of Washington, DC. We talked about the look of the store—something chic and sexy, yet cozy. We talked about the target market—young women between the ages of eighteen and twenty-eight. I don't understand why that is such a desirable target for so many retailers. Then we came to the topic of brands. I could have guessed it; she wanted to carry La Perla. If you're not familiar with the brand, it is designer lingerie; bras start at $250 and panties at $90. I asked her why she wanted La Perla, and she replied with the typical wrong answer: "Because all my friends and I love it."

"Are you opening a personal closet for you and your friends, or a business?" I asked. She didn't quite understand my question, so I answered it for her. "You're opening a high-end lingerie store in the most conservative part of town as a hangout for your friends and as your personal shopping closet. This is not a business — this would be a very expensive hobby." She was shocked that I had spoken to her so matter-of-factly. All of her friends had told her it was a fantastic idea. I explained that she was going into the business with the wrong mindset and that I couldn't work with her.

Let me explain something about this industry. You will have many successes and many failures, but the only thing that stays with you is your reputation. I will not take on a client I know won't be successful. I need to be able to sleep at night. After I told her I wouldn't work with her, Amber admitted that without our support her husband would not fund her new store. That's when the compromises began. She gave up the $20,000 crystal chandelier and the $8,000 gold-leaf mirror that she thought were crucial to having the perfect store. That was the easy part. I told her to add shapewear to the merchandising mix, and she looked at me like I had grown a second head. She asked me, "Who wears that?" I told her that everyone wore shapewear. "Well, my friends and I don't." I gave her a hard look. Yeah, she was right, she probably didn't, but the rest of the world did!

"We need to add some sleepwear," I added.

"So like, chemises and teddies?"

"No, I mean T-shirts and pajama pants."

She scoffed at me. "Who wears that—that's why they can't keep a husband!"

I tried to talk down in her language. "Honey, these are all first wives who have babies."

"Oh, right. Now I get it. I don't want them coming into my store. That's not my customer."

"It is your customer. You're opening in a conservative stroller town."

After a knockout, drag-down, virtual hair-pulling catfight, she threw in the towel. I won everything, except we had to buy La Perla. My plan was simple: we would buy as few La Perla pieces as the brand would let us get away with, and at the end of the season we would take a look at the numbers. I had a feeling these bras and panties weren't going to sell unless they were deeply discounted. We would move on once I proved my case.

Using Peter to Pay Perla

The store opened with much pageantry. If I had to guess, I'd say she spent more money on the opening than on the inventory of the store. Champagne flowed freely. Waiters scurried about with lobster canapes and caviar. Grand openings are one of my pet peeves. Who are they for? Your ego? I believe in soft openings. The rule is, the second you have electricity and a box of goods, you're in business. Amber's store opened three months late while she waited for everything to be perfect for the grand unveiling. If you are going to do any event for the opening, it should be three to four months into the business. That way you can invite those first few customers who have shopped in the store, and not just family and friends. When you open a store, you have a lot of different interests to balance—who you are, how you want to be perceived by your peers, and what the store needs—and it's hard to keep them in balance. I understand that it's human nature to worry about what your peers think of you and your business, but it shouldn't matter what you are selling. Whether it's peanut butter sandwiches or filet mignon, all that matters is that you run a profitable business. Then your friends can watch you laugh all the way to the bank.

The first season came and went. As I reviewed the numbers, my eyes went right to La Perla. It had twenty-five-percent sell-through at twenty percent off—in other words, her friends bought a quarter of the stock at a twenty-percent discount—fifty-five percent sell-through at seventy-five percent off—this from the end-of-season sale, and twenty percent were missing from inventory. That would be Amber stealing things from herself. Point proved, end of the story, no more La Perla. Not to mention the brand's minimum purchases were enormous: $10,000 each season. I went over the numbers with Amber and told her that the numbers didn't lie. We had to cut off La Perla.

She cried, saying that everybody was calling the store to find out if an advertised style was available in their size. Advertised style? I knew Amber didn't have a budget for that type of luxury advertising, so where was it coming from? Of course, my first thought was that Amber had secretly gone behind my back and made a desperate attempt to save the brand by advertising. It turned out that the brand itself nationally advertises by listing the names of stores that carry La Perla. Customers would see the ad and contact the store, and Amber would tell them if the item was available. If it was, the customer would come in, but after seeing the price of La Perla they would end up buying something less expensive. Without knowing it, Amber created a loss leader. La Perla served as a lure to create a higher perception of the store's unknown brands that she had a higher margin on. La Perla was bringing in customers and used very little space. After crunching some numbers, we took money from our advertising budget and used it to fill the loss from the markdowns. Ultimately, La Perla didn't hurt our bottom line because the money came from our advertising and marketing budget, not our Open to Buy. Amber got to keep her precious La Perla.

Don't Be Quick to Judge

One year later, I picked up the phone and Amber asked, "Can I be sued for discrimination?"

"What are you doing for this to even be a question?" I asked her back. Apparently, a man had called the store asking if he could make a private appointment after hours. He was very clear that he wanted to try on and purchase ladies' lingerie. I told Amber not to worry, and that this was a perfect opportunity to grow a niche market.

"This is how you handle it," I said. "Ask a girlfriend to come join you and give him his private space. Let him know up front that he cannot step out of the dressing room because you are not trained to give him an opinion on the fit."

There's a way to distinguish the fetish guys from the perverts. The perverts are creepy, want to expose themselves to you, and don't spend money. However, the fetish guys do spend money, and they have friends.

Fast forward to two years later, and Amber is running an incredibly successful business, including her extracurricular activities with her fetish fellas. She invested in a French red velvet curtain that goes up twice a year across the whole front window and the glass door. She hangs a gold-framed sign that reads "Closed for Private Party" and offers the gentlemen single-barrel aged whiskey and macaroons. She had to sign a non-disclosure agreement and shut off the cameras, because no one should know that our judges, senators, and congressmen are walking around in ladies' lingerie. It's at least a $20,000 night.

The best part is that they're the only ones who buy La Perla full price. The bestseller is a little lace trim silk slip that we buy in 2X. La Perla makes them special, just for us.

Who you are and what you like has nothing to do with your business. Your store exists to fill a need, and it never pays to judge another's lifestyle or taste.

In Amber's case, many things changed during the first few years she has been open. The original target market she had in mind was young, affluent, and dating. It turns out her base consumers are middle-class, thirty-five-to-fifty-five-year-old divorcées back in the dating game and looking for much-younger men. Amber's consumers were married before internet matchmaking and Brazilian waxing. They are looking for sexy, flattering lingerie that can offer some shaping, support, and comfort. I remember when Amber told me she would die if she had to offer shapewear, and now it is her bestselling item. Amber now hosts lectures by sex educators and divorcée parties complete with a cake topped with a miniature groom hanging from the gallows.

Your store is always a work in progress. Think of how many retailers have changed their original concepts. Barney's started as a men's discount store, Gap sold only Levi's jeans in their denim area, and Wet Seal was a diving shop. Amber, once just arm candy, is now a self-sufficient divorcée. Running a successful business, she feels a sense of satisfaction from helping women take charge of their own destinies and gain confidence.

THE EXPRESS LANE

$\mathcal{I}$ started working in Russia just a few years after communism fell. Retail was shockingly rudimentary. Goods were sold mostly in open-air markets out of the back of containers. It reminded me of the idiom: "In the land of the blind, the one-eyed man is king." I was the queen.

I met the Russian, as we affectionately referred to him in the office, at MAGIC. Dmitri (his real name) patiently waited after the workshop I had just given, while the crowd approached with their questions. He was a tall, lanky man with a severe, mysterious look about him. He brought Boris, a small, round man with a bright red nose, as an interpreter, who didn't speak to me until he was instructed to. Boris began by explaining that his boss was a wealthy and successful businessman who wanted his company to become the Gap of Russia.

As a genuinely jaded New Yorker, I have found that when people brag about how great they are, they usually are not. "Sure," I thought, "Who wouldn't want to be the Gap of Russia?" However, I did like the idea that he wasn't trying to make anything from scratch. When you find a niche that works, the idea is to make it better. No need to reinvent the wheel. Starbucks, for example, didn't invent the café or drinking coffee. They merely took drinking coffee to the next level by making it more social. Starbucks realized that people needed to be in one of three places: home, work/school, and somewhere else—and that somewhere else was going to be Starbucks. Pretty brilliant thinking, right?

Dmitri and his interpreter spoke in rapid-fire Russian, and each time Dmitri said something to Boris, he pulled his jacket collar up over his mouth like he had a microphone in it. I started to get a creepy feeling about them. It was getting really weird. Were they some type of corporate spies? That wasn't unheard of in the world of fashion.

Only later did I learn the reason for the sinister-looking jacket behavior. Dmitri had been involved in the black market during communism and spent ten years in prison. It wasn't until the Soviet Union fell that he was released. It's my understanding that to survive in a Russian prison for ten years while supporting your family, you had to be some type of Super Kingpin. He covered his mouth while speaking as a precaution against someone reading his lips. Once I had gotten to know him, I asked him why he went into the denim business. He said it was the most American, capitalistic thing he could imagine. His black-market business had been built on selling Levi's jeans.

A couple of emails and a wire transfer later, I found myself on a flight to Moscow. Except for a few east Asians and four or five American women, the passengers were all Russian. It didn't take long for a flight attendant to ask me if I was adopting a Russian child. I answered no, but perhaps too quickly, because I soon learned that Dmitri was the biggest baby of them all. He was short tempered, chauvinistic, and rumored to strike anyone who dared to disagree with him. It would have been helpful if Boris had given me a heads up before I had my sit-down with Dmitri and his international staff of yes-men several days later. Boris was also a yes-man, and the worst of them all.

I spent my first two days in Russia visiting Dmitri's stores and learning about the business. I visited his factories and learned about his supply chain. We traveled by car through some of the poorest neighborhoods in Moscow, but they didn't seem poor to me, with their brick houses and everyone looking chic in their fur coats and hats. The covering of February snow made everything look crisp and pristine.

Dmitri's empire was actually quite impressive. It wasn't all smoke and mirrors. He had a $90 million business and ninety percent brand recognition, but Mango and Zara had just opened several doors. The international competition was moving in and offering clean, modern stores with well-trained staffs. Dmitri understood that this kind of retail in Russia was the next big thing. Meanwhile, he was still selling from container stores in the open-air markets.

At a container store (not the Container Store) a person would stand in the front of the open container and shout out what they were selling to people passing by. "I've got jeans, I've got T-shirts, I've got potatoes!" You get the idea. The stock was kept in the back of the container and was separated by a wall of boxes. It was hard work standing all day in the cold, and it wasn't much easier for the consumer, since there was no fitting room or return policy. People were accustomed to shopping this way, yet with the opening of the new malls, they were starting to demand more. This was why Dmitri hired me; he needed to modernize his operations.

A Ship of Fools

On the third day we had a group meeting. I walked into a cold, sterile, old military uniform factory. I felt like I was in a bomb shelter bred with a Gothic cathedral. Dmitri's chair was regal and threatening; it looked like it belonged in a Russian Orthodox Church, not in a conference room. Dmitri sat down and shot me a "What the heck are you doing sitting there?" look. Mistake no. 1: I had chosen a seat next to the head of the table. That chair was for someone much more important than I, a mere woman. I channeled my inner Rosa Parks and held my ground.

There was a Dutchman who handled Dmitri's operations. He sat to the right of Dmitri and across from me. To the left of me was a German who handled logistics, and next to him was an Australian, who handled sales. Dmitri's bookkeeper and an assistant rounded out the group at the far end of the table. I genuinely felt sorry for everyone. There wasn't a fun, friendly air of team spirit. In fact, everyone seemed a little sad and beatdown.

"So, Mercedes," Dmitri began, "What are your first impressions of our organization?" He spoke via Boris, who stood behind him. I first complimented him on how vast and fast growing the business was, considering he had established it just a few years ago. I told him that I was impressed by the whole business and its future potential. That seemed to please him. The group breathed a collective sigh of relief.

Then I started with my checklist of everything that needed to change. "The first thing you need to do is change the windows of your stores. They are too tiny and have bars covering them." I noticed that Dmitri wasn't speaking behind his collar anymore, and Boris stopped interpreting what I was saying to him.

Boris, interpreting for Dmitri, said, "That's stupid. If people can see everything inside the store, they won't go inside to shop."

"Wrong," I corrected. "That's what makes people want to come inside. You have to have interesting visuals that draw them in. There are people called visual merchandisers who do only this type of work." I assumed Dmitri asked Boris to clarify what I just said, because it might have seemed unbelievable to him. Everyone at the table tensed up.

Dmitri shot straight up, slammed both hands on the table, and began to yell at me in almost perfect English. "Did you just say I was wrong? How dare you even consider I am wrong when you have been here three days? Already you are insulting me with a list of everything that is wrong! I had an important English company study my business for six months, and they never said one word about the windows."

"Well, Dmitri, what can I say? I must be smarter and faster than the Brits."

When I started my consulting company, my husband told me there were two types of consultants: people who don't have jobs, and people who steal your watch and then tell you what time it is. I am neither. I like to get right to the point. Problem, solution.

I thought I was being pretty clever, but Dmitri, catching on to my sarcasm, thought otherwise and slammed his fist on the table. Oh, no, that was mistake no. 2. For the first time, I felt a little afraid of the guy. He turned bright red and a vein in his forehead started to throb. I looked around the table to see if I was going to get a little backup, but everyone else was looking down, desperate to avoid eye contact with me. Then I thought, "What am I afraid of?" I needed to take control of this conversation. I was right, and there I was, in his best interest. If he wanted me to be another yes-man, it would cost him double. I explained to him that I was on his side, and that we needed to follow the retail examples of the United States if we wanted to beat the European chains that were on the move to take over. That seemed to calm him down. Now, we had a common enemy.

Dmitri composed himself as best he could and condescendingly gestured for me to continue. Picking my words very carefully now, I turned to the German logistics guy and asked him about the pricing of their jeans. I had found the same products in every store, but the price point was different from one town to the next. The German explained that this was a matter of shipping costs. Since the cost to ship to each location was different, it was necessary for each store to price the product accordingly.

"Well, I disagree with that system of pricing," I said. "People travel, and if a person sees that a price is lower in another town, they will stop shopping in their local store." I went on to explain that soon people would be able to look up the lowest price on the World Wide Web—that got a condescending chuckle from the group. The air was getting thicker and much harder to breathe, and I wasn't making any friends. Dmitri seemed intrigued, though, so I continued.

"The idea is this," I explained to the German logistics guy. "You have to average the cost of freight and add it back to the jeans. Otherwise, you'll have one store cannibalizing another."

Since I was now reprimanding the German instead of insulting him, Dmitri seemed pleased, and turned to me and said, "That is a very good point . . . "—wait for it—"for a woman."

"Ugh," I thought, "Don't roll your eyes. Did he really say that?" I put on my most serious face and continued with my observations, always making sure to direct the problem to one of the overpaid yes-men and not directly to Dmitri.

That night, I had dinner with Dmitri, Boris, and a woman named Ana, who was educated in the United States and did marketing for the company. She was my roommate at the corporate apartment, because she lived in St. Petersburg, and had come to Moscow for the meeting, acting as my tour guide on the store visits. Dmitri was showing off his American consultant while toasting with bottle after bottle of high-octane vodka.

He had invited some friends to the dinner. One of them was the owner of a high-end supermarket chain. The man was pleased that I knew of his stores; I had shopped in them with Ana to get some things for the apartment. Then he asked me what I thought of them. I hesitated, since he wasn't my client, and I was there on Dmitri's dime. Reluctantly, I offered one small observation, "Have you thought about adding express lanes?" I asked. "I think you should have at least two of them for every store. The line to check out was over thirty-five minutes long."

He turned to Dmitri. "What, is she joking with me? This stupid girl wants me to reward the people who buy little at my markets and punish the ones who buy a full shopping cart?"

Dmitri put his hand on the man's shoulder and said in perfect English, so I could understand, "For every three stupid things she says, one could be a good point."

I rolled my eyes, and this time I didn't give a shit that they saw me. Ana caught me and said in a whisper, "Don't roll your eyes. In our country, it's the same thing as giving someone the finger."

"But I am giving him the finger," I told her. I calmly tried to explain that if people did not have to wait so long when they came in to his markets, they would come back more often. At the end of the week, they would probably have spent as much, or more, than the person with one full shopping cart. The putz just waved his hand in front of my face. His loss.

Bumper Cars

Fast forward six months: I had returned to Russia to see the progress of a new mall store Dmitri was building. I was pleasantly surprised to find that all my suggestions, including big, bright windows and hiring a team of visual merchandisers, had been implemented. I was excited to see the mall store, but my heart sank when I arrived. It was a big, beautiful storefront without one single sign with the company's name on it!

When I asked Dmitri about this, he proudly said, "With ninety percent brand recognition, who needs to spend any money on a sign?" "Oh, lord," I thought to myself. I couldn't help it. But that was Russia. So much potential for growth and innovation, but so hard to get them to change.

While I was there, I also visited his friend's supermarket location. I wasn't surprised to see that he now had two express lanes. I should have sent that rat bastard an invoice.

What were the odds of getting another client in Russia, especially in the remote corner of Siberia? The gig was in the third-largest city, called Novosibirsk, to work with a mall developer. We had met at the opening of Dmitri's mall store. The mall developer had invited me to give a workshop at a shopping center. I was invited to speak in February, of course. It's not only cold there, it's fucking COLD. Like, minus twenty degrees . . . is the warm day.

I cannot even begin to explain how typical it is for them to be that COLD. It's just life. There are no snow days. The strangest thing I discovered was that there are no weather or traffic reports on the morning news. I asked my liaison, Nina, to explain. She said in a very typical are-you-kidding-me tone, "Because the traffic is always bad, and it's always cold." Point well taken.

I love the way people adapt to their situations. The cars all have bumper guards, and not like the ones you might see in NYC with just a rubber mat to protect the back bumper. No, these wrapped all the way around the car, more like the bumper cars you see at a carnival. Cars just slip and slide all the way to work. I found myself using the ever-so-popular imaginary passenger side brake several times on our way to the mall. Nina would start to brake way before we would need to stop, and the car would just glide down the road in slow motion. I would be bracing myself for the unavoidable impact with the car in front of us and the argument that would follow. To my surprise, they would greet each other in a friendly manner and make a gesture that I could only assume meant "oh, well." It happened several times on the short ride to the mall. As we drove along, we passed mothers with sled strollers—yes, imagine a regular stroller but with rails instead of wheels—and a group of Nenets, the nomadic indigenous people, who were riding in their reindeer sleds.

We parked at the mall employee parking lot and plugged in the car. No, this was not a hybrid. This was way before the electric vehicle. If we didn't plug into the electrical socket, we ran the risk of the car's oil freezing. It felt like getting to the mall was like crossing the Siberian tundra. Oh wait, we really did cross the tundra. I don't know how the hell Nina could talk and walk. Each time I tried to whimper out a word, I immediately felt the cold air rushing into my lungs, shrinking them to the point where it was hard to breathe . . . forget about speaking. Of course, Nina thought all of this was funny. She pranced in her high-heel boots like a graceful ballerina while I trolled behind her.

I wondered if I could get her to pick me up at the front door when we were done that day, or maybe I could just stay overnight at the mall . . .

"Why was I warm all of the sudden?" I thought. "Did I pee my pants? I can't feel my feet . . . am I going to lose a toe? Take the pinky toe, but not my big toe . . . I hope these aren't my last thoughts . . ."

I had made it. I had expected some type of warm rush of air to return my body back to a normal human temperature, just like in the States when you walk into the mall and immediately complain about the heat. That wasn't going to happen here.

The workshop was about how to compete with international retailers with just a little adjusting. Even back in the States, so many retailers complain that business is bad because of online sales. They blame Walmart and Amazon. They blame the weather. But they never take action on the open niches that are made possible because of these large retailers. Business isn't bad; they are merely an outdated business.

After the workshop, a mall developer asked me if I would do a case study with one of the stores. They suggested a footwear retailer with stores in their other malls, because the developer didn't want them to go out of business.

I should stop here and mention how insightful this mall developer was. Back in the States, so many malls don't support or even want independent retailers in their centers. The malls all end up looking the same, hurting their businesses.

Yes, I did survive the walk back to the car, and I am telling you, I am a winter person. I ski, I had on the right super performance clothing, but I just didn't have the right attitude. I was fighting the cold and not embracing it. It's all about the mindset.

The meeting was quick, and the goal for the day was to see how she ran her operations and how her competition stacked up. The stores were tiny for the number of shoes they had on display, and it turned out that the same style of shoe was displayed in many different areas of the store. It just looked overcrowded and confusing; there was hardly any place to sit, and the store didn't have a stockroom. The workers had to run down the hall and a flight of stairs to get to the stockroom. This took about eighteen minutes, and they weren't even trained to bring additional styles, or even sizes. Taking a walk down to Zara, Sketchers, and Rockport, I noticed that they offered ample sitting areas, engaging visual displays, and quick turnaround times. What they did not provide was customer service, and they didn't have an understanding of Russian fashion. Did I mention they wear high-heel boots in the snow? They were more expensive than the local brands, yet they were selling more. We found our niche.

Meeting with the store owner the following day, I proposed the concept of stack and rack. We take all of the stock and stack them up on each other by size, leaving one open box on top so the customer can see the styles. When I asked her why she had so many of the same styles in different parts of the store, she said that people didn't like to shop in half-empty stores. There were a lot of profound psychological reasons why this could be true. It might remind them of the days of rationing clothing and footwear, and of half-empty government-run stores. To see a full store is a sign of prosperity.

Since we were keeping the stock on the floor, it cut the waiting time to zero. We walked over to IKEA, the largest one in Russia, and bought some cute chairs to sit on while trying on shoes. Besides doing very basic training in sales and service, we also added the service of measuring a person's shoe size. The store quickly increased sales, and since they didn't need as many runners to get the stock, they were able to pay a better salary and have a smaller, better-trained staff. One person commented that she had been wearing the wrong size shoe since she was in the military. The military had mismeasured her, and who was she to argue with the government? She had been wearing one full size too small. She thought it was normal for everyone's feet to hurt.

The Gift

The government took note of my excellent work and asked me if I could help the Nenets open some type of commerce. They explained that Novosibirsk was a boomtown because of its natural-gas resources. The Nenets are nomadic people who move their reindeer herds for summer and winter grazing. They are also very skilled artisans when it comes to making embroidered reindeer-skin boots and clothing. One of their concerns was that many Nenets were being killed every day on the dark superhighways because they were driving in unlit sleds. Also, much of the land they previously used as migration paths is now privately owned and closed off to them.

Their future as a group of indigenous people was grim if they didn't plant roots in one location. Taking all of this to heart, I knew I could make a marketplace for their goods. It would be the best example of fair trade, since I would teach them how to get it to market themselves. I had grand illusions of opening direct-to-consumer retail locations in the newly developed airports. I, for one, would totally buy hand-embroidered, fur-trimmed hats.

I was astonished by how short a distance beyond the city the Nenet camp was set. The landscape was vast and empty. It was barren, blank, and just bleak. I wondered how anyone could live there. Once I got to the camp, I started seeing the beauty in the vastness. The color of the sky, with its endless horizon, turned the color of the snow a silvery blue. The tents were lined with intricate stitching. The fur trims were warm and inviting. There was an odd placement of an IKEA plastic chair in the center with a fur throw over it. This is where I was invited to sit.

I was also surprised that the tribal leaders were twin sisters. I love that—the hand that rocks the cradle runs the world. I had learned over the years that it was always a nice gesture to bring a gift. I wasn't prepared to meet them, but I did have a large stash (don't ask me why) of M&Ms with me. I gave one of the packs to a young boy who seemed to be the oldest son, around ten years old. Never taking his eyes off me, and receiving a nod of approval from both leaders, he took one out, studied it, smelled it, and then popped it into his mouth with much hesitation. First came a look of surprise, then the crunch, and finally the look of joy. Everyone knows chocolate in one form or another, but that candy coating brings it to a whole other dimension! That look was worth everything in the world. He quickly shared the candy with the other children, and I gave him a few more packs. To this day, I couldn't tell whose children were whose and which ones were brothers and sisters. It was one tribe, one family.

I sat down with the sisters, who showed me all of the incredibly beautiful things they made. These pieces could have been a part of any Dolce & Gabbana, or maybe Valentino, or even Gucci collection. It was on point and on trend. I asked why so many pieces were covered with embroidered flowers (not seeing flowers anywhere), and they said they embroider flowers only to remind them of the spring when winter is upon them. Oh, my freakin' Jesus, Mary, and Joseph, I thought, are you kidding me? The US market would eat this story up.

We started a conversation about how difficult and dangerous nomadic life had been for them. "I believe you were told about my reason for meeting with you. I would love the opportunity to develop your collection and retail supply chain." I am sure the interpreter did a great job of translating that, because her answer to me was loud and clear.

"We are not a poor tribe. We have over five thousand heads of reindeer that provide us with milk, meat, and skins to make clothing and boots. We trade reindeer for dry goods and other products we might need. We don't trust the government to act in our best interests, because during Stalin's regime people were banished to Siberia to die. We thrived because we never depended on the government. By heritage and agreements, this land is ours to roam freely. We have no interest in settling down or being a tourist attraction. We are happy and free."

Isn't that what life is all about?

THE EMPEROR AND
HIS NEW BOOTS

$\mathcal{T}$he new owners of a well-known Spanish shoe brand with a hundred-year-old history had just signed a lease for a flagship store in NYC. I was to meet the owner at the bar in the W Hotel in Times Square. An industry friend of mine recommended us to do the hiring and sales training for him. After weeks of appointment switching and canceling, you know—his secretary telling me over and over that he was a very busy man, we made an appointment for noon. I was a few minutes early, so I took a seat, making sure I could see the front door and telling the hostess that I was waiting for a man named Raúl. Half an hour went by with no call and no email, so I called his secretary. It must have been ten o'clock p.m. in Madrid, but she picked up the phone.

"Oh, he's not there yet? He is staying at the hotel; I'll make sure he comes down." I figured my time wasn't of value to him. That is when you feel the truth in the saying "time is money." If I can't make my spa appointment, they still charge me for a visit. If I'm late, they deduct the time from my visit.

The bar at the W is always so chic, considering it's in the middle of Times Square chaos. The bar is my little haven for a pre-theater drink and interesting people-watching. It is the crossroads of the world. I love to guess where people are from, and, I admit, I like to play Guess the Hooker! They are dressing in Gucci now, not like what you would imagine a Times Square hooker would look like, in ripped fishnets and *Pretty Woman* red high-heel boots.

I could tell it was him when he entered from his typical European dress. Not much of a man, a little wiry, with a twitching eye that made him look like he was continually winking. In fact, he ended almost every sentence with a twitch/wink. We went through the polite formalities and I asked him how New York was treating him. He asked what my nationality was. Not such an odd question— in Latin culture, there is definitely a hierarchy. Don't ever call a Puerto Rican a Dominican, or a Mexican a Guatemalan. The Spanish, through genocide, often believe they are on top of the totem pole.

"My parents are Cuban," I anwered.

"You speak Spanish very well." Spanish, not *Castellano*, which is what they speak in Spain and considered the superior language.

"Well, that's because I grew up in New York City." That seemed to confuse him. If he was playing the I-am-better-than-you game, then I just won.

I knew nothing about his retail situation, and even our acquaintance didn't have many details. "So, Raúl, tell me about your store. I understand you are in the footwear business." He took great pride and his time telling me about the history of the company and his family. This man loved to hear himself speak and often repeated himself by saying the same thing in a different way. The founder, his great-grandfather and the original designer, had lived in Texas for many years in the late 1800s. He came, like many immigrants, looking for a better life. After years of working on a cattle ranch, he had fallen in love with the cowboy boot. When he returned to Spain, he started making American-style cowboy boots, replicating the mass collection he had compiled over the years. He hired only the *best* artisanal cobblers and used the *best* skins and leathers, which he got from the *best* tanneries, which he got from the *best* regions in Spain. Ay, I get it, I said to myself.

Raúl's generation felt it was time to return to the United States and promote the family's legacy here. The strong family heritage was critical to him. He was the new keeper of the brand, and strong family hertiage was critical to him.

"Where will the store be located?" I asked. Suddenly, he became as giddy as a schoolgirl after her first kiss.

"In Times Square," he announced. Jesus, Mary, and Joseph, that's a bad idea, I thought. My knee-jerk eye rolling betrayed my feeble attempt at composure.

"I know, isn't it amazing that we were able to negotiate such a great location?" he boasted. He was definitely not picking up the right vibe from me. In his mind, they had just commandeered the center of the retail universe, but I sat there with a look of dismay, hoping that I hadn't heard him right. He winked . . . maybe it was a joke.

"Where in Times Square?"

"Right in the center!" My God, Times Square is a monster. They call anything from 42nd Street to 48th Street Times Square.

The meeting quickly spiraled downhill from there. He was getting very defensive after any simple, fundamental question. He must have realized that I wasn't impressed, and this insulted him to his very core. He started throwing numbers at me.

"Three hundred thousand people cross my corner every day," he said. "The W Hotel is just across the street, and rooms start at $800 a night."

If you've ever been to Times Square, he would've been located across from the half-price ticket booth, right next to an Olive Garden.

"The investment banking offices of Morgan Stanley are right there on the opposite corner," he said, pointing out the door of the W bar. "This is the best location for retail, in the best city, in the best state, in the best country of the world!" He proclaimed this like the most patriotic New Yorker.

He wouldn't stop. I don't think he could stop. "We only have to sell twenty pairs of boots a day to make the numbers work!" That was a heck of a lot of $900 boots to sell in a day. I could see where that number came from. Three hundred thousand people a day crossed that corner, and let's say one percent could afford this price point. That's three thousand people, of which only one percent of them might like cowboy boots. That meant thirty people a day would have the possibility of buying his boots. That's ten more than his projections.

But numbers lie. I was so floored I didn't even know where to start, and I was stuttering! I never stutter! I tried to talk and collect my thoughts at the same time, because I could sense that he was already blowing me off. I hadn't even started my full-on spiel on demographics!

"Times Square is not a shopping destination, and it's most definitely not a luxury shopping destination. Tourists are overwhelmed by all the stimulus. They are sightseeing, going to the theater, or to dinner. Shopping isn't on the Times Square agenda."

"Not true," he said. "I have hired the best people from around the world on this—the best consultant to find me this perfect location, the best architects to design the store, the best construction crew to build the custom fixtures. Who are you to tell me this is a bad location?"

Now we were in a pissing fight. "I'm the best," I said mockingly (he loved the word *best*). That was my attempt at breaking the tension with humor. It didn't work. Well, at least I thought it was funny.

I hate having to spell out my accomplishments. When you are

hiring someone, shouldn't you have already done a "background check" on them? To loosely quote Sun Tzu, "Know your enemy." Right then, I could have said anything with a convincing tone, and I felt like he would have bought it. Maybe a little name dropping, too. "I have worked for Lucchese, opening their flagship store in New York," I could've said. I didn't, and they don't have one. I don't think that would have mattered, but I tried with facts.

"I'm a native New Yorker who grew up in the retail business with a degree in economics. I sit on the board of fashion and merchandising departments in two universities. I have opened more stores, including my own, than you have opened fancy cans of Spanish olives, but most importantly, I have had to close hundreds of retailers that came to us in a distressed situation all because of poor location. So, I might know a thing or two about opening a store in this location."

"Give me fifteen minutes," I then demanded, "and I will prove to you that this location is not only a bad idea, but it's possibly the worst location in all of New York City."

We took a short, awkward walk to the storefront. Why do tourists insist on standing in the street while waiting for the light to change, and then not move when it does?

"Let's stand right here in front of the store and count shopping bags." The simplest and easiest way to see if there is shopping or pedestrian traffic is to stand in front of the store and count shopping bags as people go by. Ten minutes passed. Silence. Twenty minutes passed. He was wringing his hands, but still not a word. Half an hour passed.

"Raúl, do you see my point?" I was shouting over the noise, but really I wanted to wake him up.

"That you have so many ugly tourists?" he said, trying to avoid the subject. He understood my point. He knew I was right, but he was in too deep to admit it to me, and maybe even himself.

"No," I said, pointing out the shopping bags. The only bags that went past us were from the M&M store. God bless that M&M store. They sell a heck of a lot of M&Ms in there. And it's not like you can't find them in any corner bodega, but at the M&M store, they give you a full frontal retail experience that a bodega just can't. The only other bags we saw in that half hour were I LOVE NY plastic bags holding I LOVE NY T-shirts that sell two for $10.

Shopping traffic is very specific. This is why so many malls have become entertainment malls. People go to see a movie, eat at the food court, and go home. The new mall strategy of upgrading the dining experience is not going to help the retailers. It's just putting lipstick on a pig. It's still just a shopping mall.

He couldn't be convinced. Still adamant and arrogant, he told me, "Well, we never counted on the tourist trade. We are targeting the eight million New Yorkers with their two billion in disposable income." More stupid demographics.

I was seriously cracking up. Not an "lol," a full-on belly laugh that I was thoroughly enjoying. Tears-running-down-your-face type of laughter. "This guy has his head up his ass," I could hear Manolo saying from the great beyond. He was completely delusional. I wondered where he was getting this.

"Where is your best location consultant from?" I asked. He knew I was mocking him, but at that point, I didn't care! Let him hang himself with his own rope. I was trying to help him, and I was doing it for free!

"Boston," he answered.

"Yep, that's what I thought. Any New Yorker would tell you they would rather have a root canal than go shopping in Times Square. On the rare occasion that we must even go near it, like going to the theater, we know every side street to avoid this particular corner." I could tell he was trying to take it in. I had just bitch-slapped him verbally. Maybe he was trying to compare Puerta del Sol in Madrid to Times Square. It does, in fact, resemble it, in that it's full of tourists looking for bargains.

I will note that since Raúl's store opened in Times Square, it has become one of the most successful Forever 21 stores in the world. In its four floors that are open from 8 a.m. to 2 a.m., yes that's right, they generate $400,000 a day in sales. Yes, that is also right. The store doors take up almost a whole New York City block. It's bright and engaging. Trends are prominently displayed on multicultural mannequins. It feels like there is a party going on and everyone is invited! Walking past it, I have found myself accidentally sucked into the store, and before I know it, I am on the fourth floor shopping, when my sole intention that day was to quickly and without incident get to my destination. Brilliant merchants, they are indeed. Go across the street to American Eagle, and you can hear the crickets chirping in the store.

"Call me after the build-out," I said as we parted ways. Kind of like when you go on a blind date with a dud, wondering what the heck your friend was thinking, but hoping there might be some correction, and today was just a bad day. "I'll call you!" He wasn't going to call me unless it was to gloat about the store. And we both knew that wasn't going to happen. I was OK with letting the project go. He would never make it in that location. If I had done the sales training, he was the type of person who would've blamed me for the store's failure. Maybe I didn't get it because the person who recommended me didn't say I was the best.

Then the emails started coming in. He was so adamant that he was right and I was wrong that he forwarded me emails he was receiving from other retailers and friends. The first one was from the Stetson Hat company. "You are the Rolls Royce of Cowboy Boots." Nice compliment, I thought, if only it helped to pay the $100,000-per-month rent. No joke—the rent was $100,000, not counting the $30,000 billboard the landlord persuaded him to take after the first month in business. Then there were emails from Camper and TOUS, fellow Spanish retailers, congratulating Raúl on the opening of the new store, and on the quote "great location!" Let it be noted that Camper and TOUS have their stores in SoHo, a popular trendy shopping area, and not in Times Square.

Remember Raúl's team of the best industry professionals? They oversold him, cheated him, and ripped him off. The architects? Well, they were not retail architects; they were home architects with some restaurant experience. They had failed to design bathrooms into the space, and the store had an odd hostess podium in the front. "Hello, please wait to be seated, your shoe salesman will be right with you." No. The poor staff was stuck using the bathroom at the Jamba Juice next door.

Then there was the ongoing situation with the sprinkler system— they didn't follow the New York City fire codes, since they were the best architects . . . from Spain. Raúl had to hire a fire marshal to sit in the store at $100 an hour if he wanted to open the store. The store had only a temporary certificate of occupancy, pending the sprinkler system. He owed the architects the balance of their fees, but a colossal battle formed over what he should pay for, and what they should have done. I guess bathrooms were extra and the sprinkler system wasn't in the agreement, because the architects never finished the rendering for the bathrooms or filed for the sprinkler permits.

Meanwhile, his business consultant advised him on an insurance policy that covered up to $1 million—of jewelry and furs, that is. Typical coverage for a store like his was around $8,000. It cost him

$30,000 a year.

It sounds like Raúl was a stupid man. Perhaps you could have sold him the Brooklyn Bridge. But he wasn't stupid, actually. He was paying top dollar for the best advice. You know the adage "you get what you pay for"? It's all bullshit. He thought he was paying for experts in their field. He had fallen for two classic pitfalls in business. One: he ran the business with his ego, not his pocket. Two: he had relied on big fees offered by bad consultants. He'd thought it must be good if it was expensive.

What he did was hire yes-men. This is a fear we all should have. Friends and family are the first ones to encourage us, and also the first ones to ask for a discount. They say nice things about your business idea mainly because they love you. This was the classic case of the emperor's new clothes, or in his case, new shoes. Everybody was blowing smoke up his ass. Side note: Did you know that this saying comes from an actual medical procedure from the 1700s to revive drowning victims? Now Raúl was the one that needed reviving from all the smoke.

How can people be prevented from hiring and surrounding themselves with yes-men? One: find the Negative Nellie or Chicken Little of your group. Two: be your own devil's advocate. Three: trust your own gut feeling. They all make valid points.

I Told You So

I was in Spain when I was referred to Raúl again, and now it was to fix his retail situation. "What comes around goes around," "what a small world," and "I don't believe in coincidences," were all clichés that popped into my head.

Our paths had recently crossed once again. We had seen each other briefly on a flight we shared to Madrid just a few months ago. That's how I knew about the thirty-thousand-per-month billboard, a bargain the landlord had given him since the landlord personally loved the brand so much. True, that is a bargain for Times Square, since some billboards cost that much per day, but he failed to tell me why he got the good deal.

Business was horrible.

He was now a broken man, and I was now his confidante. He was humbled by all the problems the store was having, starting with its design, which didn't fit the image of the brand. It was too sleek and clean. He had hired an interior designer (not a floor planner) to update the place. She said it needed a mirror to reflect the outside walking traffic inside the store to fill it with the illusion of people shopping. Ay. So, $75,000 later, she hung eye-level mirrors that seemed to reflect only the cartoon-themed panhandlers into the store. They didn't have a single floor mirror for people to see what the shoes looked like on the customer's feet. I would have suggested elements of something rustic and personal. Maybe the original collection of his great-grandfather's boots on display.

The store had to open. They were bleeding money every day they didn't open. In the lease negotiations, they failed to ask for a free month's rent to build out the store and have a month of sales before they started paying rent. That is a very common lease agreement, considering he had put six month's deposit on the lease. Yes, that was $600,000 US.

The staff that was hired came from the Coalition for the Homeless and wasn't trained (nor looked the part) to sell boots that cost from $900 to over $5,000. Before you get your panties in a tangle, we are in the fashion business. In this case, the high-end fashion business. I am all about hiring people that need opportunity, but without proper training and grooming, they should have started in the stockroom or back office. I don't care what a shallow person you might think I am for saying this, but we all judge a book by its cover. Fire Marshall Tim was better at sales than anyone who had been hired. That was my first fix, and the easiest.

The daily goal of selling twenty pairs of shoes wasn't even a pipe dream; they were barely selling fifteen pairs a month. One of the reasons was that many of the high-end, exotic-skin boots were stuck in customs. Those had the wow factor, and it would've been easy to get some editorial on them, which would have been free PR. He didn't have the fish-and-wildlife license to get them out of customs, but we did, and all that took was a little switching of paperwork.

He was still paying a fire marshal to do nothing but sit in the store all day because the new sprinkler system was installed incorrectly and wasn't passing inspection. I was able to call the New York City inspection's office and get an expediter to procure the needed permits and hire a contractor to finish installing the sprinkler system correctly. I got all of that done, and I hadn't even left Spain, nor did I have an agreement with Raúl about the scope of the work and my fee. Since I knew what fires had to be put out immediately, I could do everything that was needed within a couple of weeks. We agreed on $15,000 to fix the situation. Just like a mob job, I was a different kind of hitman and took a $5,000 deposit on the project.

Back in New York, I met with him and his lawyers at their office. I had gone over the lease with a fine-tooth comb, trying to find any exit clause on his ten-year lease. His attorney turned out to be a divorce lawyer, recommended by a friend from Spain, who had married an American and won a large settlement in her divorce. How do you hire a divorce lawyer for a New York City lease? Leases are so complicated that just the scaffolding clause alone could be fifteen pages. You wouldn't go to a cardiologist if you had a brain tumor, would you?

After trying to find any loophole I could think of, I found that the lease was unbreakable. Who agreed to leases like this? The lawyer said that the landlord had told him it was a standard lease and it wasn't negotiable. So he didn't question it. I thought, of course you didn't, dumbass; you don't know a thing about commercial leases! It was so freaking frustrating! There is no such thing as a standard, non-negotiable lease! The only way out was to find someone to take it over, but considering that he was overpaying in rent, it wasn't going to be an option. I had spoken with the manager at the Jamba Juice next door to see if I could get any inside intel about the landlord and the building. The manager complained to me about how much rent he was paying. It was a third of what Raúl was spending, and their space was double in size. *Mother!!! F'er!!!*

As we were gearing up to meet with the landlord and his attorneys, I planned to ask for mercy. Raúl had rented the space in good faith. He was up to date with the rent. I would take a jab at their price gouging by mentioning that we couldn't even sublease the space since it was above market value. I was mentally on point to handle any of their objections and to break the lease in good faith.

Their legal team was massive and confrontational. There were maybe eight of them in total representing the landlord. They started by noting all of the code violations that were contingent to the lease, and how they were the nice guys by not enforcing the penalties that were in the rider. I never saw a copy of this rider. They went on to say that the insurance, which was mandatory, had lapsed and Raúl had five days to reinstate it, or they had the right to close the store while he would continue to pay rent.

I looked at Raúl. "The money was wired this morning from Spain; it will just take a few days." What else wasn't he telling me?

There was an uncomfortable pause after their list of unresolved issues. I guessed that this meant it was our turn to speak. I glanced over at Raúl's lawyer. I saw he wasn't capable of adding to the conversation.

"Gentlemen," I started, "thank you for your time this morning. As you know, this is my client's first attempt at opening and running a retail location in the United States, and the sales projections made by one of the top US consulting firms verified by your office have been significantly dissimilar." I was using all my fancy words, and I was trying to include the landlord in the blame.

"I believe that since Raúl brought my team and me onboard, and with some cooperation from you, we will be able to, in a short amount of time, run a profitable business. We will then continue to grow and use some of your other properties throughout the country." Emphasize the long-term vision.

"In just two weeks my team has overcome some significant challenges that have increased sales." I had poached a seasoned salesperson from a Madison Avenue footwear store, and she was killing it with calls from her client list. She was offering photos of the boots and free delivery so they could test them. Madison Avenue does not shop Times Square.

"Gentlemen, nothing can be established without your corporation. We are asking for a rent reduction equal to our neighboring tenant, and we would like a six-month grace period on the rent equal to the value you have on deposit."

One person stood up. "It's not that we don't want to see this excellent brand be successful and continue a long and mutually beneficial relationship, but unfortunately you have a signed non-negotiable lease."

"But."

"There are no buts. These are the terms of our agreement as signed by the owner and his legal counsel. At this late stage we cannot make any exceptions."

"Do you have any questions?" asked another of the attorneys.

"Yes, I do. How do you sleep at night knowing that you willfully deceived this man and gouged him with the rent cost?" I could feel my blood boiling. I could have shredded their $10,000 custom-made Brioni suits with my bare hands.

"It's called business, honey." With that, like a group of well-choreographed chorus boys, they stood up and left us in the room.

"Take all the time you need," said the last guy walking out the door.

As we were leaving the lawyer's office, Raúl's lawyer took me aside. "You know," he said, "I never did think that was such a good retail location." Were you fucking kidding me? Now he spoke up? I had an urge to grab him by the neck, but instead I made him tell Raúl what he had just told me. Raúl just shook his head, like it wasn't the first time he was told something after the fact.

Meanwhile, back at the ranch, things were getting worse. Raúl was running out of money, and he wasn't making payroll. The store had never been entirely completed, so it still had no bathrooms or storage.

But the sprinkler system was up and functioning. Amen.

We had received the first shipment of goods that had been held up in customs, by using our fish-and-wildlife permit. Double Amen. They were delivered to our offices, and what an extraordinary collection of exotic, handcrafted boots they were. They really could have been art-quality museum pieces.

My colleague wanted us to keep enough goods to cover the cost of our fees that had yet to be paid. It wouldn't have taken many boots to cover the cost, since some of them had a retail value of $5,000. Unfortunately, you can't pay the rent with boots, I told her. We were not some country doctor collecting our fees with chickens and eggs.

An aside on my colleague: I like to refer to her as the Oreo Ninja because she's quite the stealthy person and she really loves her Oreo cookies. She loves Oreo cookies so much that she had written a secret business plan, without consent, for the grand opening of a flagship Oreo cookie store in New York City. That might've been one of the few interesting retail situations for Times Square. She is the Yin to my Yang, the bad cop to the good cop, and we're constantly switching roles.

She insisted that he was never going to pay us. Not pay? We were the only ones to have done any worthwhile work for them. We had already put out a dozen fires. We had kept him from getting roasted, even with the fire department.

The next thing I knew, Raúl was having new cow print leather rugs made for the store. One of his designer buddies had convinced him that doing so would make the store look more rustic and authentic. Are you kidding me? He was rearranging the deck chairs on the Titanic! I had been begging for a tiny advertising budget, but instead he spent $8,000 on those ugly tripping hazards! I got it. He didn't want his friend to know that things were desperately bad, until there was no more question about it.

We took several dozen boots. I've never even worn a pair of cowboy boots, but I picked a pair made out of rattlesnake as a nod to my younger sourcing years. The Ninja had taken matching ostrich boots for herself and her husband. Even my husband got a pair, and he had not worn a pair of cowboy boots since his disco-dancing days in the '70s. We also took several pairs of boots to sell on eBay to compensate us for some of the money owed. Sadly, they did very well on eBay. I say sadly because if he had a better location, I believe the company would have done exceptionally well in the United States.

The mirrors, cowhide rugs, and his ego were all left behind when the store closed its doors eight months after it opened with the highest of hopes. Raúl was sued for the balance of the rent. The boots had to be reshipped back to Spain, which cost more than the goods themselves. Of course, he said he was sorry that he was not able to pay us. At least that's what he thought.

The number one reason stores go out of business is because of poor location. New retailers often pick the up-and-coming area or the little space around the corner, near the Main Street, upstairs, or even downstairs basement locations to save money. When we work with stores that have been around forever but are doing just about everything wrong, the common denominator is that they all have fantastic locations. Not suitable locations, but amazing ones. The money you think you are saving by not being in the right spot will be spent trying to get customers. You will spend money on advertising and by offering discounts. In Raúl's case it was different. He paid for what he didn't get. He paid top dollar for a poor location.

I was reminded of an old joke that I love to tell about the industry, and how getting the best advice from the best people sometimes doesn't work.

The joke goes like this:

A man receives a letter from the IRS. It's always very distressing, even though you know you haven't done anything wrong, to get a letter from the IRS. The first thing he does in the morning is run over to his accountant's office, sit down with him, and show him the letter.

The accountant looks at him calmly and says, "They're sending these to everybody these days. Don't worry about it too much. I'll go with you to the meeting. I'll present all your paperwork that is in one hundred percent good order and everything will be fine. But just in case, I want you to dress in a shabby suit. Go a little unshaven. Don't wear your good watch, and make sure you have a scruffy briefcase with you. I want them to see a poor, hardworking man when you walk in that office door."

The guy goes home, thinking about the advice the accountant has given him. It seems like pretty decent advice. It makes sense not to show off wealth while being audited by the IRS. But he still has this unsettling feeling about the whole situation.

He decides the next day to visit his lawyer. He explains to the lawyer that the IRS is auditing him. He is very nervous, but confident that the accountant has all the paperwork in order. He wanted his lawyer's opinion and advice about handling the situation.

The lawyer is outraged. "I'm tired of the IRS chasing down the small business owners. We should take them to court! We should sue the IRS! I'm going to go with you to this meeting. Here is what I want you to do. Go dressed as sharply as possible. Wear your Rolex watch, wear a Tom Ford suit, and make sure you have a custom-made attaché. We are going to show the IRS that you are a savvy businessman and they had better not mess with you."

Now the guy is downright hysterical. He has gotten two perfect pieces of advice, yet completely different. He talks to his wife about the situation, and she suggests that he call a neutral party. "Ask the rabbi. He'll know what to do." Now you know rabbis always have a good story to tell when it comes to conflicts.

The very next day he goes to see the rabbi and he says, "Rabbi, what am I going to do? I'm being audited by the IRS! My accountant wants me to show up as a hobo, and my lawyer wants me to show up like an industrialist. It seems like both opinions are very good ones, but I need to make a choice. Could you help me make a decision?"

The rabbi leans back in his chair and starts to stroke his beard, thinking out loud. "This reminds me of the story of the young bride. She was very nervous about her honeymoon night, so she asked her mother what should she wear on the first evening with her new husband. The mother turns to her and says, 'Child, you should look like your pure virgin self. You should wear long flannel pajamas with long sleeves, and a high neck. Then he will truly know who you are.' Not liking this advice, the young bride goes to her friend who has been married and divorced twice. 'Hey, what do you think I should wear on my honeymoon night?' 'Oh, honey, you need to make an excellent first impression. You need to wear spinning tassels and peekaboo panties so this guy will never wander or want to ever again.'"

Now the guy is completely freaked out. "Rabbi, what are you trying to tell me? What does this story have to do with my situation?"

"Son, it doesn't matter what you wear, at the end of the night you're still going to get fucked."

Raúl had been royally fucked.

NICKELS AND DIMES

$\mathcal{S}$ome of the work I do is training new store owners on how to buy. It's so much more than just picking out pretty things. To keep the flow of merchandise turning every month, there is a ton of math and systems that need to be learned. The best way to train someone is by having them go to market. So much of it is gut feelings and situations in which there are no dress rehearsals for. The math I can teach in a class, but to get the actual feel and skills of a buyer, you have to do it in real time, in a showroom or a trade show situation.

One of my favorite showrooms to visit during training is a children's showroom on 33rd Street in Manhattan. The Garment District in New York City is broken down not only by the geography of streets, but also by product. 1400 Broadway, where my uncle had his showroom, was known as the dress building. 1407 Broadway was the sports building, and 110 West 33rd Street was the children's building. There was a great sense of ownership by the brands to be in the right building, which is not so defined today, with tech companies moving into the dress buildings and hotels being built out of the factory loft buildings.

Before we go in, I tell my client that no matter what happens, just stay seated. It might get a little loud, but it's all going to work out. I have to say, I do have fun making them wonder what is going to happen next. The owners, two Hasidic Jewish brothers named Schlomo and Moshe, greet us at the door. No handshakes—their culture doesn't allow them to touch women. We sit, we catch up, and then Schlomo starts to hang pieces on the grid wall behind him. Moshe has more important business than to be a yenta all day, so he excuses himself and goes back to his office. His office is to the left of us and has a small two-way mirror where he can see everything that goes on in the showroom. We pick the styles we like, and the ones we don't, Schlomo puts away. Once we get the final picks together, I take out my order form and start to write up the order. He begins to quote me a price. Upon hearing the first number, I look up and put my pen down. I try to do this with a touch of drama.

"Schlomo, really?" I ask. Using the universal hand gesture of "come on," I say, "Is that the best you can do?" in a secretive, hushed tone.

He looks at the garment in his hand. "You know, Mercedes, this is all one hundred percent brushed cotton made in Peru. This isn't cheap Chinese shit."

"Schlomo, you know the customer doesn't care. They want price."

He takes the garment off the wall. "This isn't shit; this is worth ten times what I am asking you for." Placing it on the table, he demands that I feel the Peruvian cotton. "No one has this type of quality at this price. No one."

"Schlomo, don't get upset," I say. "I am trying to do my best for my new client. Can't you do anything for me?"

He takes the garment and throws it on the floor, then kicks it across the room. He is good at getting the sample all the way across the room. Years of practice.

"Are you saying my goods are shit?" he barks. "This is how you treat shit. Get out. I can't work with you. You are completely unreasonable." I start to gather my things.

As I'm walking to the door, his brother Moshe pops out. "Mercedes?" he says in a long whine. "Where are you going? Are we finished with business?"

"No, Moshe, your brother is throwing me out of the showroom because I am trying to do my job."

"That doesn't seem fair," he says. "Let me see what I can do." We walk back together; Moshe stands in front of the grid, talking to his brother in Hebrew. I can only imagine they're chatting about what to have for lunch. From here, Moshe takes over the sale.

"Mercedes, can I get you a cup of tea?"

"No Moshe, but thank you." I know that the cup of tea is the kiss of death in these negotiations. They give you something, and now you have to give something back.

"Mercedes? Tell me then, what you want to pay."

"I want to pay the right price."

He grins. "Mercedes, the right price for you may not be the right price for me."

I should have known better. I try again. "Moshe, give me the price that would be fair to both of us. My client is new, and we need all the mitzvahs we can get."

Moshe smiles again. He can appreciate my understanding of Jewish culture. "How's about half a dollar off the line price?" By saying "half a dollar," it makes it sound like more than just fifty cents.

"Thank you, Moshe, but that doesn't even buy a cup of coffee; I need a dollar."

"Then you should drink some tea." He is cracking himself up. "You're right, so meet me halfway. Seventy-five cents off. Deal?"

"Deal."

We get to work writing up the order, and seamlessly Schlomo is back working with us. No hard feelings. Regardless of whether I am with a client or not, Schlomo always makes me work to get my discount. At times I have come to the showroom alone and asked Schlomo, "Let's get right to the point. What's the best price?"

"What?" he says, shrugging his shoulders and raising his palms up in the air. "You think I waste your time? You think I enjoy this?"

Yes, I secretly think to myself.

"You, Mercedes, are very difficult to work with."

"Well, Schlomo, that might be true, but I am just doing my job."

We do our song-and-dance routine. Moshe joins in the chorus, and it's curtains.

I find that too many buyers want to win homecoming queen. They want all the vendors to like them, which is human nature. But the truth is, salespeople are not your friends; they are salespeople. I am not saying you shouldn't, or won't, have a friendly relationship with them, but this is work and not a popularity contest. I would much rather have you respect me than like me. I am sure the brothers think I am a super pain, but they respect me. In fact, when prospective clients ask for a reference for our buying services, I just tell them to go to a trade show and ask if any vendors have worked with my company or me. "If the vendor has anything nice to say about me," I tell them, "don't hire me." If they say something about how I'm nice and easy to work with, then I am not doing my job. Most likely they'll all say something about how bitchy I am and how I nickel-and-dime them to death. That's who you should hire.

I just want to point out that these gentlemen are some of the most generous people I have ever met. I have been in their showrooms on a Friday morning, when there must have been a hundred rabbis waiting in the reception for their turn to meet with Schlomo for a donation, or mitzvah, which means a good deed. Some of the rabbis have been known to lose their patience waiting their turn, since many of them travel from as far away as Pennsylvania to collect their mitzvah, and since it's Friday, they must get home before sundown.

On a given Friday, I have seen Schlomo write out hundreds of checks. I remember one time a rabbi asked for a double check. It seemed a young man was getting married and asked for some money to start his new life, and another man was ill with cancer.

Schlomo said, "No, pick one. The one that is going to die a long, tortured death, or the one that has cancer."

RICH OR FAMOUS

$\mathcal{T}$he email started with "I think it will be important to document our first meeting. You should have a camera crew, or at the very least a photographer. You will want to have this for when they do a Lifetime movie about me."

Oh dear, I thought. This was going to be a winner. I politely answered (must have been in a rare form that day), "Sure, and you can even bring a posse with you, if you like. I have time available this week, and I recommend the $250 feasibility consultation that is about two hours long. We should be able to come up with a clear plan of action during that time."

He answered, "There is a fee? You are going to make a lot of money with me! You should just sign on as my partner and financial advisor." Then he went on to insist that I had a notary sign off on a nondisclosure agreement.

As our virtual conversation went back and forth, I gently told him that before I made any financial agreements, we would have to have the first consultation. I wasn't signing any agreements, because honestly, I'd seen it all before. Fifteen emails later (I'm not joking), I finally put on a very short tone and hinted that I was getting tired of his bullshit, and he needed to pay up. While he understood about me not wanting to sign the agreement, he couldn't understand what would take two hours. Remember, I was going to fall in love with his work instantly. Why should he have to pay me $250 when all he needed was fifteen minutes of my time? He gladly offered to pay me $31.25 in cash. He did the math.

I wasn't going to waste any more of my time, so I answered, "I'm not interested. It's not the cost of my time, but the value of the information I offer, the years of experience, and the network I have built."

I thought that would be it, but one early morning, catching us all off guard, a thick cloud of cologne burst through the door, followed by the one and only Tyler himself. He made his way in, and with a flick of the wrist, he handed Lyn $250 and told her I was expecting him. This really pissed me off! How dare he think that the world stopped because he entered a room, or assume that the fee was still $250. I charge more if you're a pest or need me to sugarcoat things. But there he was. Truth be told, I did want to meet him and his massive balls.

He was strikingly handsome. The type of handsome that made you look twice and stare. He wore a vested suit with a bow tie and pocket square way before it was fashionable. At least he made an effort to dress well. He had a slight southern accent, with a Brooklyn "Fuhgeddaboudit" nasally tone. Yet there was something awkward about him. He calmly sat down without even looking around to familiarize himself with my office. There was no formal introduction.

He got right down to business, knowing he was on the clock. "I want to tell you something, Mercedes," he started, "I don't show my work to just anyone. In fact, I show it only to paying customers." Are you kidding me? I thought. I hoped he didn't think I was going to buy something. It didn't work that way.

Then he began his show with a very well-rehearsed pitch. "You have never seen anything like this," he said, waving his hands in the air like he was ready to do a magic trick. "It's so avant-garde, edgy, couture, and chic." All the adjectives that for a buyer translate to unsellable. Trust me, it's all been done before. The trick is to give the consumer something familiar, but new.

Now he was twirling a sample fabric in the air. "See how this glides and drapes like the wings of an angel? This is couture silk chamois; it's a very rare and expensive fabric." It's not.

"See the color and depth of hue as the light hits the fabric?" Seeming a little irritated, he continued, "These bleak office lights don't do it any justice. I personally mix the colors for each of my clients to make them look a fierce finger snap."

"Excuse me," I interrupted, "you personally mix the colors? Are you hand-dying the fabrics yourself?"

"Why, of course, every couture designer does," he said quite snobbishly while tossing his imaginary hair off his shoulder and wrinkling his nose at me.

"No, they don't," I said matter-of-factly.

"Can't you see I am the next Versace? The next Valentino? The next Roberto Cavalli?"

"OK, Roberto."

"My name is Tyler," he corrected.

"I know," I said dryly. "Show me some of your work."

"Well, you see, I am not a trained designer. I am more of an artist. I work abstractly and I have trained couture seamstresses to sew the garments for me."

"OK, enough with the damn couture business. Did you know," I asked, "that you can't even legally use the word *couture* without a certification from the Fédération Française de la Couture?" That seemed to hurt him. I toned it down. "The word you want to use is bespoke."

"Of course," he said. "I just use the word couture because Americans don't know what bespoke means."

Eye roll. Put a fake gun to my head and pull the trigger. "OK, honey, I got you; let's move on."

He opened up a giant portfolio that spanned my entire four-person desk. It barely fit. Then he pulled out the first sketch. It was done on tracing paper. You could see the rub lines where he copied the sketch and added his own.

"Déjà vu," he said. I think he meant to say *je ne sais quoi*, which translates to "I don't know what." In other words, he didn't know what the hell he was talking about.

"This can't be it," I said, unamused and underwhelmed. To his dismay, I asked to see all of the book. He tilted the book away from my view so I couldn't see the pages as he flipped through them.

"Oh no," I said firmly, standing up and standing behind him. "You brought this humongous book for me to see, and I want to see it all." I could barely contain myself. It was hilariously bad. I mean, it was ridiculously amateurish and reminded me of preschool drawings. There was no artistic value. There was no edgy point of view. It was horrible. He was right—all we needed was fifteen minutes, but I knew he couldn't take fifteen minutes of me being brutally honest.

I knew if he had gone to one of the many industry predators out there, they would've just blown smoke up his ass and milked him dry. Yes, I have been accused of being a dream killer, but I think I am someone who prevents dreams from becoming nightmares. I could see that I was hurting his feelings, and I hadn't even said anything yet. My God, I hate crybabies, but I had to endure this crybaby for a little while longer.

"Please tell me how you are producing your collection," I asked calmly. Surprised that I hadn't lost interest, he started up again.

"Well, I have only made a few dresses for friends of mine. They get so many compliments, and it's always been my dream, so I thought you could help me make it a business."

"OK," I said, "but how did you make the dresses for your friends?"

"First, I go to 37th Street to the wholesale fabric stores." They are not wholesale. I swear, people watch one episode of *Project Runway* and think they are designers that know everything about the business.

"Then I choose the color I want for the dress."

"Oh, so you are buying greige (pronounced "gray") goods?"

"No, they are white," he replied. Not the question I was asking, but I let him continue.

"You dye the fabric at home?"

"Yes, in my tub?"

"With Ritz dye?" I asked sarcastically.

"Yes, but the liquid one," he said smugly, implying he was using only the best. Stop for a moment and just picture how difficult that was. Imagine what a mess it is to hand dye anything, let alone six or seven yards of fabric.

"OK, that seems like a lot of work, but we can easily digitize your handmade sample and have it printed in China. Who is doing the pattern and sewing?" I asked.

"Well, I ask my friend to come over, and I do a fitting on her."

I corrected him, "You mean a draping?"

"Yes, of course, and I get usually a Chinese lady to come and pin it before she does the sewing."

"God bless those Chinese ladies; they really know what they are doing," I responded.

"Amen," he said. He was southern, I'd guessed it.

Now that it was finally getting interesting, I asked, "How and where do you find them?"

"It's a secret, but I'll tell you," he giggled, and you could tell he was so proud of himself. "I go to Chinatown, and I ask the guard at the community center to write me a note in Chinese for a patternmaker/seamstress. In a few hours, I usually get a call from someone's child who is translating for his or her mother or grandmother asking about the job." I had to hand it to him. That was pretty genius, and now I understood why the dresses were so simple—the deep V back, the one-shoulder drape back, and the long Grecian.

"How much does each dress cost to make?"

"Well, given that they're couture—"; he then hesitated and corrected himself, "I mean, made with luxury fabric, the dyeing" (which was just the cost of the dye, not valuing his time), "and the cut and sew, which I pay $12 an hour for—around $300."

"That seems like a reasonable price for a sample. Since we can digitize the print, buy the silk in rolls, or even switch to a Japanese poly and have a garment factory make them for around $30, you can have a very nice business. I mean, the designs are dumb" (an industry term for basics and not an insult), "but the depth of colors in your print, the ombre tones, and the dying is genius."

The colors were deep and contrasting. There were shades of peacock, sky, and robin's-egg blue intertwining into a colorful ménage à trois.

"Usually, in production, there is a standard for continuity, and this would have been considered a dyeing mistake, but in mass production, we can keep the beautiful artistic value by digitizing the print, making them competitive at a contemporary price point." I swear, I was trying to be complimentary by explaining all of this to him, and yet he was having a meltdown.

"This is not how you describe Oscar's (de la Renta) work or Carolina Herrera!"

"Well, Tyler, how much did you want to price your dresses for?"

"Well, at the very least $3,000!"

"Brahahaha, are you joking? No one is going to pay three thousand for a simple dress by Tyler from Brooklyn. For that price, they will buy an Oscar or Carolina. Do you want to be rich or famous? Because in this business, it's tough to be both."

So many designers are household names, yet they are in financial jeopardy any given day of the week. Even Michael Kors went through a bankruptcy. Here's a tip—become rich, and you'll become famous. Just ask Bill Gates or Mark Zuckerberg.

"But someone has to buy it!" he cried. "Everyone loves them!"

"Yes, when you make them for your friends for free. I seriously doubt anyone will buy them. Do you know there are only forty retailers in the whole country that buy dresses at this price point?"

He was dead serious about his $3,000 price point, and he was furious. He packed up in three seconds, called me a bitch several times, and warned me I would regret it. I thought that would be the end of Tyler. Then it happened.

Are You Kidding Me?

First, it was *Town and Country Magazine*. I saw a socialite wearing a simple dress, and the print reminded me of Tyler. No, it couldn't be. Ombre was in fashion. It was just a coincidence. Then *South Beach Magazine*: a short little number worn to the opening of the Bass Museum. Again, I dismissed it, but I thought about Tyler and how right on trend he would be with a few styles at $398 retail. Then the avalanche hit full stride. *Scottsdale, PaperCity Magazine* in Dallas, *New York Magazine*, *Vanity Fair*, the *Hollywood Reporter*. Those were just the ones I happened to catch. After a full year of watching his dresses worn by all the top American socialites, I saw it! He was in a photo next to the wife of an international cosmetic brand for the premiere of an Oscar-winning movie. Son of a bitch! How was he dressing the elite? Let's face it, Tyler from Brooklyn did not go to the right private school. He did not vacation in St. Bart's, nor did he live on the Upper East Side. How the hell was he meeting and dressing these women? I had only an old AOL email for him that no longer worked, and he never gave us a chance to collect his information after rushing out. This was irritating the shit out of me, keeping me up all night. How could I have been so wrong?

Lo and behold, we met at a CFDA (Council of Fashion Designers of America) cocktail mixer, which I had bought a ticket for. I mention this because it's not a cheap ticket to purchase, but it is THE fashion fundraiser of the season. He was at the far end of the room when we made eye contact. It was like a cheap Harlequin romance novel, except it wasn't love at first sight. It was the evil eye of death that he shot over at me.

I walked right up to him, not even saying hi to people I knew, and said, "Hello, Tyler, remember me?"

"Of course I do. You're the bitch that told me no one would ever buy any one of my incredibly fabulous dresses," he said a little too loudly, so everyone would hear.

"Yup, that would be me, but I'm here to congratulate you. You can't imagine how happy I am for you. I even have to say that I'm glad that you proved me wrong." We kissed.

"I have to thank you. If it wasn't for you, I don't think I would have had a fire lit under my ass to prove you wrong. You were my motivational muse."

"Well, thank you, I will take the credit for that." I was also speaking a little too loud. "Let's toast to success!" Picking up our drinks,

I leaned over and in a whisper asked, "How did you get to meet these ladies? No disrespect, but I am almost sure you are not from the same social circle."

"Oh, I can't give away all my trade secrets, but once you are in and they adore you, it's all word of mouth from there."

"Yes, but how did you get IN?" I was now asking in a strong voice.

"Oh, darling, a girl doesn't kiss and tell."

Oh, I thought, you ARE going to tell me, bitch. "Let's have another drink!" I'd been drinking from such a young age that it was basically a sport for me. There are two types of drunks: the sailor who wants to pick a bar fight with everyone, and the "I love you, man." Lucky for me, he was the second one. Just after that first drink and a sip of the next one, he was fully intoxicated. He started the story with his early childhood. His story was going to take some time, I could tell, but I was in it to win it.

"At the age of nine, I was sent to live with my grandmother because I was bullied in school for being a sissy, and it had gotten to the point where my mother was worried." He talked about how he hated Barbie's outfits and would make Bill Blass and Dior clothing for his cousin's dolls. Come on man, fast forward. "Grandma spoiled me. She told me my dresses were the most beautiful things ever and I was going to be fabulous. That I was perfect in every way and could do no wrong." Well, la-ti-da, that's where he got his ego.

Finally, we got to real time. He is a private male nurse at Lenox Hill Hospital—the number one hospital in the country for major plastic surgery. "When all of the society ladies go for plastic surgery, they don't stay at the hospital. They are sent home with a private nurse. Yes, you're looking at him. Yours truly. And when does one get major work done? On the eve of a big event, a significant birthday, anniversary, wedding, second wedding, third wedding, whatever it may be?" He had captured an audience.

"While they are all drugged up with draining tubes coming out of their necks, I would start a very polite conversation about the event and end with 'Do you really want something off the rack, or would you like me to design something for you?'" Fucking brilliant!!!

People often ask me what makes a great designer. Is it talent or money? The truth is, I have worked with both. Some are people with extraordinary talent, and some are Saudi princesses dripping in diamonds with Bulgari snakes around both wrists. Neither improves their chances of making it. Do you know what the common denominator is? Drive.

But not just any drive, the kind of drive that is painful, that causes you to lose friends and offers only a modest lifestyle. The type of drive that feels like you can't breathe until the moment you make it!

With dollar signs rolling in my eyes, a cash register ringing in my ears, and the taste of champagne and caviar, I began to hemorrhage with ideas for scaling!

"Tyler, do you realize what a gold mine you are sitting on? You have financial backing from these ladies, a signature look, and brand recognition. We will take your samples to China, dummy them down (again, this is a good thing), and let's talk to David's Bridal about doing a hundred-dollar prom dress rollout. We can put them in every store. This could be a million-dollar business!"

He looked at me like I was Medusa with a hundred venomous snakes coming out of my head.

"Are you insane? Don't you know I am living the life I always dreamed? I am invited to the best parties. I had dinner with Andre Leon Talley just before coming here. I was flown on a private jet last week to keep a client company whose husband had to work. The darlings find me charming. I am going to retire as a nurse in eight more years. I will have a full medical package and a pension. Plus, I sell about three dresses a month. I am set. I am happy. I am fabulous." End of discussion. He sashayed away.

He chose fame over fortune, and that is incomprehensible to me. You might argue that he is happy. But no one was ever sad laughing all the way to the bank. He was thinking small and didn't see how much more money he could have made.

Fast forward a few years later. Tyler and his cologne dropped by the office—déjà vu. It seemed just about everyone had a unique ombre dumb dress and his look had hit critical mass. Even H&M had a little summer number that retailed for $48. Now, he was ready to scale. But the market had left him behind.

I saw him recently at the memorial for Bill Cunningham. He had moved back to Atlanta to care for his ailing grandmother and had taken a nursing job at the care facility. I asked him if he was happy, and he said yes. He had lived the life he had always dreamed.

I wish he knew how much more life was left to live.

DOVETAIL

If my husband were to tell this story, he would say, "She started Dovetail because she had nothing better to do." After twenty-plus years of marriage, he has mastered my sarcasm.

At this point in my professional life, I had been working with clients on developing new brands for more than a decade. The failure rate for an emerging designer we preselected in our emerging designer program is ninety-eight percent. Some brand concepts do not make it past our feasibility consultation. Concepts like tracksuits with pictures of cats, for the homebound cat ladies. A line of jumpsuits, an item that wasn't on trend at the time and hard to fit (turned out the guy had a fetish for them). A dress that had a bib built in so you could wash your neck during the day and not get your dress wet (sounded like a personal problem). A scarf line made of a material that claimed to repel ninety percent of radio waves to protect your brain cells from being read, and was inspired by the designer's leader who unexpectedly passed away.

A stoner with glazed-over eyes presented us with a collection of one pair of swim shorts made out of waterproof velvet, which he would spend hours scotch guarding, himself. All this so he could look like a pimp on the beach. Or how about a collection of transparent clothing for nudists who wanted a little layer of protection when they sat down? I actually liked that one, but I couldn't find enough retailers to make it more than just a hobby business.

Once we determine that the concept has legs, we pick four designers a season to assist with the development of the samples and support for sales. Some concepts never get past the sampling stage. People want these perfect samples the way they see them in their mind's eye.

It never turns out that way. It's not about making a perfect sample; it's about making a sellable sample.

Some designers make a great first collection, get frustrated with their first-season sales, and quit. It takes at least three seasons to really gain traction. Most designers make a fantastic first collection, and then their second collection is monstrous. You never have the luxury of time like you do for your first collection, so it's a good idea to plan several collections at a time. If not, the seasons will seem to sneak up on you. Some who have had great success burn out of creativity. Some become huge drama queens begging for sympathy because it's such a torturous process. Some even become physically ill.

This is where my husband puts everything into perspective for me. No one dies in my business. The worst that can happen is that someone will be disappointed. They might feel like they want to die or they may want to kill someone, but no one physically dies. My husband works in many environmentally hazardous situations. His job is to make sure that people are safe while doing remediation work. At least that's what he was doing at the time; he now does international business development for his company, but when he was working in these hazardous situations, dinner conversation might have gone something like this:

"Hi honey, how was your day today?"

"It was great! I was able to save the drinking water of a small town."

"Good for you, honey. I was able to find a supplier who can get me underwear for under $6 a dozen."

We both had great days. Nobody died.

I wish, in addition to a feasibility consultation, I could also do a personality test. It takes so much focus and determination to continually create. It does wear you out, especially when results are so slow. I compare this business to gardening: "The first year it weeps, the second year it creeps, the third year it leaps." No one in fashion is an overnight success. Unless, of course, it's all smoke and mirrors, and we have a million examples of those. Even Marc Jacobs has said, after being hired by Louis Vuitton, that it took him only twenty years to be an overnight success. You have to be in it for the long run. It's more of an endurance marathon than it is a sprint.

Some of my clients do a lot of complaining. They might not have enough money or time to focus on the collection, so they quit their day jobs to dedicate their time to the project. I find that this mostly works against them. They worry more about money, which adds to the stress, and it seems the more time you have, the less you do. I have been known to give some harsh criticism to my clients who make excuses. I absolutely hate excuses.

One of the excuses I constantly hear is, "I'm a one-person team." Why are you telling me this? Everyone starts as a one-person team. Is that your excuse? If I took you on as one of the brands in our emerging designer program, it means you have something that makes me think you will be successful. I take it personally when you fail. Or should I say when they give up, because most of them don't give all the time that the development of a brand needs?

Personally, I detest consultants who lecture me on what to do when they might have had a failed business twenty years ago. Now let me be clear, you can learn a great deal from people's successes and failures, but their experiences need to be current. My own experience in developing a collection for my uncle was now twenty years old, and in truth, it wasn't my own. To honestly be relevant, I had to put my money where my mouth was. I needed to start a brand while keeping my day job and maintaining a humble budget. This should be easy, right? I am industry. First, I needed a niche, and a dress is a dress, a pant is a pant. I'm not a designer who was going to make beautifully detailed clothing.

Stand Up or Shut Down

Only once in my lifetime, so far, have I met a designer whom I am comfortable with using the word couture. She had quite a fascinating look, with crystal blue eyes and dreadlocks. She came to my office because after studying to be a sculptor, she had become very interested in fashion design. She went to one of the most prestigious art schools in Rhode Island and had dabbled in many art mediums, including textiles. When I looked at her portfolio and saw some of the samples, I knew I was looking at something great. Something that had yet to be discovered. Something that was extraordinary, relevant, engaging, and stunning. This was a once-in-a-lifetime opportunity. I was discovering the next phenomenal American designer. I would be the Diana Vreeland to Houston. The Anna Wintour to Alexander Wang. Not that all of the sudden I had become the editor of *Vogue*, but in the sense that I had discovered a raw talent.

I was fully committed to whatever it took to see Janice reach the new levels of a true American couture designer. My heart was racing—

becoming a couture designer would take an incredible amount of financial backing. We would have to be approved by the chamber of commerce of the industry in Paris to even use the word *couture* for the collection.

I said to Janice, "You have what it takes creatively to be one of the next household names in fashion design." I couldn't believe that those words were coming out of my mouth. It went against every grain of my existence. I don't think there's a couture designer who single-handedly makes a living from his or her couture collection. All of the big houses, like Givenchy, Chanel, Gucci, and Fendi, make a considerable amount of their income from the cheapest products they sell, such as accessories and fragrances. The other obstacle we were facing is the fact that all of these houses are heritage. Some, like Louis Vuitton, are almost a hundred years old. No overnight success story there.

Janice, who could see my concern, was all about the financing and not at all about her creative direction. Let me tell you a little more about her collection. If I had to describe it abstractly, it was bittersweet. It wasn't androgynous in the sense that it had no sex; it was feminine, yet strong and bold. It was a balance of light and dark. It was Rick Owens meets the architectural simplicity of Zaha Hadid.

She looked at me with a hint of hesitation, then in a soft voice said, "My father is a private banker." "No, I take that back," she said, "My father owns a private bank. He does very well investing and selling commodities in privately held companies. He just donated twenty million to the rainforest in a project that he and Sting put together. Financing my collection would be an insignificant amount of money for my father. But my father is a businessman, and he is expecting a detailed business plan—this is why I need your help."

I absolutely loathe business plans. One of the components of a business plan is a five-year sales projection. How can one possibly project five years of retail sales when we don't even know what's going to sell this Christmas? Instead, I was going to write a concrete industry plan of action, not a traditional business plan. More like a concept book with budget goals and objectives that can orchestrate an influential group of very specific industry people. To be acknowledged as a couture designer, you could not show the collection in New York, London, or Milan. It had to be shown in Paris, during Paris fashion week. It could not be shown in an off-site location. It had to be shown on the best runway. You couldn't have just any publicity or public relations company make your guest list. You had to use the right companies. You couldn't have any model walk the catwalk. You had to have top models, which run about $10,000 for one twenty-minute show. You couldn't send paper invitations. You had to go to the most exceptional advertising and marketing company and come up with a unique way of presenting your invitation. You had to have the press, the celebrities, and the industry trade papers at your show. Basically, this was done by gifting—a fancy industry term for bribing people.

In my plan of action, I noted that it would take at least two full years of doing two runway collections each year. Each collection needed more than twenty different styles. Each sample could easily cost thousands of dollars just in fabrics. You had to work with various skilled and expensive seamstresses who, of course, had insufficient time to dedicate to a new designer. You had to pay them extra to fit you into their busy schedules. My low estimate of what all of this would cost, without Janice even eating a tuna sandwich, would be around $2 million. I didn't think it was a lot of money, considering some brands have spent $2 million on just one runway collection. I was very frugal in my calculations. In her case, she needed to have some fame before she could make a fortune. The strategy was that once she got all the press and notoriety, creating a specific credibility within the industry, we would go to the house of Vivienne Westwood and ask for a job.

Sounds ridiculous, doesn't it? All those years, and all that money, and the best strategy I could come up with was for her to get a day job. Have you noticed that every top designer has a day job? Karl Lagerfeld—not only does he have a day job with the house of Chanel, but he also designs no fewer than four collections for Fendi a year, on top of his line.

The day of truth arrived. Janice had already been in my office for a little while, had a cup of tea, and was able to relax enough to crack a smile. Whenever she spoke about her father, she had this intense look on her face, an uneasiness that I took for "he is judging me for being an artist."

Janice's father walked in, and Janice greeted her father in the same manner I did, despite the fact that I had just met him. After a polite shaking of hands, a quick conversation about traffic in New York City, and how hard it had been to get a taxi, he got right to the questions.

"How much is this hobby going to cost me?" I liked that he used the word *hobby*—I assumed that he felt the same way I did when people started a business. It was going to be an easy conversation about how this was a detailed action plan with a very clear objective.

"Well, sir," I said, "Janice has extraordinary talent. I've traveled all around the world; in fact just this year I've been in eight different countries, and it's only March. I have never in all my years seen anyone whom I can honestly call a couture designer." This in no way whatsoever seemed to impress him. I moved on. I explained that it would be a two-year project with four seasons. I broke down our budget by season, focusing on the importance of each segment, which would cost $500,000 each.

"We don't expect to get any sales." I was being as honest and as realistic as possible. "Couture collections are bought by just a handful of women in the world. We might get lucky and dress royalty or a celebrity, but most likely they would want it for free. The goal is for Janice to establish credibility and a signature DNA for her brand so that she may get a position." I made sure not to use the word *job*, since that seemed so insignificant.

"She would work under Vivienne Westwood, a most highly regarded designer." Vivienne Westwood, in her late seventies, is the godmother of punk and has had a very long and respectable fashion career. Westwood was the prime house for Janice's aesthetics to apprentice. I made an excellent case of how every penny was going to be spent and what the end result would be.

He stood up suddenly. He had seemed like he wasn't even paying attention to my pitch. But now he was very intensely looking at me. Crystal-clear blue eyes (I see where Janice got them) were piercing me while hers were still blue waters. "Let me get this right," he said. "You want me to spend $2 million so my daughter can get a job?"

I knew how ridiculous that sounded, so I used the example of Stella McCartney. "Did you know Stella McCartney had to intern for free at Christian Lacroix? Her father is a Beatle. You cannot get more money, more prestige, more doors opening, than when your father is a Beatle. Yet she too had to go to work for free. Stella then went to work under the house of Chloe before she was able to establish her own brand: Stella McCartney. But she still has a day job designing activewear, which pays very well, for Adidas."

"Yes, I know the story very well; Paul told me himself." Why didn't that surprise me?

"So this is what I want you to do," he said, speaking a little louder. He was still standing, but now in the middle of my office, making sure that he had a full view of Janice and me but totally giving us an awkward amount of personal space. It was almost like he wasn't even in the room. "I want you to call Vivienne Westwood's people and tell them that I will pay them $1 million to hire my daughter."

"No, sir, it doesn't work that way. Janice needs to establish credibility in the industry, and the only way to do it, at this level, is to follow the plan that I just laid out before you." The conversation was getting aggressive and uncomfortable.

I looked over at Janice, waiting for her to jump in and maybe acknowledge that she could do this, but she had physically shrunk down into a tiny child. She could not defend herself. The father saw this, and I saw this. It would take only one callous review of her collections to crush her. The father and I, without saying a word, saw the reality. Janice was too emotionally fragile to handle the pressure of this level of design. Look at all the greats. Yves Saint Laurent had to be institutionalized after his runway shows due to exhaustion and alcohol abuse. Alexander McQueen was a genius who ended up taking his own life. There would be no alcohol abuse or suicidal thoughts in her new position as a barista working in Williamsburg, Brooklyn.

Back to my collection: I needed an emotional connection for this new brand in the way people are emotionally connected with Apple. Apple does not have the most advanced technology and even runs some ethically shady factories. The loyalty of their consumers is incredibly solid. This was one of the differentiators needed to be competitive: emotion.

Divine Intervention

While watching the news, there was a story about the Westboro Baptist Church protesting a military funeral. I was sickened by the festering hate they oozed. All I kept thinking was how the hell can they call themselves Christians? This is not the peace and acceptance that Jesus taught us. They were worse than any radical extremist of any religion. In fact, they are extremists. Yeah, I am a Christian. A whiskey-drinking, foul-mouth, gay-loving, it's-your-own-choice kind of Christian gal. To be exact, I identify with being Methodist.

My family became Methodist when I was in the first grade. We were Catholics, and we all went to Catholic school. We all grew up in a brownstone on 99th and West End Avenue in New York City. When I say we, I mean my whole family lived in this brownstone. One uncle and two aunts from my father's side, my cousins and their spouses, and of course my mom and dad, my two sisters, and my little brother. It was an open-door building with each family living in their own apartment, and we took turns cooking dinner and watching the smaller children.

The youngest of my aunts was pregnant with her second child. We were all old enough to understand that a baby was coming soon to our family. We all planned how to pitch in and help with the new baby. I was going to be in charge of teaching her how to roller skate, since I was the best one in the family. My brother pledged to share his books with her. I remember sitting on the stoop of our building the day the taxi came to take my aunt to the hospital to give birth to our newest cousin. We were so excited we could barely eat dinner, and we had so many questions: Would it be a boy or would it be a girl? What would we name it? Names were voted on. It got too late for us to stay up and wait for the news of our new little cousin, so we all had a sleepover in our apartment.

Morning came, and my mother gathered us all around. In the most cheerful voice, she proclaimed that we should all rejoice because a baby angel had been born to our family. She had gone right up to heaven and was there to protect us all. They even named her Angelica. We laughed, we hugged each other, we held hands and danced around in circles. We chanted, "An angel, an angel; we have an angel named Angelica!" I felt superior to all my friends who didn't have a guardian angel born into their family. My aunt, thinking back, probably emotionally healed faster because we all spent a considerable amount of time hugging and kissing her, stroking her hair, and thanking her for our baby guardian angel. Can you imagine how she must've felt?

A few weeks later, I was sitting in Sunday school with my brother. We were in the same Sunday school class since we are only eighteen months apart. The nun, an ancient, cranky, bitter nun, was talking about baptism. One of the things she stressed was the importance of being baptized as an infant to protect us from Original Sin. This made no sense to me. What Original Sin? I knew that we had all been baptized; I'd seen the pictures. But baby Angelica wasn't baptized, and she went right to heaven. I quickly wanted to prove that nun wrong. I knew you could go to heaven without being baptized.

"Excuse me," I said, raising my hand, and told the story about how in my family we had a baby guardian angel who went straight to heaven. The nun was outraged. Her face flushed, and red angry blood cells pulsated on her forehead.

"It's a lie," she said as she stared down at me, "they lied to you. No baby is born an angel, and if that baby wasn't baptized, it is sitting in hell."

She said this with the most authoritative voice. My God! Oh my God! I turned to my brother. He was shaking and tears filled his eyes.

I told him, "I don't think it's true. I know it's not true. This nun doesn't know what she's talking about. She's crazy. Let's just forget this and pretend it never happened." I was whispering to my brother so the nun couldn't hear us. "You can't tell anyone this. Tía will be so sad. No one needs to know. It's not true. Do you understand me?"

My brother's face was pale and had no expression.

"Please," I said, "she's lying to us like Pinocchio. She's just mean. It's okay." I was trying hard to shake it off so I could be more convincing to my brother. "Please, please just forget it. Okay, okay, okay." I held his hand, and he was crying. That made the nun smile.

It wasn't okay. My brother stopped talking. He started wetting his bed at night. My mother tried to coax out what was wrong with him with gentle conversation, but I would shoot him the meanest stink-eye and it would shut him up. He was throwing up anything he ate. My mother was about to take him to the doctor when he reached the point that he couldn't keep the secret anymore. He told my mother what the nun had said through swollen eyes and sobs.

My mother was beyond livid. I don't think I'd ever seen my mother this angry before or since. If you knew my mother, you would think of her as a mouse of a person: very reserved, very proper, extremely soft-spoken. She grabbed my brother and me by the hand and marched us right to the church, demanding to speak to the priest immediately. We sat down in the priest's office, and he seemed defensive and standoffish as my mother asked me to explain what the nun had told us during Sunday school.

"She said that all babies go to hell if they're not baptized, but I know that's not true," I added. I was hoping that the priest would back me up so that my brother would be okay.

"No, it's absolutely true," he said. "All children need to be baptized in the eyes of God to remove Original Sin."

My mother slapped her hands on the desk. "What kind of church tells children that babies go to hell?"

"A church that preaches the absolute gospel of God as written in the Bible," said the priest.

"Then I need to find myself a new religion." My mother stomped off with us in hand. She stopped for a second in front of the church, looking around, and remembered that on the opposite corner of our Catholic Church was a Methodist Church. We went up the steps of the rectory, and she knocked frantically on the door. The minister opened the door and greeted us warmly.

My mother was yelling at him, "Do you teach children that babies go to hell?"

"I don't understand your question, but why don't you come in and have a cup of coffee with my wife and me?"

"You're married?"

"Yes, I am."

"And you're the priest?"

"No, I'm a minister."

My mother, the minister, and his wife spoke about what had happened. He briefly explained the Methodist belief system, and how they believed you should be baptized as a teen, when you felt you were old enough to understand the word of God.

"What about babies going to hell?"

"We believe that God is love, and if you love something, it wouldn't be in hell." Amen!

That night during dinner, my mother said in the same tone you would use if you were going to go see a movie, "We are Methodist now." My father began to ask a question, but my mother interrupted him. That was something you rarely saw, and she said, "It's not open for discussion." She went to every apartment the next day, made the announcement, threw out all the Catholic icons, and pulled us all out of Catholic school. I smiled thinking about the nun.

In a very Oprah-esque "aha" moment, it came to me. I should develop a Christian clothing collection. It would consist of classic bestsellers, no need to reinvent the wheel, be modest in its styling, and focus on genuinely being made ethically. It would be for similarly minded people who don't want to be identified as a crazy Christian and were proud of their beliefs.

Step one: Who is the retailer?

Southern boutiques would be an easy sell. I looked up several, looked at the brands they carried, their price points, and started to follow them on social media. Now I needed a name. It should be something with meaning, something symbolic, without being in your face. In a moment of divine intervention, which I feel comfortable saying, I came up with the name Dovetail. Dovetail in carpentry (Jesus is said to have been a carpenter) is the joining of a corner without using nails or glue. I took it to signify the relationship you have directly with God without any assistance.

I needed a logo that was modern and catchy. Something that when you saw someone wearing it would produce a little head nod acknowledging that you were from the same tribe. I was inspired by Tory Burch's logo using the T as a focus. I was able to design a very clever logo where the Ds intertwined to form the symbol of Christianity, the fish. And if you looked at the logo from a different angle, it looked like a Celtic cross. The whole logo was so minimal that it just looked pretty.

The next step was to develop a collection. This was the first time I didn't take my own advice, and I designed a full collection of twenty pieces each, for both men and women. Usually my advice is to start with just one product category and one department, such as women's dresses. One of the parameters I had set for myself was to try to source everything domestically. One of the items I wanted to source was a men's polo shirt—ready for this?—that had the Lord's prayer printed inside the pocket. The tagline was "Keeping the Lord close to your heart." I know, corny . . . but it was clever!

Getting this polo sample made became an ordeal. I sourced a knit manufacturing company in Los Angeles that quoted me a twenty-dollar production price. I based my price study on my competition and where I wanted the collection to be placed. I came up with a retail price of $48. Not the cheapest, not the most expensive in the market, but right in the middle, and I was offering the retailers a 2.5 percent markup, which in Men's is generous, considering that most brands offer a 2.2 percent markup. That is outrageous, I told the factory in California. I wrote an email asking for the cost to be itemized. They wrote back and said $9 for fabric, $3 for printing the Lord's prayer, $2 for the embroidery of the logo, $5 for labor, $1 for trim and packaging.

Ridiculous.

I found a factory during a trade show in Peru that made only polo shirts. They make polo shirts for everyone, from the high-end brand Psycho Bunny that retails for over $120,000, to American Eagle that retails for $12. Fantastic, I thought, and asked them if they could make me a polo shirt with the Lord's prayer printed on the pocket. The guy at the tradeshow booth thought for a moment and said to me, "Of course we can, that's brilliant. You should also consider printing it in Spanish."

Mental note: rollout for the second season.

I needed the samples rushed, as I was about to launch at the emerging designer showcase during the MAGIC show in Las Vegas. For all of the other samples, I called on designers I knew and factories that owed me a favor—the second time I didn't take my own advice. I advise designers not to invest in trade shows in their first season, since it's challenging to get any traction without the brands already having some type of market recognition. Days before the trade show, I got the first sample of the polo shirt. This was the third time I didn't take my own advice. I advise my clients never to freak out when they get their first samples, because they will often need corrections. But I completely freaked out. They had printed the Lord's prayer on the outside of the polo shirt's pocket! Jesus Christ, I guess I wasn't specific enough. But it was too late now to resample or even photograph the polo shirt for the line sheets and look books.

One of the traits that you have to learn in this business is to be a spin master. At the tradeshow, I advised my sales team that I had to hire people to run the booth because I was working my day job of buying and speaking during the show. The polo shirt was an exclusive item— that was why it wasn't on the line sheet. And we had intentionally printed the Lord's prayer on the outside of the pocket so that they could see what would be on the inside in its entirety. Once again, I thought of myself as so clever.

We didn't write a single order. While it was very disappointing, it was typical of a new brand. The buyers first buy the brands they know are making money. Then, if there's any budget left over, they buy from new brands they have had some communication with. This could be done by email, by phone call, by social media, or even at a trade show. But you have to be relentless. You cannot stop communicating for one second with the retailers that you want to sell to. It can be borderline stalker-psychopath if it's not done with great care. Or worse, you could come off as desperate, and no one wants to work with the desperate. One hour each day, which is significantly less than the four hours a day, three nights a week I dedicated to developing a collection, I would send out personal emails and make phone calls to the retailers I want to sell to. They all had lovely encouraging things to say. But no one placed an order.

I came up with the idea to put an ad in the local church bulletins and use a service to place ads in local newspapers across the country. The ad read something like this: "Keep a parent in every household working from home! Sign up today for sales training in America's new hottest Christian clothing line. We are looking for regional independent salespeople. Training and sale samples will be provided free of charge." Guess how many phone calls we got? Zero.

During this time, I received my second sample of the prayer pocket polo. This time the pocket was so big that you could fit an iPad mini inside. What the heck? I Skype-called the factory, showing them the pocket.

"What the fuck are you thinking?" I said in the most unchristian way. He explained that he wanted it to be legible, so he used a bigger font and, in doing so, needed a bigger pocket. "Oh my God, no one's going to read it! It's just symbolic. I'm running out of time in the selling season. You have to make me another sample with the corrected pocket this week."

I got the third sample. This time, the pocket was correct, but the pocket color and the polo color did not match. The color difference was so slight, but it was still a production mistake. If I were to have sold these to a department store, they would have returned them. I called the factory. They needed to use the same dye lot to print on the pocket and on the polo shirt. He told me that this was a problem because they had to send out the pockets to be printed, and by the time they came back, a new batch of the dyed fabrics was made. When this was done, the tone, even under the best circumstances, were never a hundred percent match. This was an issue.

By the fourth sample, I could correct the dye lot situation by holding the fabric on the side until the pockets came back from the printer. This was a production nightmare for any small factory that lacks storage space. But then a new problem emerged, since the gold color ink was bleeding through the other side of the white polo. The solution was just to print all of the Lord's prayer on a thinner fabric that then would be sewn into the pocket. This would've avoided the dye lot problem and the bleedthrough on the white shirts. It added to the cost, but my landed cost was just $7.75.

You would think that making a polo shirt was a simple process, since they are a factory that makes only polo shirts. But there were so many choices to make: How many buttons do you want on the collar? Do you want the sleeves banded or not banded? What buttons would you like—natural buttons, plastic buttons, dyed-to-match buttons, or clear buttons? How many holes do you want in those buttons, two holes or four holes?

"I need to make these decisions like I need a hole in my head. Just make me a high-end polo shirt. Enough with the questions!"

"Hold on, do you want a split side or a square bottom on the shirt?"

"Please," I said to the sales guy, "just make me the best polo shirt you can with the Lord's prayer printed on the pocket." Those were my exact words at the trade show when I introduced myself to the factory.

I'm losing count; how many times does this now make that I didn't follow my own advice? I could've avoided all of these sampling problems with the polo shirt if I had given them a tech pack or at least a CAD calling out all of the things that I wanted to be featured in the polo.

Fifth time's the charm. I got my polo shirt. I asked him to send me ten of each color in each size, because I was down to the wire and I needed to get some sales. It seemed that all of the interest was for just this one item. I was a little crushed that I wasn't selling my magnificent collection, but I was okay with this one item, since I really came up with it on my own. We sent emails to the retailers saying that our polo was such a superior product that we were willing to give them one for free. Every retailer that accepted my offer wrote us a generous opening order. Thank God, Dovetail was now a real business!

If It Was Only That Easy

We shipped the first collection in early spring, just in time for graduations and Father's Day. It was an immediate hit, selling out at full price within three weeks in all of the stores. In fact, retailers were upset that we didn't have any back stock for them to reorder. Advice not taken number six: always overcut your production after your break-even, so that you will be in an in-stock position with positive cash flow.

We designed a fall collection. This time, the polo shirt was updated with long sleeves, and I added a women's polo dress with the same prayer pocket concept. Guess how many orders were placed with our emails? ZERO. Not following my own advice once again, I had failed to follow up, in a timely manner, with my fall emails. I was so close to the production closing time that I put the fall collection into production without receiving any orders. I skipped the dresses. I was frantically calling up the retailers, asking them to please place their orders since I was very limited in my production, and I didn't want them to be left out for the holiday season.

I got my orders. Once again, it was an incredible success, selling out six weeks before Christmas. We had added a pocket flasher, a little cardboard sign that read "Putting Christ back in Christmas." I was clever again. I had some back stock to replenish a few stores, but not enough for all of them. Some people will tell you that this is a good thing, keeping the retailers hungry. It's a terrible situation. When a retailer doesn't have your product to sell, they're not likely to leave an empty rack for you. They will buy from another brand, filling that budget and space, often quickly forgetting you.

Next season, once again, I was preoccupied with my day job, and frankly, a little burnt out from making these polo shirts. You would think my third season would be an automatic system. You still have to send out the emails, make the phone calls, update the line sheets, keep up with the social media, negotiate with the factory on your production delivery, deal with the shipping, deal with the warehouse, make sure that the customers are invoiced, make sure that you've paid the factory, and ship out the goods. I am just one person, I'd say to myself, sounding like all of my clients (#ifeelyourpain). I didn't take my advice once again, I should've been paying someone to handle the Dovetail production and sales. But I didn't.

I got a phone call from the Military PX. The Military PX is an international chain of stores that are located on US military bases. It seemed a soldier was given a Dovetail polo shirt as a gift when he was deployed to Afghanistan. His captain had seen this polo shirt and called the PX to ask if they were able to supply them in their shops. That's who was calling me to place an order for the next spring.

"Sure, I would love to sell to the Military PX. I'm not sure how to go about it, though; could you walk me through the procedure?"

"Oh, it's easy enough; I will send you a purchase order and the shipping guidelines that you'll need to follow."

I received my first order for 40,000 units. They wanted it shipped directly to their warehouse as a bulk shipment, and they wanted sixty-day terms to pay the invoice. I quickly did the math. Holy shit, I realized I needed over $300,000 to go into production. It would've been easy enough to find a venture capitalist, or what I like to call a loan shark, to lend me the money at fifteen percent, but I didn't want to give away $45,000.

Up until then, I'd become really, really good at not taking my own advice. Why quit now? So, not only did I finance the production by remortgaging my home, but I also gave them credit terms. That was an interesting dinner conversation.

"Oh, honey, do you mind signing here?"

"What's this?"

"Oh nothing, it's just our future."

I have a very tolerant and trusting husband. Besides, it was the US government! What could possibly go wrong with giving them credit terms? I didn't even bother making a single phone call to any of the boutique retailers we had been selling to. This time, screw them for making me chase the order every season. I figured that if they really wanted some, they would call me. Are you tired of me pointing out how many times I didn't listen to my own advice? In any business, you never put all of your eggs in one basket. My ego was starting to take over.

I spoke with the factory and asked for credit terms on half of the production cost. I would send them a wire for half the amount, and in ninety days, considering that the US government was asking for sixty-day terms, I would send him the balance of the payment, +2 percent. He agreed. Production went without a hitch. The best part was that I didn't even have to warehouse the goods. This saved me money. It went directly to the military's own warehouse distribution center. I received confirmation, as noted on the purchase order, and now all I had to do was sit back and wait for my money. Picture me sitting back in my chair, legs up on my desk, hands behind my head, daydreaming of all the things I was going to buy.

Reality check: I woke up to the news that the government had shut down. They were not making any payments. Congress had stopped working. All government agencies had stopped working. My heart had stopped working. My payment was due last week.

I was literally on my hands and knees, praying that my check was cut. No one was picking up at the PX office (duh, they were closed). My husband noticed that I was fidgety and anxious, but had not put the two things together. In my mind, I was scrambling to think how many credit cards it would take to cash out the $150,000 I still owed the factory. It was more than $150,000. The mortgage payment on my home was manageable, but what wasn't manageable was losing my reputation in the industry. I had to come up with this money! Could I go back to the bank and remortgage some more? Could I take out a personal loan? Could I go to the loan sharks? I had thirty days to make this work out.

Then . . . there it was. The check. It had been cut and sent out on time, after all, but the stupid post office had taken its time in delivery. Whew, I was laughing and skipping all the way to the bank.

The government shutdown didn't last long, and neither did the polo shirts at the Military PX. They quickly put in for a replenishment program. That meant that as the product sold, each month, a computer system would send me an email placing an order to replenish the amount that was sold by color and size. I had to invest in continuous stock and warehousing, since they wanted replenishment within ten days. That was fine. I took the profits that we had made and invested in the replenishment program.

I also gave money away like it was going out of style. I bought my husband a fancy car. I paid off a couple of our nephew's student debts. I helped my brother with a down payment on a house. I also self-funded some trips to speak in Africa at trade shows. I spent the money like the gravy train was never going to end.

That train came to a screeching stop when they hired a new procurement officer who was an atheist. He had a massive problem with a religious item being sold in a US military base. The first thing he did was cut off our replenishment program. I had the name of the captain who had initially recommended our product, and reached out to him to see if he could help. I'm not sure if going over the procurement officer's head made matters worse. The captain did help me establish direct relationships with some of the individual stores. The size of the order was minuscule compared to the corporate orders and replenishment program. Unfortunately, I had let the sales of the boutique business ultimately die off, and it would take a full-on effort, with a team this time, to dedicate itself to Dovetail.

Old Catholic habits die hard. Like some type of penance, I used the profits from Dovetail to help other people start businesses. It's not a vast Goldman Sachs million-dollar women's fund, but it helps a few people out. Not that I wouldn't jump-start Dovetail again with a good kick in the pants, but like my husband would say, "She'll do it when she has nothing to do again."

IT TAKES US TO
MAKE THE VILLAGE

*T*hat's odd, I thought to myself. Was that pigeon trying to get into my office? Was it actually knocking on my window? Was it trying to tell me something? Now it was flapping its wings like a shoulder shrug that says, "Hey man, let me in." I cracked open the window, and it plopped right on top of my desk. It was doing a little chicken dance, like the ones they do at weddings. How bizarre is this, I thought to myself. Wait a second, there was a note attached to its leg! The pigeon stood perfectly still as I unwrapped the note. "Let this be a warning," it said.

I certainly wish that really would have happened. It would have prepared me for what was to come. It was the start of a new millennium, but I was going to go back a thousand years in time.

The phone call was brief, with just a few questions to qualify me as an expert in footwear manufacturing. It wasn't the first time I had done some work for the World Bank, so they had all my credentials on file.

"Have you ever been to a leather shoe-manufacturing factory?"

"Yes, I have, many times in Mexico."

"Are you familiar with the different machinery needed to manufacture shoes?"

"Yes, I am, they need leather-cutting machines, stitching machines, and different kinds of shoe lasts." I knew the person I was talking to was just clerical, going through a checklist of questions. If I gave anything more than a yes or no answer, she would be lost entirely. I tried to keep my answers simple.

Recently, I'd wanted to apply for a consulting position with tribal weavers in Nepal. The forty-page questionnaire had many abstract questions. For example, "How do you feel your experiences in working with indigenous people would impact the emotional well-being of any person you might have interacted with?" Huh? I don't know how I am emotionally impacted myself half the time. I once applied to a US government agency for a consultancy program in Haiti. The amount of paperwork I would have been required to fill out on a daily basis would have been more significant than the actual amount of work to be done. The bureaucratic system, with all its checks and balances. has gotten entirely out of control. The goals for the common good that you're supposed to be accomplishing get lost in the paperwork shuffle that is required.

The World Bank, despite all the sinister conspiracies you might hear, actually gives a tremendous amount of grants and low-interest loans to developing countries. They provide hundreds of millions of dollars in healthcare grants so that these developing countries can have a stable workforce. One outbreak of malaria can cause an economic crisis on a grand scale. But with each Yin, there is a Yang. For example, the World Bank was one of the driving forces behind the antipollution laws in the Rio River in Brazil. Then they went and financed a very toxic paper-producing mill that borders the Rio in Uruguay. It's not that I turn a blind eye—and I will use this term loosely—to the evil shadows that lurk within the World Bank, but that those rays of sunshine they do offer to so many are opportunities that make a significant impact. It's not a matter of choosing the lesser of two evils. It's a matter of using the opportunity to do good.

The job was an easy one, and the World Bank is notorious for paying very well. The full scope of the job was to fly to Karachi, visit a newly retooled footwear factory, and confirm the fact that they were, indeed, just making footwear. When I told my friends what I would be doing in Pakistan, just for a bit of drama, I would add "to make sure that they were making footwear and not bombs." My compensation would undoubtedly make up for the boredom I was planning on facing. I was just a girl trying to make an honest buck.

I stayed in a luxury hotel suite. It had a very interesting Indian motif in its architecture and design. But don't make the mistake of confusing Indian and Pakistani architecture. The suite was large, with a separate living room and what we would consider in New York City a full kitchen. I was to stay ten days, visiting the factory at random times of the day, and check off endless boxes of observations on a clipboard.

The checklist had a mundane list of things I was to note. The time people arrived, the number of people working. Were the machines operational? Did the people using each machine appear to be trained?

How many pairs of shoes were being produced within one hour? Was there adequate ventilation? If not, please, describe the type of smell you believe is causing the disruption. I wondered if you could check off BO. The list went on and on. Basically, any person could have figured out the checklist and gotten this job done. A trained expert was unnecessary. The World Bank reports to the United Nations, so I guessed that it was vital for them to have credible experts as boots on the ground giving accurate reports.

Karachi itself was a very international port city. For being such a patriarchal country, I found it to be very current with its treatment of women. Women were working in very ordinary aspects of life. I had even seen women police officers. In Saudi Arabia, my layover coming to Pakistan, the women were not even allowed to drive. It was a surprising contrast.

I hadn't been in Karachi for more than twenty-four hours, and I was waiting for a taxi just inside the hotel lobby to take me to dinner when an incredibly well-dressed young man turned to me and said, "Excuse me. Are you a Bollywood actress?"

That was the first time I'd heard that pickup line. I said, "Yes, I am the most famous Bollywood actress in all of Cuba."

He looked a little puzzled, and then he realized that I was making a joke. "You're not Indian?"

"No, I'm not." One good thing about my complexion is that I can blend into many countries. I have been told I look Moroccan, Italian, Greek, and Turkish, to name a few. I might've made a great spy, rather than a footwear observer of mechanical procedures. Such a snore.

His name was Mahoor. He was a popular DJ and established menswear designer who designed many of the Bollywood costumes for the movies. His family owned an important shipping company, and while he was obligated to work there, he spent most of his time designing and spinning records. His Gaydar is on full alert. He's testing me to see if I'm a friend of Dorothy. He started to feel a little more at ease when I told him that I was also in the fashion business. I started a conversation about markets like London and New York.

He was more interested in my friends than any business affiliates. I told him about my dearest friend Tito, and how he is an incredible patternmaker and a jack-of-all-trades when it comes to production. A funny story came up about how insane the New York City factories can be, and how when Tito is in total panic mode he breaks out into full Broadway showtunes.

"It's showtime, it's sew time, it's so good to be here." I start singing with jazz hands, imitating the way Tito might sing.

Mahoor starts to laugh, saying, "So do I, except I break out in Bollywood songs! Is your friend a homosexual?"

"Yes, he is."

Endearingly, he says, "I would like to be his friend." No kidding!

"Well, where do the girls go for dinner around here? It seems like my taxi is never coming, as we've been talking for twenty minutes."

He smiles, we have an instant connection, and he says, "I'll take you to the best supper club you have ever been to," and like the magical timing of a Bollywood movie, his driver pulls up in a new Mercedes Benz.

"I didn't tell you my name. It's Mercedes," I said, stepping into the car.

When I tell my husband this story the following night, this is where he goes completely nuts. And he is one hundred percent right. "How do you jump into a complete stranger's car?" You know, I feel like I should have died at least a thousand times already. Growing up in New York and riding the subways at two in the morning during the eighties was as risky as being on any battlefield. Believe it or not, I did take some precaution. I told the hotel that I was going out to dinner, and the hotel seemed to know my new friend quite well. Nowadays when I travel, I've developed a safety protocol: I snap a picture of the license plate of the street taxi and text it to my husband or the office before taking the ride. Then we have evidence of the last person that was with me if I am not heard from the next day.

We passed this impressive shrine that sits high on a hill. "That is the Abdullah Shah Ghazi shrine," Mahoor told me. "It's the best gay cruising spot in Karachi."

I'm paraphrasing a little, because he used a different word for cruising which I can't remember, but I do remember what he meant. Never in my wildest dreams would I have thought that Karachi had a place for gays to cruise.

The supper club was indeed spectacular. There was a small stage that metamorphosed from performer to performer. There were drag queens who sang old Sylvester songs, trapeze artists who swung from ropes hung from the ceiling, and burlesque dancers with old-fashioned, velvet-tasseled, feathered costumes. There were dancing go-go boys who hopped from table to table. You held your glass over your head to ensure they wouldn't make you spill a single drop of booze. Reaching out to tip one of the dancing boys, I was told there was no tipping allowed. This is a cheap date, I thought. There were women dressed like men and men dressed like women, and both were a stereotype of each other. The women were overly feminine, and the men excessively masculine. It was a mix of Cirque du Soleil and South Beach, Miami, on a hot Saturday night. I loved this supper club. I wanted to come back every night. In fact, I wanted to live there, with its animal print rugs and wild tapestry walls. If you had an eccentric French gypsy grandmother, I would imagine this is how she would've decorated.

By my second day at the factory, it was already feeling like *Groundhog Day*. Everything was exactly the same as the first day. It was a little unsettling that nothing was even the slightest bit different than the day before. All of the workers wore uniforms, so no change there. The routine and the hum of the machines provided nothing different to report. I left after a few hours, thinking I would have a "long lunch," which translates into taking a long nap and coming back in the afternoon to check off more boxes. The factory was only a half hour away, and a cheap cab ride.

Mahoor had left me a message at the hotel. "I have another business engagement this afternoon at your hotel; would you like to meet me for dinner afterward? If so, just meet me in the lobby at 7 p.m."

I met him at the lobby door with bells on. "How was your day?" he asked like an old friend would when you got a new job.

"Boring and uneventful." I'll make sure to mention that with tonight's phone review, I thought. Each evening, I was required to call the department officer who hired me for this job and give a verbal report of the situation, I guess partially as proof of life, since communications like international cell phones were very limited. It was all very formal and polite.

"Where are we going for dinner tonight?" I asked.

"There is an English pub that many expats like to patronize. I thought you might like some more familiar food tonight." I didn't want to argue that English food has nothing to do with American food, but I did want to share a dirty pun with him when ordering my bangers and mash.

We met up with a few of his friends at the pub. All of them seemed to be professional and around the same age as Mahoor, but it took a while for them to speak to me, or even acknowledge that I was there, since a cricket game playing in the background made it hard to get their attention. Typical gay sport, I thought to myself. I'm shocked that it isn't figure skating. Now I was just being bitchy.

It seemed they were all Pakistani men who just happened to like sleeping with boys. It was interesting how they explained homosexuality to me. "If you're a top, you're not gay," was matter-of-factly uttered by one of Mahoor's married friends. It was also explained to me that since boys and girls did not go to school together, for most boys, their first sexual experience was with another boy.

"Boys will be boys," giggled one of the friends. I was getting quite the education.

At the pub, I heard young American female voices coming from a table. You can imagine how out of place they looked and sounded in a gay (sorry, I mean relatively straight) English pub in Pakistan. I ran into one of the girls in the ladies' room. I had to ask her what they were doing there. It's not the spring break you would imagine these young girls would've chosen.

"We are here doing missionary work."

"Missionary work in Pakistan? You know they're mostly Muslim, right?"

"Yes, I know. It hasn't been easy, but we have made lots of friends and shared some pretty fantastic experiences."

"That is what it's all about; understanding each other so that we can all live together on this one little planet." I was trying to hint at the fact that no one needed to be saved.

"What are you doing here?" she asked me.

"I'm inspecting a footwear factory. Not exactly God's work, but it does help better the lives of many people." Another not-so-subtle hint.

I'm not fond of people imposing their religious beliefs, or even trying to "civilize the natives." My philosophy is to be true to yourself, and if someone needs your help, they will let you know. I've had this conversation about indigenous people before. Some people believe that it's wrong to Westernize them with the evils of electricity and running water. Of course, I am exaggerating, but some people genuinely believe that indigenous people should stay in the same place as they are. I think the choice is theirs. Some people will continue to value their traditional ways, others will adapt their cultural particulars into a more modern lifestyle, and still others will abandon their culture altogether.

I ended up bumping into the young girls several more times during that week. It wasn't hard, since the places to go were limited. I learned that the girls were Mormons, and that for the first time women were allowed to go into the world spreading the Mormon faith. I should say "girls," since they were so very young. Wow, the world was changing, and everyone was finally getting their place under the sun.

Week two was pretty much the same routine: go to the factory in the morning, take a nap, and maybe or maybe not go back to check off some more boxes. In the evening, I would go out with the boys, and at night I called in my report to the head of the department, which was his morning.

Mahoor had asked me if I wanted to go on a picnic in the mountainside with some friends over the weekend. Pakistan is a scenic country with picturesque mountains and emerald-green valleys. It was a fun afternoon with his pub friends and their families. That was where Mahoor told me about his business matters at the hotel. I would never have guessed that these "business engagements" were actually secret rendezvous, no less with the chief of police!

"Now that sounds like a gay Bollywood movie in the making! Shall we call it *Sari Not Sari*?" That cracked us both up.

He told me how he was promised to a childhood friend who knew about his secret life, which she agreed to keep out of their matrimony. They were to be married in late spring, after Ramadan. She was in school, which was why she wasn't able to come.

I asked if he was in love with the chief of police. "Oh no," he said. "I learned at a young age not to emotionally fall in love. It is all about the physical. I love my wife-to-be." That was a little too complicated for me to understand, but I didn't judge.

"Do you want to meet her?" he asked. "She's very remarkable, independent; she's a schoolteacher, and she comes from a very liberal family. She doesn't even wear a hijab."

"I'd love to meet her," I told him.

Noor was drop-dead gorgeous. We met Sunday afternoon at an outdoor café for tea and cake. It was a Persian café, so they had the most aromatic teas and rose-scented cakes. There was amazing people-watching. It seemed that all the fashionable, chic people came to this area of town. She was joyful and kind and sincere. We started a conversation about the wedding plans, a three-day event with traditional ceremonies and a few modern touches. That's when the messenger came.

He handed Mahoor a small folded card—he read it and then dropped it on the table. Noor picked it up and read it, then stood up, reached over to Mahoor, and hugged him. It seemed that one of their friends had been brutally beaten, stoned, violated, and thrown off a building.

They had carved the word *faggot* into his chest. Mahoor and Noor started speaking in Urdu. He had, until this point, spoken only in English. It was the chief of police who had sent the message, because he wanted Mahoor to know before it was on the news. Noor was crying and holding onto him. I could see the fear in her eyes. He was angry and cursing the skies. I slowly backed away. I wondered if it was one of his friends from the pub, or one of the performers from the supper club. I left them standing there in the cafe and made my way back to the hotel.

Nothing Is Fair in Love and Work

I called in my report. This time, the department head had a different tone in his voice. "Mercedes," he said, "it seems that one of our consultants has quit in the middle of a project. Would you be able to stay for a few extra days and take over for him?" Just having been shocked by the random violence, I wasn't sure if I wanted to stay in Pakistan. I communicated this to the department head, not sure why. I think I just wanted to tell someone. This was before the days that you could vent on Facebook and have your friends virtually console you. He said, "Mercedes, that was not a random act. If you are concerned about your safety, we understand, but you are not a gay male, so it's not the same situation."

Man up, I was saying to myself. It's not about you. Hear out what the project is before you act like a pussy. Ha, you think I am harsh with my clients? I am harsher on myself.

"What are the details?"

"Oh, you're going to love this job. It's observing a cottage industry. You'll get a full briefing sent to your hotel room by tomorrow morning."

"You're right, it's totally my thing," I said as I thought about the weavers I had worked with in Peru.

That project, while challenging, was gratifying. The scope of the Peruvian project was three years in the making. Part of the concept of "cottage industry" is that the workers are able to work from home, thus being able to care for their children and not have the long commutes that jobs sometimes require. In this project, the idea was to match indigenous techniques with established American designers and have them collaborate on fashion-forward pieces. The goal was for the villagers to have a more significant revenue stream from the techniques that they already incorporated in their traditional clothing.

My role in this project was to streamline the supply chain, so I got to spend a great deal of time with them, even on occasion sleeping over in the village. That's where I got my taste for *cuy*. They would also be able to send one child to Lima, the capital, to receive a university education. The first year they had sent one of the oldest boys, and after one semester, he declared he would never go back to the village. Part of the objective was that the educated child would return to the village and provide formal education to the tribal children, since a formal education, at the time, was not readily available. The next year they sent a slightly older boy, thinking he would be more responsible. He also declared he would never come back. The third year, they decided to send one of the older girls. She was happy to return and started teaching the young children the basics of math and reading that summer.

I got my attaché with a plane ticket, hotel reservation, map, some local currency, and the scope of the project. It was pretty cut and dry. I was to observe women doing embroidery work from home. My job was to note observations, make a conclusion of the situation, and provide—if needed—a solution. I was now instructed to call in to a different department head at the end of each day.

On my last day visiting the shoe factory, there was no farewell cake, pat on the back, or "I'll miss you" from someone that I might've made eye contact with. It was just the last of my checkmarks. Check, check, check, date and signature. And CHECK! Done.

Oddly enough, my new batch of paperwork did not provide me with the detailed checklist that I had become accustomed to. At least I felt like I was accomplishing something as I ticked off the boxes. I called Mahoor to tell him that I had gotten a new job and was going to Lahore in the morning. He insisted that we have our last dinner in Karachi at the magnificent supper club. This time, it was somber. The heaviness in the air was palpable. I could tell that he wanted to talk about what had happened, but all he said was, "Indeed, Allah is with those who patiently endure. That's what is written in the Koran."

I was off to Lahore. It took a little over an hour in a tiny, uncomfortable plane. My suitcase was over the limit in weight. I had bought a ton of textiles while I was in Karachi, not knowing that I would be staying a few more weeks. A few dollars to the agent, though, and it seemed my suitcase was no longer over the limit. I hoped everyone else didn't play the same game. I checked into the hotel and was told by the concierge that my escorts would be there in the morning to take me to my location. Looking at the map, it seemed to be about one hour outside where I was staying in Lahore. This whole region was famous for its embroideries, so being a textile hoarder I was looking forward to working with them.

That morning, standing outside my hotel, the hot wind kicked up. It was dry, but I was soaked in the dust. Some Western cowboy music should have been playing in the background. Where are the tumbleweeds, partner? An oversized tan Humvee pulled up. Two giant, living G.I. Joe men jumped out in full military gear.

"Are you Mercedes?"

"Yes, I am."

"We are with Blackwater. We're your escorts to the site." They gave a whole new meaning to the word *escort*. An escort to me had always been someone whom you would find in the back pages of the *Village Voice*—SWF looking to escort a gentleman for the evening. But this wasn't a dinner date. Blackwater was serious business. They were wearing vests with full metal jackets and live grenades in several of the pockets. They had submachine guns, and their sidearms were Berettas.

I was starting to feel the gravity of the situation. Inside the car, there was a local driver and a young girl who would serve as my interpreter. I was instructed to sit between them. The boys back in Karachi would have loved this, I thought as I tried to humor myself. They weren't exactly the chatty bunch inside this Hummer. The young girl was trying her best to point out different features of the landscape. It was hard to make out what she was talking about, since the windows were tinted and the guys wouldn't let me sit by the window.

"Protocol," they said.

She told me a little about the history of the region. I always find it fascinating when a country's history goes back centuries, unlike my own American history. She wore a hijab. I had brought one with me, since I was visiting village people and I wanted to be respectful. I asked her if she would help me tie it correctly. It seemed I always managed to show my hair. I also wasn't sure if the local custom was to show ears or not. God is in the details.

We pulled up to what seemed to be an abandoned town. There were rows of cinder brick houses that had openings for windows and doors, but had none. There didn't seem to be a single person walking about. There were no businesses to speak of. It was a desolate and startling place. We pulled up in front of one of the larger square cinder brick houses.

The driver looked back and said, "This is the place." G.I. Joe opened the door closest to the opening of the brick house, stepped out, looked around, and offered me his hand to help me out of the car.

The young girl corrected the scarf that I had tried to put on by myself. "Not too bad," she said with a smile, easing the tension that was so obvious. All of the sudden, a swarm of small children streamed out of the house. They ran past us, as they knew from experience not to acknowledge us. G.I. Joe put his hand on my shoulder in a gesture almost warning me that this wasn't the worst of it, and to stay calm. The children were naked, they were shoeless, they were dirty, and their mouths were crusty. They didn't seem human. Their walk and posture were primitive and awkward. They were communicating with each other through growls and gestures. They bit each other and they pulled each other's hair. The smell of human waste was horrendously toxic. It was like these children were feral, having been left to fend for themselves. I felt like I had just stepped into some *Mad Max* movie.

Only the interpreter and I stepped inside. The G.I. Joes stood outside the door, and the driver left the engine idling. It was the most unbelievable thing I had ever seen in my life. It reminded me of that scene in *Apocalypse Now* when they find the madman alone among the skulls. The room was dark, except for one beam of light shining in from the window with no glass. It was filled with babies lying on colorful rugs. The only adult that we found was a woman sitting on a stack of fabrics, a sewing basket next to her while she breastfed a baby. There was an eerie silence in the room, considering how many babies there were.

I asked the interpreter, "Is she the embroiderer?"

"Yes, she is."

"Have you been here before?"

"Yes, I have."

"Is it always like this?"

"It's not for me to say. You are the observer."

Oh, shit, I left my clipboard back at the hotel, I remembered as we walked over to her. I'd have to remember enough details to write them down later.

"Can you introduce me to her? Can you ask her her name?"

Before the interpreter could ask, the embroiderer looked up at me and said, "Fatima."

"Do you speak English?"

The interpreter answered when Fatima didn't. "No, she does not, but that's the first question everyone asks."

Everyone? I wasn't sure how much embroidery she could have been doing when it seemed that she was the only adult in the village. She was no more than twenty years old. The interpreter was avoiding my question about "everyone." It was easy to grasp the situation, but what was the solution? There was not much more to see there that day. I went back outside, and even though it must have been 120 degrees, the air was easier to breathe than inside the building.

I said to the G.I. Joes, "I guess it's a day, but I'm not sure what else to do. I need to call corporate and see what they say."

I asked the driver if he would drive me around, so I could get a better idea of the whole situation. The house we were in was definitely on the outskirts of the village. There was more life in the center of the town, with some shops and businesses running at a normal village pace. I noticed that most of the people going about their day were elderly.

The interpreter finally said something. "Most of the healthy adults go to the city as day laborers, and that's why you don't see many of them." I started thinking to myself, if it took us one hour to get here, going 140 kilometers an hour in a brand-new car, how long does it take the villagers to get to the city, work all day, and get home?

That night, I called my department manager. "Wow, that was a strange situation." I was picking my words carefully, because I didn't want to sound like an emotional girl. I hate them. I'm a professional, I took on this responsibility, and I'm going to see it through. That's what I was telling myself.

"Yes, we have had reports that these women are working in difficult situations." That's putting it mildly, I thought to myself. "Did you observe any of the embroidery being done?"

"No, sir, but I did notice that there was a large stack of fabric and a sewing basket on the premises."

"You need to make notations on the quality and speed of their work."

"Sir, do you know there is just one woman embroiderer?"

"Oh, so there is just one left?" I didn't understand what he meant by that, but before I could ask questions, he asked me to take photos and make detailed notes. Crap, I had brought a camera with me but had already run out of film.

It was impossible to fall asleep that night. My heart and mind were racing so fast it felt like they were in an Olympic competition. I had never been in a situation where people's lives were definitely at stake. I guess I had been wrong. People do die in our industry. Sleep came in the wee hours, and that's when Our Lady of Fatima came to me in a dream and said, "Don't be afraid." This frightened me even more, so

I couldn't go back to sleep. I took the time to write down all the details of the previous day.

I turned on the TV. *Mad Max beyond Thunderdome* was playing on the only English channel. Of course it was. I called my husband. I thought it would be fun to tell him how the G.I. Joes were my escorts, but I realized that the minute I mentioned Blackwater, he would question what exactly I was doing there that needed special trained forces. I didn't have an answer. Blackwater had a reputation for being vicious, merciless mercenaries. All I knew was that if it wasn't for these men, I wouldn't have been able to do my job.

Early that morning I decided to go for a walk, hoping to shake off some nervous energy. I was in a very residential area in Lahore's upper-middle-class neighborhood. I came across St. Andrew's church. Who knew I would find this beautiful cathedral here? I went right inside and lit a candle. I might've been in over my head, but I had made myself responsible for helping this woman. Were there other women? All of the horror stories I'd heard reemerged. Stories of women being chained for days, without food or water, to get embroidery done for the most exclusive haute couture fashion houses in the world. I prayed that the answer would come to me.

The entourage promptly came to pick me up at the hotel. My scarf, clipboard, and all of the bottled water that I could find at the local market (which wasn't much) came with me into the Hummer. I could not find any film for the camera, but the hotel said that they would look into it for me. The ride seemed a little longer today, as I feared what I'd find. I tried to make small talk with the G.I. Joes.

"Where are you guys from?"

"Louisville, Kentucky," said one.

"Lewisburg, West Virginia," said the other.

Silence.

"I'm from New York."

"We know; we have been briefed on you." *What the fuck?*

"I must have missed my briefing on you," I said only half jokingly. Who were these guys?

"Ma'am," he said, "our details are classified and on a need-to-know basis. All you need to know is that we're here to protect you." From what? I wondered. I saw that I had a limited amount of questions, so I decided to use them sparingly.

We were back at the brick house. Once again, I walked in only with the interpreter. Like bats coming out of a cave, the older kids charged out. Fatima was embroidering the most intricate flowers on a delicate, woven silk fabric. I didn't need to get close or even touch it to be able to appreciate the quality of the artistry. I handed her a bottle of water and asked, through the interpreter, how I could help her.

She looked at the interpreter and said, "Does she know how to embroider?" They were both laughing before the interpreter was able to tell me what she said. I joined in the laughter. Fatima's response exemplified the dignity of a person who can keep their sense of humor in a dire situation. I took notes on the hotel stationery that I had attached to my clipboard. I looked around at all the naked babies lying on their colorful rugs. They were sleeping so peacefully. It made me wonder how it was possible. I reached down to comfort one of the babies who was kicking in his sleep. The interpreter grabbed my hand and reminded me that I was here only to observe. That's weird, I thought. It's just a baby.

My tolerance for heat, dust, and wretched smells had a very short time limit. And that time was up. I wanted to be able to come back in the afternoon and see how much of the work had been done. I asked the driver what we could do to kill a few hours and not have to drive all the way back to Lahore. He suggested that we drive to see the Shrine of Shams-ud-Din Sabzwari. He was, if I understood what he told me, the ruler of the sun, and we should go to pray for cooler weather. Plus, there was an excellent place to have lunch. The G.I. Joes agreed. A short ride later, we were at the shrine. It seemed that the person buried here had been accredited with many miracles. It was colorful and ornate on the outside, and even richer in an Arabic-Rococo way on the inside. It would've made Liberace envious. It was such a stark contrast to the dusty brick row houses where Fatima lived and worked.

I learned a little more about my interpreter. Her mother was the personal maid to an English businessman's wife, who was childless. The wife took great joy in having her house staff bring their children over during the holidays. It was something that was not very typical. Seeing that the interpreter was an enthusiastic reader as a child, the couple paid for her to go to the international school in Lahore. She was the first to be formally educated in her family. This was a point of great pride, but also problematic, as no male suitor was good enough for her family. So, at the old age of twenty-five, she was still unmarried.

Early that afternoon, we went back to the village so that I could measure the progress of Fatima's work. Stepping over the still-sleeping babies, I got close enough to see how much of the silk fabric had been transformed into a strikingly beautifully detailed rose garden. My fingers felt the pain that Fatima must've felt from stitching and knotting the fabric for such an extended period of time. She hadn't even stopped to drink from the bottle of water I'd given her.

"Fatima," I exclaimed, "this is so beautiful!" The interpreter didn't have to translate. She was blushing and shaking her head. She didn't want to accept the due compliments. I wrote down all the notes, did the calculation of how much work had been done, and considered the amount of time that it took before even putting a price value on it.

I went back to the hotel that evening feeling a little better. If we could just do something with the children, it would give Fatima the needed time to get the work done. I went out to dinner at a restaurant around the corner from where I was staying. The hotel told me it was a place that many expats went to eat. I went in with the high hopes of meeting someone who might have experience with the situation that I was facing.

There was my ray of light—the Mormon girls from Karachi were now in Lahore!

"Girls! How are you?" There were hugs all around. "Did you guys give up on Karachi?"

"Kind of," said one of them. "A new group of us came from Salt Lake, and we were relocated here. It seems nice here, considering we've been here just for a couple of days."

"Me too, I just got here. I am working on a project that is insane." They were eager to hear all the details about my past few days. I mentioned the state of the children. The girls had an education in early childhood development.

"I may put you guys to good use," I said jokingly. It is funny that behind every joke there is a bit of the truth.

A week had passed, with the same routine just about every day. Fatima had grown to trust me a bit. She had started to eat and drink the things that I bought for her. But everything was going to change.

When we pulled up to the brick building one day, there was a shabby square car with a rug as the upholstery on the front driver's seat and a cracked windshield. The G.I. Joes jumped out of the car and told me to stay put. I didn't. I was right behind them. In fact, I squeezed between them and entered.

Fatima was crouched in the corner with her arms covering her face. A man a little smaller than me was kicking the living shit out of her. She wasn't even whimpering. He wouldn't stop kicking her. He turned around for a brief second and saw me standing there in the shadows of my two giant living G.I. Joes. He went on kicking her.

I started screaming. "Stop, stop, stop, you motherfucker! Don't you see I have a fucking clipboard? I am an official observer!" He didn't stop; he didn't even turn around. How much more of a beating could poor Fatima take? I am going for it, I decided. I was leaping over the sleeping babies when one of the G.I.s caught me midair.

"You can't do that! You will cause an international incident," he said.

"Right, that's what you're here for."

He had me in a bear hug with my feet off the ground and carried me back outside to the car. "We are here to protect you, not her."

I was thrown into the back seat of the car. He pinned me down. I couldn't even breathe.

"Fuck off," I was yelling at him. "Where the fuck are we going?"

"Certainly he killed her. We are going back to the hotel. Your mission is over."

"Fuck you if you think you are going to tell me what to do!" I was struggling to sit up in the middle seat. He moved over a tiny bit, making sure to block the door. My ribs hurt from him squeezing me so hard when he carried me to the car.

"You are just a piece of shit loser who couldn't make it in the real military, and now you get a hard-on playing with guns in the desert!" No answer.

I yelled at the interpreter, "COME ON! Help me! Driver, go back! He is going to kill Fatima! You will all have blood on your hands!"

No answer from anyone. I banged on the roof of the car with both fists. I kicked the driver's seat. Fuck, that hurt. I cupped my hands over my face. I couldn't bear to see that we were way out of town by now.

Back in my room, I paced back and forth. How the hell could I get back to that town? I wasn't even sure where it was. The house didn't have a street number. I still had to wait eight hours before I could call in my report.

Then it hit me. I'll call Mahoor, I thought. He is a friend of the chief of police. I was sure the chief must've known someone here who could go back with me to see how Fatima was doing and report the incident.

I called his office number, and in one ring he picked up. "Mahoor?"

"Yes, who is this?"

"It's me." I started sobbing. "It's so horrible."

"Are you OK? Did someone hurt you? Where are you?"

"No, I'm fine, I'm at the hotel."

"Should I send someone for you?"

"PLEASE STOP TALKING," I yelled at him. "Let me just tell you what happened. It's beyond horrible."

I tried to collect myself. "He wouldn't stop kicking her."

"Who?"

"Fatima, the woman I was here to observe." I had not explained my job in Lahore to him when we had dinner. I didn't have the patience or time to tell the whole story. "Mahoor, please, I need to get in touch with the chief of police here. My friend. My friend . . . she could be bleeding to death as we speak."

"Mercedes, I'm sorry. No one cares about those people."

"Those people?"

"Most likely she is low on the caste system, so she is disposable. No one will come and help her."

Disposable people? My head was spinning.

"Mahoor, you of all people should be kinder to another human being."

"It's not me. It's *jati*, it's her birthright."

"Mahoor, not even a dog."

"Mercedes, no one is going to help," he said in a much stronger voice. "Let me ask you this. Were there dozens of children sleeping in the workroom?"

"Yes."

"Do you know they poison them so that they will sleep all day until their parents come home?"

That would explain it. I had heard that gypsies do the same in Europe to collect money from tourists with a sleeping child in their arms. The drugs keep them from fidgeting.

He continued, "They will even mangle the arm or leg of a child so that people will take pity on them when they are begging in the streets." Dear God, I was thinking. The desperation people must feel to do such an atrocity.

"Mahoor, don't you use this type of embroidery in your Bollywood clothing?"

"Indeed, only the finest." He caught himself.

"You also have to share in this responsibility."

"Wrong. I buy them from a reputable showroom."

"Really?" I asked. "Was that the agent who paid a visit to Fatima today?" Silence.

"What do you suggest I do?" he finally answered. "If I knew, I would have mentioned it already."

"I will call you back with a plan."

I looked at the clock, which happened to be a clock shaped like a black cat swinging its tail. Just like *The Pit and the Pendulum* it would not stop ticking. Tick tock, tick tock, yet each time I looked up, it was still the same time.

"Director," I shouted into the phone when I called.

"Yes, Mercedes?"

"Holy fucking mother of Jesus Christ! You guys fucking set me up! You knew what the fuck was going on here and you didn't even give me a fucking little heads up!" Now, I would like to say on my behalf that while I was waiting to make my call, I had come up with and rehearsed an entire soliloquy. Professional, precise, and to the point. That all went to hell the second I opened my mouth.

"Yes, Mercedes, you are absolutely right. We should have given you a more detailed briefing. But now you have a full understanding of the gravity of this situation. Are you able to come up with a comprehensive set of standards for cottage industry that we can recommend to the United Nations?"

"Yes, I am willing, but not sure if I am able. What resources will I have?" Already my mind is racing. The kids, we have to do something with the kids. Why, why was there only one person working?

"Mercedes?"

"Yes?" I had missed something he said. "Can you repeat that; we must have had a break in the connection?"

"You have an open bank account. To be clear, you have no set budget for this project and an open timeline."

"I can spend as much as I want and take as long as I need? Is that what I am hearing from you?"

"Yes, all within reason."

"I am going to need a team."

"Just run who they are past us."

I liked this. I could do this. No, I had to do this!

"Wait, what about Fatima?" I asked.

"She is in good hands and getting the best care."

"How do you know? I didn't even tell you what happened."

"Mercedes, you only know the part that you have witnessed. We have the whole picture."

Remarkably, not only did I fall right to sleep, but I completely passed out. I was so emotionally and mentally drained. Sleep didn't last long, though, and I woke up in the middle of the night. Fuck, the Mormons! I needed to find the Mormons! I'd never asked them where they were staying. It had been a couple of days since I ran into them. Maybe they'd moved on again. Positive thoughts, I reminded myself. I called on the powers of Jesus, Mohammed, Ganesh, and who's the prophet of the Mormons? The guy they named the school after? Oh yeah, Brigham Young . . . bring your people to me, I implored.

Call me one lucky son of a bitch, but don't you know it, the next morning whom did I run into? The girls. I explained the situation to them. I told them that I wanted to start a type of nursery school where the kids could be during the day learning social skills. I had made up a checklist of all the things I needed to do to create a village of embroiderers. That was the solution. It wouldn't be a bunch of fragmented embroiderers scattered throughout the region, but a community, like in Peru. While the solution was a straighforward idea, I knew it wouldn't be simple to throw a bunch of people together, open a school, set up an independent system for their supply chain, and be able to train new embroiderers in an efficient way.

I called Mahoor. "I'm going to need you, your fiancée, and all the guys to come and help me set up a village."

"Are you crazy? How do you set up a village? You don't know anything about Pakistan, how the caste system works, how the cultures clash, the bureaucracy of the government, or the corruption of the whole supply chain."

"What better person to help me navigate through all the bullshit than someone who can lead a double life with a teacher and a police chief?" I reminded him.

"We'll be there by Friday," he said.

I had the operations office back in DC help me locate more than forty embroiderers who lived within a twenty-mile radius of Fatima's village. I wanted to set the first embroiderers' village in her town. Each one of the women had their own story and reason for not wanting to come to this new village: they were married, their families forbid them, they were of a much lower caste (social class) level. This was where the young interpreter was essential in demonstrating that the embroiderer's position in life was not determined by birth. Her mother was a maid and her father a gardener, yet she had been educated and worked for the United Nations.

It all came together. Noor worked with the Mormon girls, explaining Pakistani laws and customs when it came to preparing a proper nursery school. Mahoor's friend the police chief was able to make some phone calls and clear some paths for us so there wouldn't be any incidents when we started relocating the women. Some of the cricket fans I had met at the English pub were lawyers and accountants who helped us set up a system of certifying ethical working conditions for the embroiderers. Mahoor himself wrote the standards of what would be acceptable. Textiles with this certification would be traced back to the actual person who made it, thus avoiding any "conflicts textiles" in the supply chain. There would be a nursery and preschool that was the central part of the village. The embroiderers all would work in a clean room, which meant they were now able to do bridal embroideries. These were the most delicate and highest paying of the embroideries.

Mahoor and Noor married that spring and moved to Lahore, and now he is in charge of the Textile Federation. The Mormon girls worked at the school for almost two years before their mission was completed. They left a system in place that could be easily followed by some of the village elders. I made a presentation to the United Nations on the criteria and standards for recognizing cottage industry and how a certification program would govern each one.

What I hope to be remembered as is the woman who taught the kids how to play 1, 2, 3 Red Light!

Fatima is now the manager of all the women embroiderers. Remember how she was breastfeeding a child when I first met her? It wasn't even her own. Her child had died from a reaction to the sleeping medicine. This woman has endured tremendous suffering and pain in her life, and yet she is one of the most joyful people you will ever meet. She's the first one to praise or to sit with someone and teach the art of embroidery.

Indeed, Allah is with those who patiently endure.

RAINBOWS AND UNICORNS

$\mathcal{O}$ne of the things I emphasize when I teach a Retail 101 class is the importance of outstanding customer service. The days of having untrained store clerks satisfy customers have disappeared with the horse and buggy. Nobody would dream of using a horse and buggy for transportation, yet they think it's okay to have clerks instead of trained professionals. In fashion, it's not only about training for fit and style, but it's also about being able to address the customer's needs, crisis management, and loss prevention. Of course, it helps if they are trained in sales, too.

I did a lot of work Venezuela, a breathtaking country with breathtaking people, economic independence, and a thriving retail culture. I'd had a terrible routine of visiting these spectacular places and never taking advantage of anything they had to offer. I'd been to Peru several times and had never gone to Machu Picchu. I'd been to Egypt several times and had never seen a pyramid. I'd been to India several dozen times and had never seen the Taj Mahal. I'd been to Venezuela, even to the tiny island of Margarita, and had never gone swimming in the ocean.

That year, I decided I would start to take a few extra personal days and visit some of these iconic landmarks people often asked me about. I am not sure what set this trigger off. I think, in part, it was that I was finally comfortable in the place I was professionally, and it was finally time to enjoy the journeys.

Whenever I exited the plane and walked through the corridors of the airport in Venezuela, I saw these fabulous panoramic photos of Angel Falls. Angel Falls is about 600 km from Caracas, where I do most of my work. I was determined to get there on my next trip, so I made sure to pick up all the necessary literature, brochures, and recommendations to prepare to visit Angel Falls. With pamphlets in hand, I picked an overnight excursion midway up Angel Falls. A hike to the very top of Angel Falls would take seven days. I'm a city girl. An overnight hike is enough adventure for me. I thought about what I would need for this adventure. All I knew was that I needed a pair of hiking boots. In New York City, there is a family-owned outdoor adventure store named Paragon. I've been going to the store since I was a kid. They have everything, for every type of outdoor sport, at every price point. I figured this was the best place to start, as it was conveniently located near my neighborhood.

The store is enormous, and a little overwhelming, since they merchandise seasonally by sport. You're always caught a little off guard when you first walk into the store because of this. Finding the floor with the outdoor and camping equipment (this is a multilevel store taking up almost a full New York City block) was one thing, but finding the hiking boots was another. God forbid I would look at the directory. In the shoe area, there was a wall that had all types of hiking boots showcased from floor to ceiling. I started eyeballing them all. Who knew there were so many types of boots?

Just as I was going to reach for the first pair, this kid came up behind me and said, "Where are you hiking?" Notice that he didn't say "Can I help you?" This is because any respectable New Yorker, whether or not they need help, will always say no. I was a little wary even of starting a conversation but told him that I was going to hike Angel Falls. I wasn't even expecting him to know where Angel Falls was, but he said, "That's terrific, man; Joe from the bike department just came back from there. Let me get him over here to talk to you about his experience."

"You know, that would be pretty cool," I said, excited to talk to someone who had been there recently.

This was a time before Trip Advisor, and Angel Falls did not have any People's Choice popularity reviews. At the time, you could buy your ticket online, but you still had to depend on somebody you knew, or someone who knew someone to give you a heads-up about the trip.

Joe, a lanky, pimple-faced post-teenager, came over and said, "Hello. Are you the lady who's going to Angel Falls?"

"Yeah, I'm the lady," I said, feeling my age. "I understand you've been to Angel Falls, and I am looking for a pair of hiking boots. Can you recommend a pair?" I still didn't believe that he had been there, but I could use his advice on a pair of boots.

He pulled a handsome-looking boot off the top shelf. "This boot . . ." I cut Joe off, as this boot was marked $950. They used huge price stickers in the store. There was no mistaking pricing here.

"This is a one-time thing," I said. "I'm not a professional hiker, and I probably will never go hiking again. I just need something to get me there and back."

He smiled and nodded his head. "Yeah, I have something for you." He pulled out another pair of boots marked $98. Now, I'm no hiking expert, but how did we get from $950 to $98?

"Joe," I said, "I want to make it up the hill without the sole of the boots falling off."

He started to chuckle, "Yeah, right, and you need something a little better with some ankle support because you could be hiking in two different terrains."

"What do you mean?" I asked.

"Well, you're going to start off on really rocky and sandy ground, and as you start up the mountain, you're going to find yourself in humid tropical conditions with very wet and slippery rocks. So basically you're going to need an all-terrain boot." This made sense and was something I hadn't known.

"Okay, so what do you recommend?" He showed me a pair of leather boots with rubber soles that laced up high. He explained the benefits of these boots, and how I could use them in New York City during icy winter days.

This is a salesmanship skill we call good, better, best. He had shown me the best option compared to the opening price point. Most people will always settle for the middle price. Done.

"Well, you should also take a couple of socks if you don't want to get blisters, and you'll want to be able to change your socks at least twice a day." He showed me some $9 socks that wick away moisture and explained their benefits. In my brain, all I was hearing was yadda, yadda, yadda. I took four pairs. That's called the upsell.

Then he asked, "What are you going to do for drinking water?" I hadn't even thought of that. I knew I wasn't going to be dragging up gallons of water.

"What am I going to do about the water?" At the time, it was trendy to have a CamelBak, a water pouch you strapped to your back and used a straw to drink.

He responded with childlike enthusiasm. "Look at this. This is a Lifestraw Water Bottle."

"Explain," I said to him. As if I needed to ask him, he was already in full demonstration mode.

"You're going to be following a stream up the mountain. When you stop for a break, you take this bottle, scoop up some of the water, give it a shake, and out will come one hundred percent purified drinking water. It has a seven-layer osmosis filtration system."

"Okay Joe, you're losing me. What I'm taking from this conversation is that I am not carrying jugs of water, and I'm not going to die drinking the river water."

"Yeah man, that's right." That is called the add-on.

"Perfect, ring me up."

"Wait one second." Oh, he was going for the double upsell!

"Yes?"

"You're going on the overnight trip?"

"Yes, I am."

"The one with the hammocks in the thatch roof open-air pagoda? You know how in the brochure they show you that picture of all the hammocks?"

"Yes, as a matter of fact, I have the brochure with me." I pulled it out, and he got very excited.

"My God, this is the same one I had! Yeah man, you see right here the cotton macramé hammocks? They look beautiful. I love them, but what they're not showing you in the picture is that they're moldy." I could see that happening in the humid jungle. That could be pretty gross. "Yeah man, so I'd like to suggest that you bring a slap hammock." This was basically a travel nylon hammock.

"Okay, that makes sense, I'll take one." I wasn't even asking for prices anymore. He was a credible expert, and I started to trust him. He was genuinely trying to prepare me for the experience.

This is called selling to a life cycle. It can be as trivial as a vacation, or as life changing as having your first baby. Think about when you (or your friend) had your first baby shower. On the list was two of everything ever made for a child on God's green earth. The new mom is thoroughly prepared for every kind of complex emergency that might possibly occur. With baby number two, the experienced mom gets more practical with the things needed. Baby number three is lucky to have a diaper change more than twice a day. One woman told me that she has six children, and she had pictures of her first born's poop but had forgotten to take a baby picture of her sixth child. She would just show him pictures of his brother and say, "My, you looked just like your brother when he was a baby."

Joe started a new conversation by saying, "Don't get freaked out." I was already going to be freaked out. "That thatched roof?"

"Yes?"

"It's filled with bats."

"What?"

"Don't be afraid; they are just fruit bats. They won't hurt you at all, but the problem is when they return home to sleep at dawn, and, well you know, they poop." I imagined myself, a person who sleeps with her mouth open, dealing with a bat pooping into my mouth.

I screeched, "Gross! What the hell am I supposed to do about the bats?"

"Oh, that's easy, and it works as a double solution. All you have to do is throw a mosquito net on to cover yourself. It keeps the poop and the mosquitoes off you. Speaking of mosquitoes, did you know that they can be the size of a small hummingbird? And forget about using that natural mosquito repellent; you need a straight-up military-grade poison. They drink those natural repellents like soup."

"Okay Joe, get me the mosquito net and bring on the poison." Almost $2,000 later, I felt one hundred percent confident that I was fully prepared for my trip. I was excited to finish my work in Caracas and get over to Canaima National Park.

I flew there in an airplane slightly bigger than a crop duster. I'm almost sure I could even smell the pesticides. I woke up early, as instructed by my brochure, and went to the designated spot just inside the national park. Two American couples whom I had seen at the hotel were also there. I checked them out. They were wearing a lot of fancy clothing: pants that zipped off and became shorts, long-sleeve knit tops (made by 5.11, a tactical clothing company), a mesh hat that had UV protection, and a multicargo pocket vest that rounded off the total look. They looked like they were part of some kind of military group. I calculated that they probably had about $5,000 worth of equipment. I wasn't feeling so sorry about the money I'd spent, because I spent it on the essentials. Behind me came a group of Germans. Now they had some serious equipment. They had a GPS tracking system, satellite telephones, night-vision goggles, and all kinds of crazy photographic equipment. Shit, I had brought only a crappy little digital camera. Our tour guide came over to us. He was just wearing flip-flops, loose-fitting nylon running shorts, and no shirt. He gave us a little safety prep in what could have been either English or Spanish. It wasn't necessarily clear. What I did understand was the part where he decided that I was his hiking partner, since I was hiking alone.

Right from the start, the guide took off running like a gazelle in the forest. I was doing my best just to keep up with him. In no time, I was struggling. I was panting, I was tripping, and I was hot and exhausted. We had been hiking only for about half an hour. Oh dear, I thought, this was not going well. Was I going to make it? It was starting to feel like a terrible idea. But then, with each step, the landscape began to evolve. It was breathtaking—the flowers, the orchids hanging from the tropical trees, the parrots in single colors of red, blue, and green. Hummingbirds, not mosquitoes, dove past me as they reached into the bell jar flowers for their nectar. I found renewed energy as I realized I was walking in paradise. The guide stopped every once in a while, briefly, to point at something. Some things I saw, and sometimes I wondered what he wanted me to see. What I didn't miss was a giant anaconda wrapped around a tree, hissing, just inches away from me. You're not in Kansas anymore, Dorothy! Clicking your heels together is not going to get you out of here. Better keep moving forward fast!

A bit behind us were the Americans, who seemed to be arguing about everything. The German group was so far behind that I could barely see one of their bright-orange caps bobbing in the distance. I hoped they were okay. Our guide, or should I say my guide, had stopped in what seemed to be a swimming hole. He dove right in, without even checking for, I don't know . . . piranhas, water snakes, poison dart frogs, an electric eel, perhaps!? I'd read too much about everything that could kill me on this trip. But sitting on a rock waiting for him to swim back, I did get to see the most fantastic lizards running across the water. Yes, on top of the water! I later found out that they are called Jesus Christ Lizards. How cool is that? They walk on water!

I scooped up some pond water in my nifty water bottle, shook it a bit, and took a big swallow of the fresh water. I took it all in. I thought to myself, I'm alone in the middle of nowhere and everywhere. This was everything, and this was nothing. How could someone not believe in a supreme architect of the universe? How did I get here? Of all the paths in the world. this is where the crossroads have taken me. I started humming "Life during Wartime" by the Talking Heads. It seemed appropriate . . .

> Lived in a brownstone, lived in a ghetto
> I've lived all over this town
> This ain't no party, this ain't no disco

This ain't no fooling around
No time for dancing, or lovey dovey
I ain't got time for that now.

My guide suddenly splashed up in front of me, scaring the bejesus out of me. He shook himself off like a wet dog. No need for a towel. We set off again, not even waiting for the others to reach us.

A few hours later, with the sun still high in the sky, we reached the base camp. The gauchos had already prepared us an elaborate meal of *hallaca*, *perico*, and *pabellón criollo*. Look it up. It's worth it. In truth, I would have eaten a rattlesnake, I was so hungry.

I cleaned up the best I could. There wasn't an inch of my body that didn't hurt. I hurt down to my toes. One thing I didn't bring was any kind of aspirin. A gaucho gave me a cup of tea with some long leaves that looked like bay leaves to drink. In a very crude way, he explained that it was an anti-inflammatory. By the time the rest of the group arrived, I had already eaten and I honestly just wanted to be alone. I wanted to reflect and enjoy this overwhelming feeling of gratitude. I took down one of the hammocks, adjusted my nylon hammock, gave myself a good blast of my military-grade poison, threw the mosquito netting over me, and fell into blissful sleep until the next morning. In fact, I'm usually an early riser, but I was the last one to wake up.

"How could you sleep like a rock?" one of the Americans barked at me. I think he was a little envious. They had bloodshot eyes and dark circles.

"Did you hear all those noises?" He was trying to identify what he heard in the night. "It was a howling . . . no, more like a crackle," he said. Crackle? What the hell is a crackle? I thought.

I got three passports, a couple of visas
You don't even know my real name
High on a hillside, the trucks are loading
Everything's ready to roll.

The song was back in my head, and suddenly I was craving peanut butter.

After a delicious and hearty breakfast of quinoa, eggs, and a kind of green vegetable (I want to say it could have been herbs), and a strong cup of coffee served with goat's milk, we were back to our hike. Somehow, we made it as a group this time. From my understanding, there had been some situation yesterday that encouraged everyone to keep up with the guide. We cleared the last of the jungle foliage to find a green meadow that ended abruptly at the waterfall. The sky was the color of the Greek ocean, with one token fluffy cloud hanging above us. The mist from the waterfall cooled our hot faces and created double rainbows. Not those faded, faraway rainbows that you might have seen, though. These were so close and so deep in color that you could feel them in your heart. Gorgeous, colorful macaws pierced through the rainbows, making it seem as if the rainbows had given birth to them. I took a look around, because if there was such a thing as a unicorn, then this is where it lived. The guide told us that we had to take pictures without fear in our hearts, or our photos would all come out blurry. He said our fear made us undeserving of nature's beauty. The reason why he mentioned this was because the grassy meadow in which we were standing was quite slippery, and we were dangerously close to the waterfall's edge. I took my pictures without fear. It would be okay if this was my last day.

I had paid extra to be helicoptered back down to the city. The overnight hike was enough adventure for this city girl. The group looked at me with envy. Even the fittest person among us found it to be physically challenging. On the flight home, I couldn't sit for long periods of time because my backside hurt so much. Imagine walking to the top of the Empire State Building four times. While I'm not sure how that would feel, I doubt it would be a good feeling.

I got home to find a postcard from the guys at Paragon. *Don't forget to stop by and show us pictures of your trip.* Signed, Joe and Mike.

I was so excited that they were even remotely interested in hearing about my trip that even before my husband got home, I printed the pictures at CVS and ran over to Paragon. I went upstairs to the hiking department and immediately bumped into Mike. Mike called Joe over on his walkie-talkie as I started to pull out the pictures to show them. We were comparing notes. Was there a jerk with $10,000 worth of night-vision equipment falling asleep before the sun even went down? he asked. Well, yes to the equipment, and not sure about the falling asleep. That would have been me that passed out, I told them. While we were laughing, the manager came out.

"What are you guys looking at?"

Joe had the stack of pictures in his hands. "Mercedes is just showing us her pictures from Angel Falls."

What would you expect a manager to say? I was expecting an "OK, people, get back to work!" But instead, he said, "Can I see those pictures?

Joe has been bragging about his experience. I think I might be the one to go next."

"You're going to love it," I said. "I was so happy with everything I bought here. Joe was the expert when it came to preparing me for the trip. But the one thing that Joe didn't prepare me for was that I should have been in better shape. I'm lucky I didn't lose a lung on this trip," I said laughingly, but not really joking.

Just then, a couple was looking at the boots next to me. I grabbed the pair that I had bought and said, "You are going to love these. They are perfect for any part of the world you would want to hike. As a matter of fact, I just came back from Venezuela, and they were perfect. All-terrain, you know, you can even use them in the snow in New York City." I was selling the goods in the store. You know it's a happy customer when they do that.

"Well, I hope that wasn't your only adventure," Joe said. He put on a wrestling announcer voice, booming out "I hope you're psyched up, and maybe next time it will be Kilimanjaro, the second-largest mountain in the world."

Then he said, "You need to start training by doing some kind of exercise. You need to build up stamina. I think you should try bike riding." Remember, Joe worked in the biking department.

"Go on," I said.

"Well, you know, New York City has invested millions of dollars in these beautiful bike paths, and you can almost bike all around the island using the West Side Path." I envisioned myself going to work on my new American-made fancy bike. Of course, I would need a helmet, a bike lock, and a basket to put my little dog in. And $1,000 later, I walked out of the store with my new fantasy of riding my bike to work every day and building up my stamina to climb Kilimanjaro. I must've lost a lot of oxygen to my brain during my hike in Venezuela. If you know me, you know I consider it a full day's workout just running to catch a cab. I took the bike home, I hung it up on a fancy bike rack that I'd also bought that day, and it stayed right there for two weeks.

I was having buyer's remorse when I got home one night to a message on my answering machine. Yes, people left messages on answering machines. It was Joe, and he wanted to know how I was enjoying my new bike. Perfect, this was my excuse to return the bike. I called the store asking for Joe, and as soon as he got on the phone, I thanked him for the phone call and told him I absolutely hated the bike.

"I don't know what I was thinking. I don't have time for leisurely bike rides, and I live five blocks away from my office, so taking a bike to work is more effort than just walking. What is your return policy on slightly used bicycles?" He knew I rode it home from the store.

"Well, before you return it, I want to tell you that you will get a full refund. But you know what you need, Mercedes? You need a bike buddy."

"Joe, what the hell is a bike buddy?"

"We do this thing on the first Friday of every month called 'critical mass.' We all meet at midnight and ride our bikes down the streets of Manhattan, causing a critical mass in the name of reducing car traffic and our personal carbon footprint." It sounded a little crunchy granola to me, but I get it, and it was charming that this young kid was willing to go biking with an old lady. I was very flattered.

"Okay, I can do this. What time should I meet you?"

"Well, when the store closes at 10 p.m., we could all grab a bite, and you could meet a couple of my friends that ride together." Wow, he was pretty serious. He was not going to invite me to just leave me with a pack of strangers. I got to the store right at 10 p.m. He was just walking out when he saw me, and I could see the look of surprise on his face.

"Oh my God, what's wrong?" I asked him. I quickly realized it was something with my outfit. Was I trying too hard to be cool?

"You're not night ready."

"What does that mean, Joe?" Apparently, New York City law states that you have to have a night light and reflective taping or a vest to ride legally at night.

"Oh well, nice try, thank you anyway," I told him.

"Oh no, you're not getting off that easy." He called inside and asked one of the managers to bring out the items that I needed. "We won't be able to ring you up tonight since the registers are closed, but if you still want to return your bike tomorrow, just bring these along with them."

That is beyond excellent customer service. He had put all of those items on his account with the store. He was now responsible for my things if I wasn't going to pay for them.

We had fun at the dinner. We shared more stories about Venezuela. I told him about Margarita and the secret beaches I was looking forward to finding. His friend told me about all the places he wanted to see. Some of them I had been to, and a few were new to me. The group that started to assemble at Union Square Park grew bigger and bigger, and together thousands of us rode down the streets of

Manhattan in the middle of the night. It was intense, it was fun, and it was genuine.

Joe called me the next day. "Did you enjoy the ride? It's okay if you still want to return the bike."

"Joe, you're right, I want to keep the bike and make an effort to incorporate it into some routine. You're going to have to go with me on the trip to Kilimanjaro."

I rode that bike for years. I still haven't been to Kilimanjaro, but when I'm ready to go I know that I will find a credible expert at Paragon Sport.

HELL BOSS

$\mathcal{I}$ often work with stores in distressed situations, and many times there is a complete disconnect between the owners and the staff. The owners will give me one set of excuses, and the staff tells me another. Then, in closed-door meetings with the staff, they will tell me another story altogether. This disconnect comes from owners who don't appreciate or listen to the suggestions of their employees. I encourage daily or weekly sales meetings. These should be quick and to the point. Each season should have a group meeting to review trends, give brand suggestions, and offer training. You want to create a corporate culture where the team feels like their contributions are heard.

A morning meeting might go something like this (I take a lot of my sales-training techniques from the cosmetic companies that I think do a fantastic job of keeping meetings quick and to the point): "Jane, you sold makeup to a man yesterday; tell us about that."

"Well, this guy was hanging around the counter, so I asked if he was looking for a gift. He told me his wife had lost her purse with all of her makeup in it. He wanted to buy her something but was lost as to what she would like. I suggested that every woman needs a compact and a lip gloss. I said that he should get a gift card for her also, and I would do a free makeover where she could pick her own colors."

"Wonderful! You didn't judge the man, great, and instead offered him excellent customer service. Well done! Now, Betty, I see you didn't make any sales yesterday. What happened?"

"Well, I woke up late with a horrible migraine. Since I was running so late, I didn't think you had time to replace me. So I came in and did the best I could."

"OK, Betty, you know the rules. I don't want zombies on the floor. I need everyone to be at one hundred ten percent. You have my home number and my cell. Call me. Tell me what's going on. If I can't find someone to replace you, I will come in myself. Mary, our goal yesterday was to sell five mascaras each, but you sold twenty. How did you do it?"

"I was holding the mascara, and as each person walked past the counter, I asked them if they knew what made our mascara special. When they hesitated, I explained all of the benefits. It was an easy sell."

"That's wonderful, but keep in mind that it is waterproof. A good add-on to the sale would have been the eye makeup remover. It's excellent for mature skin because it's packed with vitamins and good for contact lens wearers. OK, team, today's goal is $1,000. Let's go get it!"

Simple, enjoyable, and to the point. It offers quick training and corrections to problems. I have been using this example for years.

During one MAGIC workshop, I taught a Retail 101 class in which I used this example.

A few months later, I got a phone call. The conversation started like this:

"Mercedes?"

"Yes."

"You are a fraud." Now, I have been called many things in my life, but never a fraud. I should have just hung up, but I took the punishment. This woman started yelling at me!

"I have been in business for twenty years," she said. "I never had a stupid meeting. After hearing you speak, I thought I would give it a try! Well, let me tell you that I lost an employee of eighteen years, and the morale in the store is dragging on the floor."

She wouldn't let me get a word in until I said, "Well, maybe something else is wrong." Oh, my God, she freaked out. Crisis management is something everyone in retail should study. I could not calm her down. I couldn't even talk. I eventually blurted out, "I am coming to visit you! Where are you located?"

"West Virginia."

I was already going on a road trip to visit clients, and I was going to end my trip at Virginia Beach. How much farther could it be? Well, eight hours later, I was finally in the parking lot of the store. I had stayed the night so that I could be on time for the 8 a.m. meeting. The store opened at 10 a.m. This wasn't going to be a quick meeting. The store was a vast open space, a family store lost in a sea of racks. It had ugly flooring and horrible fluorescent lighting. It must have been 110 degrees inside the store. The air system was on a timer and hadn't kicked in yet.

She was a half hour late when she stormed in like the Tasmanian Devil, except her head was the only thing spinning around, like the girl in *The Exorcist*. She was already in a rage about the heat and the traffic. She didn't bring a cookie, bagel, coffee, or whatever is the thing to bring in West Virginia for anyone but herself. I personally had been looking forward to a Krispy Kreme. After a few minutes of her rant, which she must've considered her staff meeting, she looked at me and asked who the hell I was.

"Are you kidding me? I came all the way from New York to be a part of your sales meeting." She huffed at me and continued, completely ignoring me. She did all the talking. I am going to put the examples from the previously mentioned meeting in her tone. This is the best imitation of what I witnessed that I can make understandable, because what went on during that meeting was unbelievable.

"Don't you know the store policy on cosmetics? There are no returns. That sucker was the perfect target for selling off all those ugly colors! And you, dear (pause, big huff, head shake)—do you not know about this modern technology called aspirin? Take two of those, because you are the one giving me a headache. And you!" She pointed to the youngest staff member in the room. "Can't you get something as simple as 'makeup/makeup remover, makeup/makeup remover, makeup/makeup remover' in that pretty little head? For Pete's sake, am I the only one who can think here? Am I the only one who can get the job done? Now let's try to make some sales. Today's goal is $100,000."

I was speechless. I didn't know where to start. I looked at the sad, beaten-down eyes staring back at me whispering, "Take me with you." She wasn't only mean to the staff, either. While I was there, a customer walked in, and she yelled across the room, "If you are planning on returning something today, you can just turn around and go, because I am not in the mood!"

Attitude aside, many retailers have harsh return policies. They say one of the reasons for this is because if they take back a return after two weeks, the chances are very high that they have sold out of that item and will not know where to hang it in the store. I don't have the words to explain the stupidity of this reasoning. If you sold all the other units at full price, then this last item can be sold at cost, and you will still be making money. As far as the merchandising question goes, just put it on a rack near the cash wrap. People will see it and ask about it, and you can say you were waiting to put it back on the floor. Someone will scoop it up.

There will be some people who take advantage of return policies. We have a client who had a woman's husband come in during March, wanting to return $900 worth of clothing that had been purchased in December. He told the salesperson that his wife had killed herself and he found these bags in her closet. Since they still had the tags, he wanted to return them. Not knowing what to do, the salesperson told him she was genuinely sorry for his loss, but she didn't have the authority to accept such a large return, and to please call the store in the morning or come back when the owner would be there.

Betty, the owner, immediately texted me asking what she should do. Google it, I texted back.

"Google what?" she asked.

"Google her death." I may be a hardcore, non-trusting New Yorker, but Scottsdale, Arizona, where Betty is from is a relatively small town. "See if you can find anything in the papers from December to now."

"Nothing."

"Is she in your client book? Call her."

It turned out she was alive and well. Her husband had threatened to kill her for overspending, and then hid the goods. She'd forgotten she'd even bought them.

I tried to speak to the Tasmanian Devil about corporate culture, but she couldn't even understand the concept. It took all of my energy not to want to hurt her physically. Even the tone of her voice got under my skin. The reason why she wouldn't listen was because she was making money. When a store is making money, even if it's just getting by, the owner often doesn't see the big picture and how much more money could be generated.

So, why does the staff stay and why do people even shop there? Location and positioning. There were not a lot of jobs in this area of West Virginia. The coal mines had started to close, and the few options included working at a minimart or being a teacher's aide. If the consumer wanted to buy anything that was remotely nicer than what the local Walmart had to offer, this was the only game in town. It's only a matter of time before the situation changes and there are other choices. They are selling million-dollar homes in the mountains with private lakes that were formed from the mining industry. I still, once in a while, call from a public phone and hang up just to see if she is still open.

She is.

THE GODFATHER
AND THE ORPHANS

$\mathcal{I}$ have been working in Colombia for some time now.

I think I have aged a few years while writing this book. A few years that I had forgotten to add up, until I wrote the memories down. All of these stories, all of these people, and all of these adventures feel like they just happened yesterday. I'm feeling old. Happy 50th to me.

It started with a phone call from the Colombian Trade Association. I get a lot of my international work from different trade associations trying to develop business opportunities for economic stimulation. Most of this economic development is in commodities, such as agriculture, raw materials, or pharmaceutical. Most of the people who work at the trade offices are responsible for many of the commodities. One person I work with at the Peruvian trade office is accountable for textiles, apparel, wine, and asparagus. This makes it a little tricky to have an in-depth conversation about a specific segment of the market when urgencies overlap, like asparagus season and spring/summer clothing deliveries.

The caller asked if I was willing to travel to Bogotá to assess a growing chain of retail stores. They said that the owner of the stores also owned one of the largest textile- and apparel-producing factories in Colombia, and it employed thousands of people in every sector of the textile industry. He even owned some of the farms that grew the cotton. The idea was that with more perception of value, a more stable economy in Colombia, and the dark years of civil war now over, the timing was perfect for significant growth. They wanted to make sure that this company stayed relevant and competitive with new international brands that were entering the market. They also wanted to showcase the pride and resilience of the Colombian people.

An unusually uneventful, boring flight down to Bogotá became quite exciting when I found a VIP agent waiting for me at the door of the plane. I'm not talking about waiting for me at baggage claim. I'm talking about waiting for me right at the front door of the aircraft. He was incredibly warm and friendly, a very typical trait of the Colombian people. He took my passport and told me to follow him. We passed the long line at immigration, we passed the long line at customs, and we walked right past security into a narrow hallway that went outside the airport but was completely covered. It was similar to an enclosed carport. This was the airport exit for VIPs. Cars would pull into this carport, completely separate from people waiting for their family and friends outside the airport. No one could see who was getting into the VIP cars. This was done for extreme security reasons, in order to protect the identities of VIPs coming in and out of the country. At this time there were still a few incidents of people who worked for high-profile companies being kidnapped. I was advised not to wear a wedding ring, not to have any pictures of my children (easy, as I don't have any children), and to just have a name card without a title or important American business name. This technically made me worthless. I wasn't married, I didn't have kids, and I probably didn't have a job.

I was taken directly to the offices of the man whom I would soon start to call the Godfather. His office building had a double security system. We drove up to a thick, tall concrete wall with a metal sliding gate that had prison-style barbed wire running across the top. The underside of the car was inspected with sliding mirrored yardsticks, and the trunk was visually inspected. The driver was instructed to type a keycode into a digital pad. I guessed it was an employee code. After parking our car in the assigned spot ordered by the first security detail, the driver used his thumbprint to enter a concrete foyer. Pretty cool, I thought. I had never seen anyone open a door by using their fingerprint. I mean, I'd seen it in the *Mission Impossible* movies, but never in real life. It would be a decade before Apple thought about using this type of technology on cell phones. In the concrete room, a female and a male security officer came out and politely, very politely, almost apologetically politely said they had to frisk us before we went through a metal detector. This was done efficiently, without any feeling of degradation. She spoke to me during the whole process, informing me of what to expect next. I was then taken into a beautifully decorated modern office. The receptionist greeted me like we had been friends for years. She offered me coffee and again apologized for making me wait a few minutes while the Godfather ended his call. I was shortly ushered past meticulously carved sliding pocket doors.

Godfather was talking on the phone with his back facing the door. He sat on a huge leather chair. It was sort of like a Henry Miller midcentury office chair, but more classically detailed. The desk could've been a partner's desk. It was abundant with lion clawfoot details, all in rich mahogany. The room was filled with art in gold-gilded frames and with vintage global maps hanging behind his desk. He was speaking in perfect Spanish about nothing important. It seemed to be a conversation about dinner that evening. He turned around, and cue the *Godfather* music . . . he was wearing a suit vest with a white button-down shirt, unbuttoned just one button too many. He was holding an unlit cigar. I would have expected the room to smell like cigar smoke, but it didn't. There was a decanter, filled with an amber-colored liquid, and a crystal-cut glass on his desk. I was almost sure it was whiskey. I already liked this guy, and we hadn't even had a conversation.

He greeted me in perfect English. Well, actually in a very familiarly accented English. Specifically, New York Brooklyn Jewish English. How could that be? The Colombian government had told me I was working on a project with a Colombian company. Certainly an American couldn't be the owner.

I had to ask him straight out. "Hey, where did you learn English?"

"What do you mean where did I learn English? I'm a Jew from Brooklyn."

Of course you are, I said to myself, laughing.

"What's a nice Jewish boy doing in Colombia?" I tried to say that in my best Brooklyn Jewish mother accent. I didn't even imagine that there was a large, thriving Jewish community living in Colombia.

"I'm Sephardic, and fifty years ago I was introduced to my beautiful Colombian wife, who was visiting New York City. We quickly got married and lived in Brooklyn for a few years. She didn't like living in New York City, and I didn't like living without her, so I've been living here for the past forty-eight years." Sephardic Jews are Jewish people who mostly come from Spain and have moved globally to most every Spanish-speaking country.

The conversation quickly turned to business. After all, that was why I came. He was revamping his business completely—a vertical overhaul from seed to yarn, all the way to final garment. This would give him a competitive edge, especially with pricing, since there would be very few middlemen in the costing of the final garment. It seemed like the company was having trouble with keeping up with the trends, making it impossible to be competitive with brands like Zara, which already had several stores all over Colombia. He needed to streamline the way that trend information was being communicated and executed. To make a clear assessment of the full situation, I needed to understand all of his operations.

"Let's get started right now," he said.

"I'm game. I've been in the country for only about two hours; what's the holdup?" We started with a tour of his office, which had a safe room. I had heard of these rooms but had never actually been in one. Things are much better now, he said, but not so long ago this was an essential element of being able to do business in Bogotá. The safe room was adjacent to his office. It was made out of eighteen-inch concrete blocks and lined with bulletproof steel. It had a satellite telephone, a small pantry, plenty of bottled water, a cot, and a toilet. Most impressive of all was his floor-to-ceiling arsenal of military weapons. There were just a few that I could identify, not being a military expert myself, but he had a couple of Glocks, an AK-47, an AK-74, a QBZ-95, and a few Jericho-941 semiautomatic pistols, which I knew was the favorite of the Israeli special forces.

Okay, so I do know my way around guns. I grew up hunting with my dad and his brother. I am my father's son. I do have a younger brother, but I was always the tougher one, and I would love to go out hunting. I started hunting with them when I was too young to use a gun. You have to be at least thirteen and pass a safety test. My dad gave me a job that he said was more important than actually shooting the gun, which was to help find the deer. Much of my important role was to find deer droppings. Despite it being winter during hunting season in New York State, I would take off my gloves and feel the droppings for warmth and texture. That would be an indicator of how long ago the deer had passed by. Creamy and warm meant the deer had been there recently. If it was hard and cold, it could have been as long as an hour. I took this job very, very seriously—it was a huge responsibility to the deer finder. Of course, later I'd hear my uncle laughing about how funny it was and how seriously I took my job. In another life, I would have been a military strategist. But in this life that would have meant going to military school and doing pushups in the morning. No, thank you, sir!

"Do you know how to use all of these things?" I asked.

He shyly answered, "No, I have people for that." He then told me with a little hesitation that there was even an escape hatch.

"Oh, you need to show me." This was really freaking cool. He stepped on one of the floor tiles near the toilet, giving it a double-click like a computer mouse opening a program. The tile flipped open to reveal a shiny metal slide.

"It's faster than a fireman pole," he added. "Want to take a slide? It goes right into the garage."

"No thank you, I think I'll wait until next time." I wanted to, but I just didn't think it was appropriate, as I was wearing a dress.

We took a walk around the main factory. The facility was over 100,000 square feet. It had yarn-spinning machines, textile-weaving machines, and a full industrial laundry, complete with a drying area. There were many safety features, such as an emergency eyewash station, that I hadn't even seen in an American factory. It was just after lunchtime and the workers were all getting back to their machines. There was a small area that seemed to be a classroom-style workshop. I asked him what was going on in there. He said that many of the retirees still came to work, but instead of working on the machines they spent their free time training the younger seamstresses. They offered them lunch and car service, but they were happy to volunteer since it gave them a sense of purpose. The retirees lived on their full pensions. I loved this guy more and more.

The next day, I visited the sample room and design center. It was a chaotic mess run by one of his cousins, an older woman who I would say was around the same age as Godfather. She had a short bob haircut that seemed very modern and current, and she was dressed in a shirt dress that I later realized would be her standard uniform. She had one in every color, in every print, and in every variation you could imagine.

Godfather owned more than 200 retail stores, and he had sold sixty more of them to this cousin years ago. I would say that all of his family, in some capacity, worked at the company. His daughter ran advertising, his oldest son ran the wholesale textile company, and his brother operated and managed the farms. This one cousin had a lot of control over the distribution of product, since she worked in product development. Product development is where you take the retail client's request and you start developing samples, until the samples are approved and go into production.

I went to visit some of the stores and had a flashback to Sid. They were all a hot mess. The stores were merchandized by size, meaning all the small sizes were on one rack with all the styles mixed together. They did this with all of the sizes. When you looked at the store, it seemed like a giant rainbow that would have made any participant at a gay pride parade happy. The logic, the cousin told me, was that people wanted to shop by size. I understood that she could think that way, but I tried to explain to her that people actually fit in more than one size. For example, I might be a large in some styles and a small in another style. And it's really that random, so that was why we should merchandise the stores by style, encouraging people to try on something that may not have been "their size" but still fits! Plus, the stores would look more put-together. The clothing was so jammed together that it was hard just to pull an item out to get a better view of the style.

"That's how Godfather does it in his stores," she said. I realized that we had been looking only at her stores. Her stores, in general, were stark white with typical aluminum fixtures. The only decorations were posters of products they no longer had in the store because they would sell out faster than they could replenish the POPs (point of purchase). The stores were brightly lit, to the point that my eyes were straining. They also had a mishmash of hangers with other brand names on them. It seemed they were using leftover materials from all the stores they sold wholesale.

Their own retail locations were an afterthought in the supply chain. They were feeding their stores with product that had been made for other brands and sold throughout the world. If there was an overcut (too many units produced that the client didn't want) or a cancellation of the style, they sold that merchandise in their own stores. Any leftover fabric was then cut into different styles and also put into their stores. There were so many locations, but it seemed that the cousin's stores always had the first pick of merchandise. I realized this when I went, on my own time, to the mall and saw the Godfather's stores. They were all half empty, with just one person working in the shop. They were dated with old fixtures and poor lighting. There was a stark difference between the two types of locations.

Now, let's get technical: my idea would have been to help them develop their own collection that they could have wholesaled to other stores, plus feed their own stores with fresh current merchandise monthly. Like most brands, they would make five to eight collections or shipments a year. They could presell the collection by showing samples to the retail buyers. Once the buyers placed their orders, they could add them all up and see which styles would hit the breakeven point, then put those styles into production. Breakeven point is when you meet the requirement on the basis of fabric consumption or factory minimums.

For example, a factory might have a minimum order known as MOQ of 300 units. Since I advise that the minimum markup from costs to wholesale be three times, in theory, you would need to sell only one hundred units in order to be in an inventory position with positive cash flow. In this case, those extra 200 units could go into their retail stores. Anything sold at retail would almost be one hundred percent profit, since the cost of goods had already been paid for and the risk of inventory is managed, because other people paid for the cost of goods. That sounds complicated, but it's very simple. That's why I can write a business plan in three lines. Make samples. Show the samples. Sell the samples. Then you'd have a business. If they don't sell, you don't have a business.

Back to Godfather: I had to clean up the way the goods were allocated. I wanted to send the goods on the basis of store location. Rural town stores and urban shopping malls have different consumers, and the product mix should reflect the right demographic.

The merchandising of the stores was the easy part of the project. I came down with my merchandiser at the time, a very tall and handsome Brazilian, who got everyone pumped and excited about the changes in the merchandising layout. It's so important to make staff part of the change. They have to feel ownership. If not, the minute you leave the stores they will go back to old ways. It's easier to merchandise by size than to create environments with displays and strategic placement of the goods. He was an amazing trainer, and since they had this new know-how, they could do it on their own. They took great pride in showing off their new skills.

Convincing the cousin who worked in product development to change the way she was doing business was a different story. She would take notebooks full of notes from our conversations, always nodding in agreement after each new point in the plan of action. She assured me that the steps would be taken when I went back to the States. But time after time, when I did return, nothing was started or implemented. She always blamed someone who had just been fired, or claimed she didn't have the time to get it done. After a full year of working with them, I realized the cousin had no vested interest in changing the way product got to the stores or developing her own brand, since it would be more work for her department. What I found instead was that she hadn't been paying for the goods going into her stores, and accounting never caught on because all of the fabrics had been bought for other brands and were left over during production.

This is a big problem for some designers. They don't know their fabric consumption, so some factories actually use their fabrics to resale other goods. We had a situation with a children's company that was buying their fabrics from Liberty of London. Those are really beautiful but expensive prints. She was shipping the fabrics to Peru in order to make little-girl dresses. She always came up short with the yardage of fabric needed to finish her production. This forced her to then buy more fabric at the last minute and ship it by air to Peru, or short ship the retailers that placed the order. This was not good for her business reputation or margins. Then, just before Christmas, while she was scrolling on her Facebook feed, she found pictures of her dresses in the window of the factory store she was using. She could tell that they were her dresses because of the custom prints from Liberty of London. The factory had taken all of the shorted fabric, which actually wasn't missing or short at all, and made it into their own little-girl dresses. They were selling them to the local public at the factory production cost. How do you prevent things like that from happening? You have to know the exact yield of each of your styles and do the calculations. You also have to make sure the factory assumes responsibility for any shortages.

Family Business

This wasn't an easy thing to report to Godfather. We had become very close friends. I was even invited to their home for Shabbat dinner with the family. His apartment sat on top of a long and curvy road that led to a ten-story apartment building. He laughed as he told me the story about how he and so many of his friends decided to move out of their estates for security reasons. It was just too costly to manage all the high security needed to prevent home invasions during the civil war. What was making him laugh was that nobody stopped to think about how ten of the richest families could easily be found in one location. It could have made it extremely easy for kidnappers to take over the whole building and demand incredible ransoms. So they had to build an elaborate security system that started with the long, winding road. He pointed to a rock as we drove past it.

"That's not an ordinary rock. Behind it there is a robotic automatic assault machine gun that flips out and can gun down any car in its path with armor-piercing bullets." He was saying this is such a matter-of-fact tone that it wasn't even slightly alarming to me. If there was an unidentified vehicle on this road, security would know about it before it got to this first checkpoint. There were surveillance cameras just before the entrance to the private road that read all the license plates and red flagged any that were not in the system.

"See all of these obstacles and speed bumps on the road? This is to slow down any incoming vehicles, giving the team time to prepare a secondary vantage point where the best ex-military Israeli soldiers would take the necessary measures." Ex-military Israeli soldiers were used as commonly as we might use ADT home security systems. They were considered the best when it comes to personal security. The building also had a helicopter landing pad on its roof, which could evacuate a hundred people in less than ten minutes. The minimum amount of time it would take the intruders—that is, if they could make it past the two interventions—would be twenty minutes.

"So, I think that we're all safe."

Riding in the car with him was an adventure. There was a massive amount of security protocol. They would never park on the street. A restaurant, his factory, his home, any place that he would go all had to have underground parking. He had two identical Humvees with the same license plates that left the garage at the same time going in two different directions. He had no fewer than two motorcycles or dirt bikes riding a short distance in front of his car. The bikes would be able, in real time, to report any roadblocks or situations that might be ahead of the vehicle so it could quickly turn around and go in a different direction. Roadblocks were a very common tactic the narcotraffickers would use to hand pick their victims. Their preference was to kidnap the famous or the rich, but a politician was the grand prize. It was all very systematic. They would ask you to roll down your window, ask for your ID, and see if you were of value, and if so, they drove off with you in the car. It was fairly quick, taking just a few minutes. It was also very random, and that was the reason Godfather had the bikers driving ahead of us. The Hummer itself was made of reinforced bulletproof steel that made it so heavy it needed a second gas tank in order to make it feasible to drive.

I once asked him if anyone in his family had been kidnapped. This was a touchy subject. He responded not by answering the question, but by saying that the public loved him because he always kept the factories working. Many ex-pats left the country during the war, but his family stayed. It's amusing to me that I never felt in danger while working in Colombia. All the security details, even when going to the shopping mall, were done so elegantly, gracefully, and seamlessly that it didn't feel invasive.

It was unlike the TSA at any American airport, which is beyond rude and degrading. I feel like every time I go to the airport I have to calm myself down and let the stupid run free. I have been stopped for having a lip gloss. "That's one liquid too many in your bag." I have been stopped for having a silver-colored pencil. "That could be a sharp object." I have been stopped for having one too many bags. I always travel with carry-on. I have my wheelie suitcase, my handbag, and a tiny crossover bag where I keep my money, passport, boarding pass, and frequent flyer card. It's tiny. I'm often reminded that I have one too many personal bags, so I simply take my crossover bag off and tuck it into my handbag.

I take a lot of joy in complimenting them on a job well done. "I feel like everyone is going to have much more room on this plane now. Thank you!" And you already know that comes out super sarcastically. Keep watching that five o'clock news, because one day I am going to be the person they drag off the plane. Thank goodness my husband has the bail money saved up. These TSA requirements provide a fake sense of security.

One of Godfather's Israeli security guys told me that the best weapon you can bring onboard an airplane is your humble CD. Think about it; you step on it, crack it in half, and now you have not one but two of the sharpest weapons possible. "Just in case, you know, you ever need a weapon on an airplane," he told me. Thanks for the safety tip.

Before I could lay out the whole scheme that had been going on, Godfather had begun to be investigated by the FBI. He was being accused of money laundering. This was completely ridiculous. Even the president of Colombia got involved in this investigation. Since the Colombian government wouldn't extradite him to the United States to answer the accusations in court, he was banned from ever coming into the United States. This pained Godfather immensely, since he loved New York and still had family there.

The FBI sent agents to our NYC office to collect every invoice and every payment ever made from his company. They came to our office one bright, sunny, carefree morning and asked for any and all documents related to this corporation. The weather didn't correspond to the ugliness of the situation. Since I ran a legitimate business, and Godfather also ran a legitimate business, it wasn't an issue to hand over the documents. I did make sure I photographed everything they took. It's not like how you see it in the movies. There is no "Where is your warrant?" or "I'm calling my lawyer" or "I am American, you can't do this." It's more like, "I'll be right here if you need me, sir." It was not uncommon at all for the US government to use these raids to make a point about drug trafficking and money laundering that was still happening in Colombia. The war on drugs was costing the US taxpayers millions of dollars, and every once in a while they had to try to pin blame on someone.

Godfather's health took a terrible turn during this time. He wasn't a young man, and this investigation was heartbreaking to him. Our business together had to stop since he was banned from wiring money out of the country until the situation could be resolved. It never was. However, the investigation revealed that his favorite cousin had embezzled millions of dollars over the years in undeclared production overages. I was so happy that it wasn't me that had to deliver the bad news, but I was upset that most likely the news wasn't delivered in a gentle, kind way.

Fashion Can Pay the Rent

Over the years I continued to work in Colombia, mostly with emerging designers who had interest in entering the US market. They needed help with their placement, their production capacities, and their sizing. As far as fashion direction, they have incredible taste and are forward thinkers so that isn't even an issue. I had the privilege of working with a designer out of Barranquilla who was extraordinarily talented and came from a designer heritage. Her mother was also a very famous Colombian designer, and the first Latin American designer to dress Barbie. Her costume is displayed in the Barbie Museum, along with Donna Karan, Oscar de la Renta, and Karl Lagerfeld. My biggest issue with working with some of these designers is that they are used to being a big fish in a little pond. Rejection, I guess to any artist, is tough and painful. So why subject yourself to the anguish when you're already established and have a successful career? One reason is to become a global brand. I think about how so many American brands take advantage of the stories told by others.

One of my favorite examples is Tommy Bahama. He is not a guy who grew up in the Caribbean. It is my understanding that he lives in Seattle, Washington. Not exactly an authentic Caribbean designer with a tropical lifestyle. He even has restaurants that serve Caribbean-inspired cuisine. Another example is yoga clothing. It all seems to be coming out of Los Angeles or China. Wouldn't it be more authentic if there was a yoga brand that came from India, you know, the genuine home of yoga and yogis?

How about Ralph Lauren? When you think of him, you think Americana: his Native American influence, the traditionally printed blanket coat, and the use of turquoise in his accessories. Have you ever seen a Native American dressed in Ralph Lauren? There are endless opportunities for brands to create a story into a lifestyle. Ralph Lauren will sell you anything from dresses, to footwear, to paint, to furniture, to towels, to just about anything. I often wonder why he doesn't have a licensing agreement for toilet paper to make the Ralph Lauren bathroom experience complete. He started as a humble tie designer. It's the big picture, it's the ten-year plan, it's the scale that some designers cannot even wrap their heads around that made him excel. It is also about getting out of your comfort zone.

Back to the Colombian Barbie designer. The mother and daughter design team were very involved with their community. They were often hired to design elaborate costumes for Carnival. I have to say that Carnival in Barranquilla is wholly underrated and something magical and fantastic to witness. Oddly enough, they still have people completely paint their bodies with black paint to represent the African influence during Carnival. I find that to be such an interesting juxtaposition of cultures. I know they still practice blackface in Holland during Christmas. I believe there is even a documentary titled *Black Pete* accusing the tradition of being quite racist. But in Colombia, especially in Barranquilla, I feel that they're embracing the culture to prevent it from being lost.

The women are very involved with charity work and give a lot of money to a local orphanage. I was able to accompany them to an event they were hosting there. This orphanage was different from the ones that you might imagine. It specialized in older children who probably would never be adopted. They taught vocational skills and independence at a very young age, knowing that this might be their reality. We attended a fundraiser there. The children took turns serving, running the kitchen, cooking, and even bartending. This was all to show off their vocational training in hospitality and culinary arts. I must say, it was an enjoyable experience and meal, despite the fact that it was being attended to by nine- to fifteen-year-olds.

I ended up talking to the headmistress and asked if they were incorporating apparel fashion vocational training at the school. It wasn't something they usually would teach, because she said it was tough for fashion designers to make money, and they wanted to teach more entrepreneurial skills rather than just being a sewer in a factory. She explained that in their hospitality and culinary arts program they taught these young people to be chefs and managers, not just employees or staff. They had an impressive system of using the children's natural personalities to their benefit. If they were fidgety and lacked focus or concentration, they were immediately guided into positions that dealt with managing others. If they were loners or had introverted personalities, they were directed more into the culinary arts, where they developed recipes and menus on their own time. Kids who were compulsive or incredibly detailed were given lessons in accounting and bookkeeping. Since many children suffered from emotional traumas stemming from loss, rejection, and abuse, the headmistress made sure that they developed emotionally as well.

She was something of a badass. She told me how she grew up in the jungle. Her mother died at a very young age in a guerrilla attack during the civil war. Her father was one of the military leaders of the resistance who raised her while they were in battle. Once the civil war was over, her father won a position in the government. He wanted her to attend a boarding school to acquire a formal education and learn proper manners. At the age of eleven, she had no experience with either. Asking her where in the world she might want to study, she picked Switzerland. Why Switzerland, I wondered, and before I could ask the question she mentioned how during her father's appointment he was given a Rolex watch. It came with a massive catalog that had beautiful panoramic pictures of the Swiss Alps with blue skies and green meadows. She decided these were the places she wanted to see. So, when her father asked her where in the world she wanted to go, she pointed to a picture in the catalog.

I asked her if I could teach the orphans the business aspect of the fashion industry. To start, I would like them to make simple knotted bracelets that looked like a rosary with a small cross at the end. I could teach them the mathematics involved with return on investment and scalability. I had bought some of these bracelets at the local market in Medellín and was using them as a gift with purchase for the Dovetail collection. I wasn't actually going to teach them how to make it myself; I could barely sew on a button.

The first lesson would be about outsourcing. I was sure I could find someone to teach them how to make the knotted bracelets, and I told the headmistress that I would pay a quarter for each one. Then they would have a revenue stream. See, some designers do get paid, I thought to myself. It was easy enough to find someone in the nearby village to teach the kids how to knot the yarn to make the little bracelets in a timely fashion.

I would visit the orphanage about twice a year, once in January when I would go to Colombiatex, and once in July when I would go to Colombiamoda. They're conveniently scheduled six months apart. During my visits, I would give short business classes teaching them about marketing, operations, supply chain management, and all the things needed to run a fashion company. In turn, they impressed me each time by growing a little savvier. They established a board within themselves to delegate responsibilities on their own.

By law, children can work only four hours a day. This is done to avoid any child labor—let's say—misunderstandings. The kids got very good and very fast at making these little bracelets, but my orders were increasing faster than their four-hour-a-day capacity would allow.

Realizing they couldn't keep up with demand, they started to outsource some of the bracelet production to the local village women. I was paying them twenty-five cents for each bracelet, and they would pay the ladies ten cents to make the bracelets and about one cent in yarn. Basically, for not doing anything but managing the project, they were making a fourteen-cent profit on each one. They understood the mantra I tried to teach all of my clients: do as little work as possible for the most amount of money. They got that. Oh, they got it too well.

It wasn't long after that that they asked me to attend a board meeting. The children wanted to enlighten me with the fact that they were very grateful for all of my training and support, but they could no longer sell me the bracelets for twenty-five cents. "Business is business," they said.

They quoted me. It seemed that an Italian nonprofit had discovered these bracelets and their socially responsible, fairly-traded, goodwill, orphan story and were willing to pay a euro for them. Due to my long-standing relationship with them, they added very somberly, they made me an offer that they would continue to supply me first if I was also willing to pay one euro for them. Why, those stinking little brats! I was so proud of them. But I was outsourcing my bracelets to China. That's another lesson for you.

I'm incredibly happy and proud to report that today this orphanage has been able to have a steady revenue stream with many products. They even make enough money to afford plane tickets to Bogotá to see soccer games. The oldest of the original group now travels to other orphanages, teaching them the skills they need to start their businesses. Of course, he charges a hefty consulting fee. Business is business.

I'M WITH THE BAND

"*L*oad out!" yelled a big guy, who was kind of scary, but not intimidating. The concert had just ended, and the band had played one song too many. This wreaks havoc with the roadie's timelines, but they never seem under pressure. A roadie's job is not a glamorous job, and yet it has to be one of the most intimate jobs when it comes to working with the world's top talent. The stars depend on the roadies not only for their brand image, but for their safety and well-being.

I was in awe, standing backstage watching Madonna rehearse in appropriate dance clothing but wearing very inappropriate high heels. She was a professional who knew the routine better than anyone, even the choreographer, yet there she was, doing a dry run for her performance that night. Watching from backstage, you can see all the little things that the audience can't. There was a part of the Sweet and Sticky Tour where she sang with a projection of Justin Timberlake. The roadies spun the projection platform around while Madonna stepped on the back of it and disappeared from the audience's view while Justin sang his part. Standing on the back of the platform, she extended both arms out. She was handed a bottle of water in one hand and a small towel in the other. She wiped the sweat from her chest and neck, making sure to avoid her face. She took a swig from the bottle of water as another person ran to touch up her makeup, full-on with powder puffs and lipstick. That took all of ten seconds. It was like watching an Indy formula racing car set up in a pit stop. Spin around, and she was back on stage. None of that could have been done without the roadie.

I started working with Mars Transport more than a decade ago. The international company is split up into four regions: North America, South America, Europe, and Asia. They are the largest entertainment transportation company, as they like to say, in the universe. They move the likes of the Boss, indie bands, and even Cirque du Soleil. My job for them was to provide a source for swag.

Swag has a lot of meanings. It's a synonym of loot, which is what thieves steal. In this instance, it refers to concert items given to VIPs, but most importantly to the dancers and roadies. It's ironic that the word comes from looting, because it was always one of the things that got stolen most often on the road. This was not your ordinary concert tee that you could buy at the concession stand; these were limited items given only to the insiders.

Some of the newer bands were easy. They just wanted a T-shirt with their logo. It was usually something high quality but under a $10 price point. Some bands were challenging, like U2, who insisted on organic cotton made in Africa. Dave Matthews Band, for a time, wanted everything to be hemp. So itchy. Then there was Madge, who wanted the most fashionable swag but didn't want to pay for it. She wanted it sponsored by somebody else. A sponsored item sponsored by someone else. Did you get that? Right.

Getting to develop the swag was a lot of fun because whenever possible, I would hang out backstage and get to know the intricacies of the different bands to really make it unique to them. I didn't need to, but I played up the importance, and they bought it. Who is going to say no to a backstage pass? That's where I got to hang out with the roadies. Movies would lead you to believe that groupies are all about the band, but I have been a witness to the fact that the roadies were getting a lot of the action themselves. It felt like a big family. The caterers made sure that the tables had different tablecloths for breakfast, lunch, and dinner just to break up the monotony. They also made sure that the dietary needs of the performers were met. Madonna, for example, ate a macrobiotic diet that she insisted her dancers followed as well. Meanwhile, the roadies were piling on layers of mac & cheese, fried rice, meatloaf, and whatever else you could possibly imagine. It was very common for the roadies to work for one band for years. Even when the band hadn't toured for a while, they always made sure to get back their original crew. Here is a book that needs to be published: *A Roadie's Tale.*

I'm going to share with you a couple of the stories told to me by some of the roadies, but I'd like to warn you that I think some of them might be the equivalent of a fish story. I heard a story about Michael Jackson being so desperate for painkillers that he checked himself into the ER of a local hospital while on tour, complaining of a horrible toothache and insisting that it be pulled immediately. Of course, the attending physician obliged but prescribed painkillers only after pulling the tooth. Sad. There was also the story of Mick Jagger being a cheap bastard and having one of his new roadies run out to get him booze. Mick would write out a check, knowing that not many people would cash a check with Mick Jagger's signature. The stories went on: the drunkenness, the wild sex parties, the narrow escapes from the police. It all seemed so damn cool.

Once a year at Mars Transport's corporate meetings, we always kicked around the idea of how we should open a retail store that would embody the cool factor of being backstage. It would be a kind of concept store that would feel like you were stepping past the velvet ropes, whispering to security "I'm with the band," and stepping into a VIP area. Everyone would feel like the rock star. It would be complete with a green room that had broken chairs stuck in the walls and dressing rooms that personified different musical genres. The product mix would be an Abercrombie meets Urban Outfitters with indie designers. All we needed was the location.

Later on, out of the blue, one of Mars' principals based out of Latin America popped into my office. "Let's do this!"

I was a little confused. "Let's do what?" I asked.

"Let's open a store in Las Vegas!"

Wow, that was unexpected, and not a small task. I knew he had been thinking about this for a long time. He had even gotten a designer that he knew to retool aluminum flight cases. Those are the black boxes with the silver trim and big handles that are used to pack and move equipment around.

"Well, I am going to MAGIC in Las Vegas in a couple of weeks; maybe we can scout locations then?" Las Vegas would be a pretty good location, as it was being marketed as a more family-friendly vacation destination and their love of obnoxiously themed hotels. I felt that a store like this would work. There weren't a lot of locations available on the strip, and we didn't want to be in the fashion mall. The only space that would meet the criteria we were looking for was in the Planet Hollywood mall, which was undergoing a major renovation. We even met with the CEO of the mall to explain our concept. We had contracted a retail design company to make us renderings of how the space would look. It was going to look amazing, and more importantly, it had a user-friendly layout for shopping.

It was a no-go with Las Vegas. Even having breakfast with the mall CEO couldn't convince him to work out a deal with the rent and the build-out allowance we needed. I knew they had a massive investment going on with the facelift of the mall, but we weren't going to be the first ones in the next up-and-coming Las Vegas mall. I would like to go on record and say that I was surprised by the temper tantrum the mall developer had when we told him no. He walked out of breakfast.

Gee.

Back in New York, I decided to work with a real estate agent. He was a young guy and knew the players in SoHo very well. You would be surprised to know that most of the buildings in SoHo are still privately owned by families. He discovered a location that still had a tenant but was a temporary lease. The building needed a tremendous amount of work, and since we negotiated the lease, it was our responsibility. New York City has strict lease clauses that make you responsible for the space you rent. Some of these buildings are a hundred years old with hundred-year-old problems. It was a huge risk that I wasn't comfortable taking, but Miguel, the agent, was. This location was a good find. It had excellent usable square footage upstairs on the main floor, and it had a beautiful white staircase going downstairs. That's where we would put the green room and have special events with our higher-priced goods. There was a second floor that could be used for office space and a receiving area. We were renting the whole building.

It was early summer, and I wanted all the build-out to be done by the middle of September so we could be part of the second annual Fashion's Night Out. It would be great timing to introduce this new concept store. It was a tremendous amount of work to do in such a short time, but I felt I was up to it.

The build-out was basic and straightforward. We didn't need to get building permits since we weren't building any walls or changing any of the electrical or plumbing. Having said that, I did get a visit from the local union asking me if I was using their union crew.

"Absolutely not," I said. "I need to get this job done on time and within a reasonable budget."

He growled at me.

"Hey," I said. "Do me a favor and put up one of those giant inflatable rats saying that we're not union in front of the store. I could use some of the publicity."

Speaking of rats, the store had a huge rat problem, and when I mean huge, I don't mean a lot of them—I mean giant rats! They were literally coming out of the walls! When you pulled a fixture off the wall, out would pop a rat. It was like playing whack-a-mole, but with live rats. We would leave poison for them, as recommended by the exterminator, and by the time I would open the door in the morning for the construction crew, there were always a couple of drugged-out rats sitting right by the front door, waiting for me to open it. Tough-guy rats were just waiting for that sailor to walk in and start a bar fight. We had a special broom dedicated to sweeping the rats out to the curb.

You guessed by now that I was in charge of the full build-out, buying, floor planning, hiring, sales training, technology, safety, and legal for the store. The actual owner of the store still had his day job moving musicians throughout Latin America. He had a huge legal and technical issue of not being able to open a bank account without first forming a corporation in the United States. A US corporation had many benefits for him, like helping him secure an investor's green card. Technically, if you invested at least $1 million in a US business that employed people, you could buy your green card. It was summer time, though, the busiest time of the year for the concert industry. He wouldn't be able to come back to the United States until mid-September, right when the store would be slated to open. I would receive money wires from a Swiss bank account to make the payments for the new store. Hundreds of thousands of dollars didn't cause me to raise an eyebrow, since I knew he was an avid skier and had lived in Switzerland while going to boarding school for many years.

Just Don't Call In Broken

We were just ahead of our high-pressure schedule when I, a native New Yorker who uses crosswalks, doesn't walk and text, and watches out for insane bike messengers, got hit by a taxi! Can you fucking believe it? I got hit by a taxi! Not only did I get hit, but I also got run over by it!

The taxi was making a turn. I saw that he was looking down and not paying attention. Move faster, go backward, I tried to save myself, but BANG, I was hit. He got me on the hip, which caused me to land on the hood of the taxi and then slide off and land on my ass, just as he ran over my foot. He slowed down when he hit me, but he never stopped. He was looking out of his window and slowly driving away when I looked up and realized that the light had changed, and I was on the ground and in the way of cars that were now coming down 9th Avenue. Then Superman (it's my story, and that's how I am going to tell it) jumped in front of me and stopped traffic. Another superhero ran up to the taxi, reached in, pulled the brake, and pulled the driver out by his neck through the window. He dragged the driver toward me while I was still lying on the ground, thinking, *gee I am filthy, it's surprising how dirty the streets are, this is why you should never wear flip-flops in the city.*

Superman II said to me, "Hey, lady, I got him."

Why thank you, young man, it seems that you do. That's what I wanted to say, but all that came out was "I'm OK, I'm OK." I was so embarrassed. I just wanted to go home.

Superman (my story) helped me over to the curb. By this time there was a crowd of people who came to help. A young couple went to a restaurant and got a bag of ice for my foot. "Oh, thank you, I don't need that, I am fine." Then I looked at my foot. It wasn't my foot, it was the Elephant Man's foot. What was it doing there? Where was my shoe? It was so surreal, like being in a Salvador Dalí painting. The one with the melting clocks. Time was going by so slowly, and it was sweltering. Another lady had picked up my bag and put everything back inside. The only jerks who didn't help, but made sure to tell me they weren't going to help, were the tourists in the back of the cab who said they didn't see anything. The police came, the fire trucks came, and, *what the fuck?*, the ambulance came. They took me over to St. Vincent's hospital, which was walking distance from the scene of the crime. Dramatic, I know, but it's my story.

I had been on my way to meet a friend for Samba class. It was something that I'd wanted to learn to do before my fortieth birthday, which was two weeks away. She came running to the hospital the minute I told her I had a good reason for not making the class. I was sure glad she did. It was disgusting how I was treated at the hospital. I was left alone on a stretcher in a hallway, and even though I seemed to be in everybody's way, no one was there to help me or even tell me what to expect. Then my Joanna showed up.

"Oh my God, oh my God. You are so dirty!"

"I know!"

"Look, you still have the car tire tracks on your foot!"

"I know." I didn't know, but I didn't want to look at the Elephant Man's foot.

"Who's your nurse?"

"I don't know, and no one has come by."

"I'll be right back. I am going to get something to clean you off with." She marched right into the nurse's station and took a bag of alcohol wipes and a box of tissues. The nurses didn't say a word. With those tiny little foldup alcohol wipes that they use before you get a shot, she started to take off the tire marks. I let her. It was comical and sweet at the same time, but then I started to realize that I was not OK. Things were starting to hurt. I told her this, and she freaked out.

"Nurse," she was yelling, "my friend is in pain and you have to give her something right now."

"Oh, so you are the doctor now, huh?"

"No, but I'll get my lawyer to call him." All of New York City came to my rescue. Yes, all of New York City's eight million people came to help. It's my story, remember.

I started to tear up. Joanna had never seen me cry. Now she was in full warrior mode.

"Who is the supervisor here? She needs an X-ray and a CT scan. She might have internal injuries."

"Joanna, you're freaking me out now. It's OK, I had a car accident, and I remember what happened to me."

The nurse came back with a clipboard and asked me for my insurance. Joanna took my bag, pulled out the card, and started filling out the forms for me. Did the nurse really expect me to do that? I thought. I had never been to the emergency room as a patient, but they could use a lot of help with the consumer experience, I thought. Wait, maybe that didn't apply here.

The nurse started squishing my belly, using two hands. "Why are you tickling me?" I asked.

She looked at Joanna unemotionally, like I was not there. "There are no internal injuries or bleeding, so we can give her some medication now."

They rolled me away to get an X-ray. My foot was still under the bag of ice the young couple had gotten me. I was stretched out under what I think was the first X-ray machine in the world. The technician put in these giant plates that were in silver frames into what looked like an oversized ray gun. He then laid a heavy lead blanket over me and jumped out of the room. He pushed a button and clink clank went the ancient X-ray machine!

"Seems like a fractured hip and broken foot," said the technician.

"Seems?" I asked. "Is it, or isn't it?"

"Well, the X-ray isn't very clear. You might want to go to a specialist." Of course, I thought.

"We should cast you up."

"I don't think so. Boot me."

"Oh, we don't have any boots here. Those are special orders that your doctor will have to order for you." It was so frustrating. I just wanted to get home before my husband did, since I didn't call him when I first got hit by the taxi. He was on a fishing trip with friends. There was no reason to worry him because there was nothing he could do for me. They gauzed and wrapped my Elephant Man leg, so now I looked like *The Mummy*. The movie, not the TV show.

I grabbed a quick bite with Joanna and her husband, who had come over to drive me home, at Benny's Burrito. I was full, the painkillers were just kicking in, and I was feeling mighty fine. I told my husband what had happened. He was not happy that I hadn't called him right away. I skipped the part about the shitty treatment but complained about not having a boot on.

"You could have just paid for it."

"Honey, they didn't even have one."

That was Saturday, and I waited until Monday to start calling around for a podiatrist. It seemed all the good ones were at the annual podiatrist convention in Las Vegas. I found one that didn't go and I didn't question why. He was pretty cool, easy to talk with, and had a boot, to boot! Sweet!

I hopped into a cab to go check out the progress of the store. To my surprise, they were two full days ahead of schedule. Brilliant! I was going on back-to-back trips in two weeks, and I wanted the pricing, tagging, and stocking to get started before I left. I would have the whole month of August to do training and a soft opening before the event. It was going to be the SoHo retailing event of the year. I had a tattoo artist doing tattoos. I had a book reading of *I Slept with Joey Ramone,* a memoir by Joey's brother Mickey Leigh and cowritten by Legs McNeil. I had a taco truck and a local rock band playing. Best of all, I was on the local press radar because Abercrombie & Fitch, just up the block from us, had to be closed down for a week because of bedbugs. I had tweeted there are no bedbugs at this new store opening, which got retweeted by everyone. Yes!

I had my fortieth birthday party at a local wine bar that we took over for the night, complete with a seventy-year-old former Playboy Bunny taking her bra off while dancing on a table and proclaiming that "you are never too old!" Never too old for what, she didn't say.

I checked in with the doctor about my foot, which seemed to be healing well, although he was a little concerned about the pain. He prescribed a stronger painkiller, just in case I needed it.

The first leg of my ten-day trip was Colombia, for Colombiamoda. It's held in the mountaintop city of Medellín, known as the City of Eternal Spring for its springlike weather year-round. The plane ride was definitely uncomfortable, but I didn't want to take the new pain medication, since I don't react well to it. My hip hurt from sitting so long. I checked into the hotel, the Medellín Royal, which had just opened. I was welcomed and told by the front desk manager that there was a hotel doctor if I needed anything. Since my birthday, I had pimped out my boot with the Tory Burch metal logo that was on the shoe I was wearing during the accident. The doctor had told me that if it had not been for that metal logo acting like a steel toe shoe, I would have lost some toes. Since the shoe was ruined, I took that metal buckle off and Velcroed it onto the boot. I wore the other shoe on my good foot, and presto, I had a fashionable boot.

The show was long and hot. I usually went during the morning when it was less crowded, but I'd had to do some buying for the new store opening. I also wanted a mix of designers in the store, since it was in SoHo and would draw a more sophisticated group. The store in SoHo was also going to have men's and a selection of vintage clothing by the curator, Misha. On the last day of the show, I wasn't feeling like myself. I thought it was the heat. I don't deal well with heat, and it seemed everyone was complaining about the unusually hot weather.

When I got back to the hotel, the manager stopped me and, right off the bat apologized, and told me that I didn't look good. "It's sweltering outside," I answered.

"No, you are much paler than you were when you first got here. Won't you let me send the house doctor to see you?"

"Yes, please do," I said, and went to my room. A few minutes later, the doctor knocked on my door.

"House doctor," he said. I sat on the edge of the bed, and he pulled up a chair and sat down. I unstrapped the boot and took off the sock. The foot looked much more swollen than the day before, and the bruise now wrapped around my whole foot. "You must be in so much pain," the doctor said.

"No, what still hurts is my hip." I raised up my shirt to show him the rainbow bruise.

"Did they scan you?"

"No, they didn't, and I never got around to getting it done, since I was coming here."

"Health first," he said, which is a common Cuban saying.

"Are you Cuban?" I asked.

"Yes, I am. I am working here for three more years before going back." In Colombia, it's a special thing to have a Cuban doctor. They are well respected around the world for their skills. It's just like having a Jewish accountant in New York.

He applied slight pressure to the giant bubble on top of my foot. "Does this hurt?"

"No."

"It feels very hot." I started to doubt the great Cuban doctor's experience. Of course it was hot, I was in one-hundred-degree weather, wearing boots and socks. I didn't need to go to medical school to know that.

"Let me take your temperature," he said while he was putting the thermometer in my mouth. I could tell his concern was growing. "You are running a fever."

"Are you sure? Maybe I haven't cooled off from being at the show."

"What show are you talking about?"

"I am here for the fashion trade show."

"So, you have been walking around all day in that boot, without a crutch?" I had been using a very cool animal print umbrella as a cane. I gestured to it with my eyes.

"That?"

"Yes."

He was shaking his head. He took my blood pressure and noted it was low. "I would like you to meet me at the clinic, and I want to run some tests, since I see you might have (I am translating what he said in Spanish to me) a deep tissue infection."

In both languages, that didn't sound good. The word *clinic* was another one I didn't like. It prompted me to think of low-income free clinics that you went to with a question for a friend.

He walked me downstairs and told the hotel driver where to take me. "I'll meet you there," he said as he walked away. The hotel driver was faster than a fire truck. The ride was quick, but I wasn't sure if we were at the right place. It looked more like luxury condominiums than a hospital. "¿Este es el lugar?"

"Sí, Señora."

All righty, I thought as I entered. I found a lovely young lady wearing a little white shift dress, holding a clipboard. "¿Mercedes?"

"Sí."

"Welcome, I am your assistant during your stay, and I am here to guide you and keep you informed. First, would you like to walk to your room, or would you like for me to call for a wheelchair?" My wrinkled nose of disbelief gave me away. She continued, "We ask this because we would like our guests to feel empowered while they are here. If we let them make the first decision, they will immediately become at ease." Point well taken, but no, I wanted to walk.

We walked past several of the private examining rooms. These rooms were set up according to the procedure necessary. She anticipated my next question.

"We have a system for each of the rooms. When a doctor is in the prescribing phase, after the questions have been answered, he enters the information into an iPad. We process the prescriptions so the medications are ready before the patient leaves. Then, we open the room for another guest. Our guests never have to wait alone in their examining room. This prevents unrelated stress and anxiety." Additionally, their version of a waiting room was called a relaxation room, where you could relax and decompress, complete with lounge chairs, dimmed lights, and music stations.

The doctor entered. "Isn't our clinic different from what you thought?" Are they all mind readers? I wondered. "I worked in Miami doing part of my training exchange." If you can read my mind, what am I thinking now? "I know you don't like to waste time, so I am just going to start the scan." Not what I was thinking. I was thinking, what do you think I am thinking . . . but he was right, I did hate wasting time.

I sat on a comfortable tufted chair that looked like it could have been in a fancy hair salon. "I am going to lay back the chair so I can also scan your hip," he said. The chair started to lean back and flatten out, like the recliners in business class. He was sitting on a wheelie stool with an iPad in his hand, which seemed to be controlling everything in the room.

The lights dimmed, and he asked,"Would you like me to play music or wildlife?"

"Wildlife, please." Tropical jungle sounds played in the background. The scanner looked more like an old, wide fluorescent floor lamp than high-tech medical equipment. It had a soft hum that went well with the songs of the tropical birds. He adjusted it manually. He scanned my hip again and turned me a little more the other way. My personal assistant, who had been in the room the whole time, helped me twist a little.

He showed me the iPad. "See that?" he asked. "That is a hairline fracture." He took a stylus and drew a circle around my hipbone on the iPad. "Your sciatic nerve is inflamed."

"Ouch."

"Let's look at your foot now." He moved the scanner down to my foot and adjusted the chair so I could sit up more and see. It wasn't good news, but it did have a solution. He showed me the iPad. He changed the settings so I could see in different colors the bones, veins, ligaments, and tendons.

"This cloud here is the infection. It's under your skin." He explained many of the ways this could have happened, like having a dirty open wound. While I didn't have a gash or anything that needed stitches, I did have a little road rash on my foot. He said that I was lucky the manager called him, because in less than twenty-four hours this infection would have entered my bloodstream and I would have become septic.

"It didn't have a way to drain, so we are going to cut it open and drain it for you. I will then place a gel strip of antibiotics in the wound, and you will be able to cover it with gauze and continue wearing the boot and sock. Good thing they didn't cast you, or you wouldn't have caught it in time. The infection would have developed faster. I would also like to give you an IV with antibiotics and vitamins right now and send you home with some antibiotics to take while you are traveling. You are leaving tomorrow afternoon, right?"

"Yes."

"As soon as you get home, ask your doctor to give you another IV within the next two days. It's imperative that you get this done. Do you have any questions for me?" I couldn't think of anything. "Your assistant will start the IV." It turned out she was a physician's assistant, not my personal assistant. But wasn't that what she told me? No, that's what I'd heard.

I did have a million other questions, like how much was this all going to cost me? I was waiting for the IV to finish. I asked her how would I tell my doctor all of this, since I didn't take any notes. "Don't worry," she said. "The scans are all in a USB we will give you, and I'll print out the doctor's notes in English for you to take with you."

While the IV was dripping, she left to get my medication, and she had filled out my paperwork using my passport and business card. Now she walked me out to a lounge. "Margarette will come and get you to take care of the bill." The dreaded bill.

Margarette walked me over to her desk, which was right outside the waiting area, where no one could overhear our conversation. "We at the clinic would like to apologize for the great inconvenience of having to pay medical bills. We know that it's an unexpected expense, but since you are not a citizen of Colombia, we cannot offer you payment terms or cover you under the national plan."

Oh boy, this is going to be a mortgage, I thought.

"Your total is $27 US."

"Thank you," I said, shocked that it was possible. "Thank you." I don't think anyone had ever thanked her for a medical bill.

I wasn't flying home. I was flying right to Las Vegas for the ASD show. I'd be speaking both mornings, doing the New Buyer workshop. I told my husband the situation.

"Come home," he said. "Let one of the girls fly out and do it."

"Honey, you don't understand. I don't feel bad, just a little pain in the hip." Pun failure. "I have some medicine for that, since I now know what it is."

"You should come home; I saw they were moving in more fixtures last night in the store when I drove by."

"What? I'll call the store from Las Vegas. I'll go to the local hospital after I check in and get the IV. That will hold me over until I get home. I get to Las Vegas at 8 a.m., so I have all day to relax."

The plane ride to Las Vegas was excruciating. I would get a shooting pain that would make me jump. It was later explained to me that when tissue and nerve endings are regrowing, you feel the pain. Mother, did that hurt. I checked in and asked the front desk if they had a hotel doctor. They didn't. Why isn't that a thing everywhere?

"Can you tell me the name of the closest hospital?" I asked her. Wouldn't you think she would ask if I was feeling OK? Nope. And I screwed up; I should have asked for the best, not closest, because she sent me to University Hospital. See why you can't go by names? Clinic = good. University = very bad.

I walked into the ER. I got handed a stack of forms to fill out. They didn't even ask why I was there. As directed by the drill sergeant, I walked to the waiting area; this was not a relaxation area. It smelled like vomit and there was no place to sit. In fact, people were using wheelchairs to sit on, and I couldn't stand for what looked like hours. I tried to look for a simpático nurse. Nothing. Screw it, I thought. It could wait until I got home. I just wanted to lie down, take the antibiotics, and rest.

As I was walking out, a Jamaican nurse called my name.

"Mercedes!" I tried to figure out how she would know me. "You are the queen of the Caribbean. You put those designers right in their place!"

I had spent the last summer living in Jamaica and shooting a TV show called *Mission Catwalk All-Stars*. I was a mentor to the designers, like Tim Gunn of *Project Runway*, but more business focused and only shown in the Caribbean with a tiny budget. I was famous in Jamaica because of my harsh critique of the Jamaican finalist, causing him to pass out (which was cut from the finale). That poor guy, he just melted into the ground. He couldn't win, and what was he thinking with his Hail Caesar Cape?

"What was Brian thinking?" the nurse asked me. "I was cheering for him, but it was all about David; he has the talent!" She was kind to me, as long as I kept telling her behind-the-scenes gossip. Let me see what the doctor ordered, I thought.

"Yes, he does, but don't you know it, he is late for the collection showing in New York."

"Oh no."

"I know." She was very disappointed.

"Come with me," the nurse told me. "What you here for?" I explained what I had been told to do.

"OK, we have that IV, but I don't have a bed. I can give it to you in the hallway."

"OK, that is fine with me."

"I see here they gave you some antibiotics from Colombia. Those are not FDA approved here, so keep taking them; they must be good. OK, now sit comfortable. I'll be back in a half hour to take it out."

Sit comfortable? I was sitting in a wheelchair outside an emergency room door where a tough-looking guy inside was having a procession of family visit him that would rival the pope. I held on to my purse with both hands.

Back at the hotel, I decided to pop a painkiller and take a long nap, which turned into what the doctor calls night terrors. They are nightmares so terrifying that people have killed themselves so they won't experience them. Luckily for me, I guess, they were a reaction to the pain medication. I had back-to-back night terrors. In my first terror, I saw a giant pink bunny with one long bucktooth gnawing at my foot. The bunny was something out of a Monty Python movie. I woke up screaming at the rabbit, covered in sweat and tears. It was just a dream, it was just a dream, I reminded myself. I was groggy and fell right back to sleep.

In my next dream, I woke up to go to the show and thought about how much my foot hurt. I didn't want to be groggy speaking, so taking the painkillers was not an option. But all of the sudden, I could feel my feet lifting off the ground. I could fly! I could fly right out of the window. Apparently, I could also go through glass. I was flying over the strip, and it was beautiful. I was laughing. This was great—I wouldn't hurt myself walking. Then it hit me. I didn't know how to land. When I tried to go toward the ground, I went too fast. If I fell at that speed, I would've broken every bone in my body. I was yelling at people walking in the street, asking "Do you know how to land?" They were ducking and waving me away. I was screaming for help; I didn't know how to fall. "Help me . . . I am going to break my legs!"

I woke up in the hallway of the hotel room. No more painkillers for me, I decided.

I did what I had to do and got the hell out of Las Vegas. Something was up with the store.

When the Party Is Over, Turn Off the Lights

It was three days before the opening of the store. We had RSVPs back from VIPs. I was excited about the book reading. We'd hired and trained a great team. I was trying out a new management system where we didn't have a manager in a store of ten employees. We were making everyone responsible all around. It seemed to be working out great, but out of nowhere, a giant stage was built into the side of the store. This display, which you could not merchandise from, was sitting in prime selling space.

"Miguel is back?" I asked a team member. The stage was so big that we had to take the windows out of the storefront to move it in. He hadn't even called me. Seemed weird, but he was the owner. I think he just wanted to say that he had done something when his friends came. He wanted the details to be so authentic, he even bought the stage curtains from Rose, the industry go-to place. Four words: not necessary, and expensive.

Miguel and I got to chat only briefly, and I gave him the full walk-through of the store the morning before Fashion's Night Out. It seemed he had spent all of his days since he'd arrived in New York with the immigration lawyer. I pointed out the items that were already selling, and how we had a few exclusive styles with some top brand. He seemed bored, but I took it to be exhaustion. He had just come off tour, had not seen his family, and was dealing with all the legal things that he needed to do for the business and his green card.

The store opened to incredible success. Fashion's Night Out was a hard sell for a new retailer, especially when you had Diane von Furstenberg pouring champagne for you in her store and Karl Lagerfeld doing a poetry reading just down the street from you. We still managed to have a nice flow of people the whole night and were the last retailer to close for the night on Broadway.

That weekend, the store was flooded with people buying and people that just really wanted to hang out in the store. One of our team members took it upon himself to print VIP backstage passes when people bought something at the store. It wasn't a discount for a purchase, but people wanted them. Finally, the routines were getting into place. I was training a new buyer to work at the store so we could stop being hands-on. The team was self-correcting, which meant that if anyone wasn't pulling their weight, they got voted off the island and the team then formed a review board for new hires. Power to the people is very rock and roll.

Miguel and I planned a sit-down at my office to start the process of the handover of operations. We at the office had been doing everything, even the payroll. I also wanted to share some news I had been holding back on about the final numbers for September. We were over our sales projection by almost $200,000. We even had an inquiry from a Chilean retailer to open a franchise.

Miguel sat down. He smelled like he had been drinking, and he had been sober for twenty years. "What is going on?" he said angrily.

"What do you mean, what is going on?"

"That's not the store I envisioned. It looks nothing like what I dreamed about."

That came out of nowhere. We had gone together to every design meeting with the company. We'd gone over every stupid little thing, like what side of the door to hang the toilet paper on. It turns out authentic backstage toilet paper is not attached from walls, but put on a mobile floor stand. Now you know. The only thing I hadn't run past him was the actual clothing, although he approved the list of all the brands.

"Give me an example of what you don't like that wasn't your idea," I said.

"The logo and the name."

"You must be drunk, because I wasn't even involved with that. You and your artist friend came to me with that when we first had a serious talk about doing a store."

"Yeah, but you liked it."

"And Miguel, I still like it. It's plastered on everything—even the 5,000 shopping bags we made."

"That's another example. I hate those bags."

"Miguel, do you not remember your wife giving me a bag to copy and me crying about how hard and expensive the bag was to make?"

"But you still made it."

"Do you want me to pull out the emails? How about this, that shitty stage you put in in the middle of the night while I was away that ate a third of my prime selling space? Do you love a margin killer?"

"You know, that was the only compliment I got from any of the roadies on opening night."

"You know what? I don't give a shit, because the roadies don't shop in the store!" Now we are full-on yelling at each other. "Miguel, what's the fucking problem? Are you mad that you are making money? The store went over its projections by $200,000, and we netted a tidy profit of $120,000 the first month in business. Still mad about it not being your vision?"

He stomped out of the office. He couldn't have even been downstairs when I get a text message from him.

"You're not with the band."

He proceeded to fire the staff we had trained, and hired untrained, non-retail workers. He rebranded everything, hemorrhaging money with new shopping bags and signage. He hired a buyer who was buying only from expensive designers who were her money-losing friends. Finally, he hired a PR firm for thousands of dollars a month without attending a single meeting.

He's no longer with the band, either.

TOO-MUCH INFORMATION

"When the hemorrhoids get really bad, I use a frozen suppository in order to cool the burning."

"For Pete's sake, could we for once just have a conversation about the collection without bringing up your hemorrhoids?"

"I thought you just didn't like it when I showed you how my hernia could pop out."

Let it be noted that medical conditions are not a welcome topic of conversation.

THE SKINNY OF IT ALL

$\mathscr{I}$t started like all internet love affairs. I found her on Instagram, and it was lust at first sight. The colors that she used, the pictures that she posted, the number of followers that was growing each day. Then I started to notice a darker side of her. She would tease me with a photo or two, and then it would all disappear. She would pull away from me and transform back into the ordinary. How could she be so cruel? Didn't I pay enough attention to her? I filled her page with hearts and heart-eye emojis. Was I coming on too strong? Did I share one too many of her photos with my followers? I had to meet her in person.

I couldn't bear for her to lose the traction she was building, and from the comments I was reading, I knew I wasn't the only one.

That skinny bitch has enough to wear. Posted @nohoehere:

M: Hi, it's your number one fan. Why did you take down all of your plus-size looks; I was loving what you're doing!

S: Hey, thanks. Yeah, it's not my thing.

M: Not your thing? I've been watching your engagement, and it jumps every time you post a plus-size picture.

S: It's only because I use popular plus-bloggers to model, but it's a hard sell.

M: That's brilliant to use the bloggers. Why don't you come into my office? I do this for a living. Maybe I can help you out.

I was completely thrown off guard when she walked into my office. "Street 509?" That was the name of her brand.

She shyly looked down and whispered, "Yes."

As I live and breathe, I would never in a million years have guessed that she was the badass plus-size designer for Street 509. For Pete's sake, she looked like a ninety-pound librarian. Pastel cardigan, pearl necklace, and black-framed glasses. All she needed to do was ask, "Would you like to renew your library card?"

I started to laugh, not at her, but the irony of the situation. Looking down, she said, "You see, I'm a phony. No one would give me any street cred if they saw me in person."

"Hold on a second, sister, is that your excuse? You are going to tell me that all the men that design women's clothing are phonies?"

"Well, that's different."

"How so?"

"Well, you know."

"No, I do not; you need to spell it out for me."

"Well, it doesn't matter, because it doesn't sell anyway."

"Fair. Let's talk about that then."

Street had a fiancé who was a computer coder. Actually, I should say he's a mad scientist when it comes to building a matrix of consumer shopping behavior. She had quite an extensive reporting system that could rival any of the big online retailers. I'm not a fan of online retailing because it's a huge money-guzzling failure, but plus sizes were one of the exceptions. She made her collection in her own two-machine workshop where she taught herself to sew. She hired one additional person to help her. She was designing her own prints and having them printed locally in New York City. Her sizes ran from small to extra large. We took a look at the turnover of her sales-through. In other words, how fast she sold something. The very painful fact to her (and the undeniable fact to me) was that all the extra-large sizes sold first, followed by the large, and finally she was stuck with the smalls.

"The numbers don't lie, Street. And your favorable online comments back it up. You don't have to change overnight, but let's drop the small and just go medium to 2X." She wasn't thrilled with my suggestion, but when I included some numbers explaining how this would increase profitability, she reluctantly agreed to. She was putting out a new collection every month. You cannot imagine the amount of work it is to design and develop, cut and sew, style and photograph, market and sell, and pack and ship every single one of your pieces. She just put everyone I have ever worked with to shame. The only help she had was an additional sewer, a shipping clerk, and her fiancé acting as the webmaster.

She launched at midnight, and I was the first one on the website to see the new collection. Fuck me! She didn't use any of her plus-size blogger model friends! Why was she getting in her own way? That was my ugly text to her in the middle of the night. Actually, it looked more like this:

M: WHAT ARE YOU DOING?

S: They weren't available.

M: Bullshit!

M: We are not going to see the sales we wanted, because the plus-size community wants visuals.

S: But this girl is hippy.

M: It's not the same. We will wait for sales reports.

Of course, I was right. While there wasn't a jump in the new 2X size, no one missed not having the small in the size run. So that was a tiny bit of progress. The next collection was going to launch ideally in time for Easter.

"Please, Street," I begged, "Let me help you pick the right models for the launch. I want it to be the biggest one ever." You secretly know where I was going with that pun. Not trusting her, I went to the fiancé for help in dropping the small and medium sizes and adding the 3X to the size run. Knowing her concern (excuse) about getting the fit right, I personally paid for a plus-size pattern grader. This person makes sure the sizes fit correctly (it's not just about making it bigger).

I should mention one thing about the data research the fiancé did: he was going back and looking at the consumer's personal Instagram page. We had discovered that it was a particular body shape. It is referred to as thin/thick; the person has a small waist in proportion to her hips. It was also mostly a black and Latina consumer.

Years ago, I had done a focus group for Nordstrom's on price point and the plus-size consumer. We discovered that there are serious emotional stigmas within the plus-size market. The Anglo (white) consumer has price resistance, because they are on perpetual diets and feel they don't want to invest a lot of money in clothing since they are going to lose weight soon on this (twenty-year) diet. The black and Latina consumer has a much different body image and self-esteem. If it fits and they feel like they look good, then "Hell yeah." That is a direct quote. They will pay "Whatever," another direct quote.

Not that the collection was expensive. If I remember, the average price was about $35, and she was making money on it, but it didn't leave a lot of room for nicer items and fabrics. I think Street was the number one customer at Spandex House, a basic Lycra textile wholeseller in the Garment District.

The Easter launch was absolutely insane. The type of wild success where sleep is optional. No one was ready for it. The website crashed twice. We had to frantically email everyone and post on social media that the website would be up in just a few hours. We had to outsource production to a small factory, which hurt the margins a tiny bit, but Street learned that she didn't have to do it all herself or watch every single garment being made. Baby steps . . .

We ran out of fabric twice, but the print house was super cool and so excited for her that they didn't up-charge the rush production. The game plan had always been to cut (produce) fifty units of each style before the launch and recut during the month if needed. We sold out of those fifty units in the first hour. 3X was the first one to sell out. *Insert smirk emoji here.* Street had no idea about the 3X since it was outsourced to a factory and the shipping clerk folded them into origami fashion, so they looked cute in the packaging.

Then, the late-night text:

S: Merc, I am in tears. This is not a "Street Bae" (how she referred to her consumers).

The picture she sent me was of an enormous older woman, not in her twenties, wearing the floral off-the-shoulder yellow Easter dress at what seemed to be a church. She topped it off with a matching yellow hat. I admit she could have used one size larger, but the smile on her face and the comments that her friends wrote on her post were seriously heartwarming.

M: What's the problem? She got 670 likes on that photo. That's 670 more people that know Street 509.

S: That's the problem; she tagged us on the photo. I don't want everyone to see her.

M: Are you joking? You need sleep. Come to my office. We need to plan Mother's Day.

She came to the office with her fiancé. It was the first time I met him in person. He looked more like a banker than a computer geek. They made an adorable couple. You could tell that she was his world. Street started to cry. Dear Lord, I hate crying. She told me her full story. She had studied and worked as a nurse. Being of Haitian descent, she had a very disciplined and strong work ethic. She would get home from a full day of nursing and sew leggings that she would sell on her eBay website. What made it different was a focus on these incredibly fun conversation prints that she was designing herself. She had made enough money to quit nursing, even though it meant she had to live a little more humbly.

She exclaimed, "I am not happy making plus-size clothing. I am super stressed with the whole situation. I have had to hire more people. I am worried about making payroll. I don't want to buy all of these prints in advance not knowing if they are going to sell. I am worried about the cash flow and not having enough money to buy the fabrics."

"You know, Street," I said in my most calming voice, "you would have all of these situations if you weren't doing plus size. Except you wouldn't have these problems, because the world doesn't need another regular legging line. There is a solution to everything you are worried about."

"After the Mother's Day launch, we will take a break in designing a new collection for the website. We will do bestsellers only for the month of June and July. This will give you the time to design and sample a wholesale collection." Street had received numerous inquiries from retailers that wanted to purchase wholesale. This would also alleviate a lot of the stress of purchasing prints that may not be as popular as others. We would put into production only the prints and styles that met our minimums with the factory. Then everything she would put on her website would almost be one hundred percent profit, because the cost of goods had been paid for by the retailers. If she needed money for production, it would be easy to find a venture capitalist to bankroll her costs. She would have the margins to pay them because of the greater economy of scale. She would also get better pricing on her fabrics and production. I also had to convince her not to continue to make any of the goods herself so she could focus on the line development.

Except she didn't do any of this. She launched a swimwear collection that came only in SML. This was a great success; I think because of the prints. This convinced her to drop the plus sizes altogether and design a collection in SML for the July launch. She sold only the large size and got hundreds of hateful posts and emails about how she had abandoned her Street base. One of the more delicate posts was "Don't take a fat gurl dessert away, sugar." Street had to start over. We weren't speaking anymore. I had dropped her as a client. I do that when I feel like I am talking to a brick wall. But I am always watching.

Her fall collection with her plus-bloggers was a success. She added some neutrals to the collection to balance out all the prints, but those didn't do as well. So, what does she do? She does a full Christmas collection just in neutrals, no prints, but all in plus sizes, which ultimately bombed!

I couldn't bite my tongue any longer. I wrote her an email. "Street, why are you trying so hard to shut down your business?" I wrote her the story of the salmon:

"When a salmon is born, it's called an alevin. It swims downstream, taking the path of less resistance. While it grows and learns, it completely changes into a full-grown salmon and goes from being a freshwater fish to a saltwater fish. It could not have adapted if it didn't go with the flow.

"After a few years, the salmon gets bored of having a great life and decides to swim upstream. Don't ask me why. It's like you insisting that the money is in the regular sizes. It has to fight the currents, it has to avoid the bears and the eagles, it can't eat because it's used to being a saltwater fish, and finally it gets fucked and dies.

"Street, don't be the salmon. Talk to me after the holidays."

We met the first week of January. She had no cash reserves, had suffered four bad months, and had lost market share and followers. For a new business, this could have quickly ended everything.

"Street, it might be time to find an investor to help you with cash flow. We can explain how you have clearly researched your niche market and have a full understanding of what sells and what doesn't." A perfect spin on "you have your head shoved up your ass and haven't been listening."

She got my attention. "Merc" (I hate when people call me that, but for some reason I let her get away with it), "I can't, I am burnt out, I am sleeping in the office/factory, I can't afford rent anymore, and I don't want to design for fat girls."

"Street, hear me out. You have come too far and given up too much to quit now. You are not the only one to sleep in the factory. Christian Louboutin also did, and look where he is now—he's the king of designer footwear. You didn't like nursing, but you did it until you could support what started as a hobby. Do the plus-size collection until we can grow it into a million-dollar business. Then you can sell it and use the money to design the collection you always wanted."

Looking down, she said, "Deal." Should I trust her? It seemed if I didn't keep her under lock and key, she changed gears faster than I change underwear. (It should be noted I change my underwear every day.)

Self-Invest

I called our legal counsel who works with CFDA designers and well-established brands. I mention this because it's such a specific industry, and I love to rattle this guy up with random questions. Like, Peter, can I get sued for telling someone to fuck themselves? Peter, can you help me sue Yelp for being shady with their reviews? Peter, what percent of production has to be made in the United States to call it Made in the US?

"Peter, Peter, Peter . . . " I said in a Marcia Brady voice. "Should I invest in this client? Should I bankroll her until we get the wholesale together and wrap it up to sell it?" After much debate, we go with the solution of finding an outside investor since Street is so emotionally drained and can't be trusted. The paperwork with contiguities could be possible, but not worth it. He recommended a client of his who was looking to start a fashion investment company and open a showroom. It sounded perfect.

I started to prepare a deck for Street 509; while analyzing the numbers, I realized that she didn't have one business, but three! The core business was the conversational prints in trend-forward items with a quick turn. She was the first to get out a lemon print after Beyoncé's *Lemonade*. I stopped and thought about the words:

"Why do you deny yourself heaven? Why do you consider yourself undeserving? Why are you afraid of love? You think it's not possible for someone like you."

The second business was the swimwear collection, which when she did it in plus sizes was another phenomenal success. There was just nothing like it in the market. She had a knack for designing the most flattering and sexy silhouettes. I strongly feel that when you have to step outside who you are and put yourself in someone else's shoes, you become a much better designer! For this division of the company, we would seek a licensing agreement with an established swimwear distributor. She would be the creative director approving all of the designs and retail placement of the brand. They would be responsible for manufacturing, selling, and distributing the product. She, in turn, would collect a signing bonus, which I was thinking in the neighborhood of $150,000, plus royalty fees of around fifteen percent with a minimum guarantee of $5 million in sales. The third company, believe it or not, was the neutral career basics. There was a massive market for this, but it just didn't translate well on the website. This would totally have to be a brick-and-mortar program.

I was going to offer the investor twenty percent of the company for $500,000 in investment with the option to pay back the $500,000 once we made $1 million in sales, and would purchase back the twenty percent at fair market value.

In our first meeting with the investor, he looked exactly what a music executive would look like. Wavy, tangled hair, scruffy with not quite yet a beard, overpriced jeans (John Varvatos, may I add), and a vintage rock concert T-shirt.

"So, what's the skinny on the brand?" he asked.

"Funny you should phrase it like that, since it's a plus-size line. But why don't you start by telling me a little about your plans? Peter tells me you started a fashion fund."

He went on to tell me that a few of his friends were kicking around the idea of starting a fund where they would pool their money and invest in fashion startups. Their idea was that they would take a share of the company's worth, the value they would project. They would also loan the startup the money needed for operations. Once that would be paid back, the fund would take revenue from the profits. Super, good luck with that, I thought.

"What else would you bring to the table?" I asked. I asked this because if you are going to take on an active partner, which was sounding more like what he was talking about, you needed to bring more than just capital to the table. Money is cheap; advice is not.

"Well, we all come from different industries: TV production, music marketing, and brand development. My friend does all the marketing for the Real Housewives!" Oh, brother, I thought, trying not to roll my eyes.

"So, no one is from the fashion industry," I said dryly.

"No, but we bring years of experience."

"Yeah, you know what, that's all nice and good, but if Street is going to take on a partner, it needs to be an insider who can speed up the process."

"Well, we can keep you on as the consultant." I hadn't even thought of that. "What are your fees?"

"5k," I blurted out. Street hadn't been able to pay me for months, and trust me, she owed me nowhere near the $5,000 I had just asked for.

"That seems pretty reasonable. So, what is the shakedown on this brand?" I told him about the three businesses of the brand that could be broken down into parts. One was a licensing agreement that could generate revenue within a year. We would need to put out two more collections, Resort and Summer, to create a critical mass to look more attractive.

By the look on his face, I knew he had no idea what I was talking about. That could work for me or against me. "Sounds great. I like having revenue after a year. I thought it took like twenty years to get a brand rolling." Thank God, at least he knew it was a long-term project.

"Not quite twenty years, especially with the momentum she has. I'm thinking more like three years." He didn't even ask three years for what. Ay.

Two weeks went by. I gave him a call. It's a delicate dance when working with investors. You don't want to seem desperate. Nobody likes desperate. Only vultures and piranhas eat the desperate, and there will be no free lunches here. It seemed he was still working things out with his friends, and since they were all so busy, they hadn't been able to get together. They would meet up over spring break in St. Barts. He was from that tribe. The Upper East Side, Hampton weekend house, can't find good help, vacation in St. Barts tribe. They can be fun, but predictable. "I'll reach out to you after Passover," I told him.

Meanwhile, Street was really stressing out, and even I had to say with good reason. It had really been a struggle to get the GURLS back, and they had been vocal about it. "Can't pay the rent bitch" posted @ canttouchthis95. There are a group of militant plus-size ladies who will cut you if you cross them. They are loyal as hell but, as Street found out the hard way, don't let them feel they have been betrayed. Maybe it was a good thing the investor was taking his time. We had a lot of cleanup to do. During this time, I felt it was important that she actually made a public appearance, because not only was she being called out as a man, but a skinny-ass boney one. They can be colorful.

Luck came during one of my therapy sessions with Street. There is a reason, other than taking naps, for the sofa in my office. It came to light that Street's whole family, including her *twin sister*, were morbidly obese. Send in the dancing boys and crack open the champagne! We got a spot on a morning talk show the day before Full-Figured Fashion Week, where Street told a sad story about how she was afraid for her sister's life. All she wanted was for her to be healthy and happy and look fierce while doing so. We even got "Amens" and "Hallelujahs" from the studio audience. The Instagram posts changed their attitude, sending her blessings and waves of hearts and kisses. Really, one person made an emoji of herself showering her with hearts.

In our second meeting, the investor sat down and started chatting away about how no one in his group—his yet unformed group—understood the process of building a brand. I began the branding conversation by saying it's about building trust and community. I talked about the increase of followers on Street's Instagram and that she had passed the 100k mark. This was all done organically and without paid promotions or buying followers. He didn't know what I was talking about, but I continued, talking about all the successes she'd had. I mentioned the morning talk show success and how this has led to more interviews. I talked about a song that hit the top forty called "All About that Bass." The white singer empowered a jump in white consumers to her website. We had crossed over. The community was growing, and it was going international. We even passed a homeland security clearance to ship overseas using the USPO for a flat rate of $12. That's a BIG thing. He looked puzzled.

"Was that not your question?"

"Well, we wanted to know more about the process. How is the collection conceived?"

"Oh," I said. I went on to explain that once the collection was on paper, we got the samples made and what I wanted to do was presell the collections.

"Hold on," he stopped me. "But how do you get the collection together so you can put it on paper?" Was he asking me about the whole creative process? That's on a need-to-know basis, and he didn't need to know.

"Well, each designer has their own DNA signature that then needs to be adopted into the current trend. I find that most designers never fully develop a signature and quickly start to look cut and paste."

"How do you develop a signature?"

This is where I drew the line. "Hey, are we here to talk about Street 509 or to give you a private class on brand development? There is a fee for the latter."

"No, it's that my wife wanted to know more details."

Wife? Oh, please man. This guy was just jerking me around, and I needed to find someone serious, like yesterday.

Street was literally a time bomb of nerves. While things were going much better, it was hard to be thinking about a collection for the month and next season. The plan to do wholesale was back in play. We couldn't afford to hire any staff, so she was even packing boxes at night.

"These are all good things," I told her every night. "It's temporary; you just need another month to build back your cash flow."

I remember meeting a South African at a conference in Ethiopia. We were speaking on a panel. He was bragging about all the money he was making with online fashion. So I called him out on it.

"What is your profitability on it?" I asked.

"About $200 million."

Fuck! "Are you serious?"

"Indeed I am."

"I would like to see those numbers."

"Well, the company has been sold and will go public soon; you'll be able to see all the numbers." B-I-N-G-O, they made money on the sale of the company, and not on what they were actually selling.

I walked over to him during the cocktail hour. He started laughing and slapped me on the back. "You had me sweating it out for a moment; I thought you were going to go for the money shot on this one."

"The reason I didn't go for it is that I put it together a second too late; the panel had moved on."

"I'm happy for your time delay."

"Must be the jet lag."

"Yeah, me too; it's been a while since it has gotten to me."

"I thought you lived in South Africa?"

"No, I've called Los Angeles home for the past twenty years." It turned out he had bought and sold more than a dozen internet fashion companies, building them up and then flipping them over. It was like the TV show *Flip or Flop,* but not with houses.

It was time to call South Africa. I had him on the phone for five minutes when I got to the part about how they were profitable, were building cash flow, and had a division that could be licensed off immediately for a revenue stream, when he cut me off.

"Listen, I'm almost done with a Kardashian deal and have some time for this. If what you are telling me pans out, after due diligence, tell her I will offer ten million for the company. She must stay as creative director for three years at $150,000, and she has to sign a five-year non-compete agreement."

"Sure, I'll tell her and I will get those numbers to you."

Had I just heard that right? Ten million for a company that hadn't hit one million in sales yet? Wait, it could happen. This was what he did. Zappos was sold to Amazon for $1.2 billion, and Zappos was bleeding money! Wait a second. Street 509 was profitable. Shouldn't we get more? Had I already agreed to ten million? No, all I'd said was I would tell her. And tell her I did, by text. She never picked up the phone.

M: Give it three years of just working on design, and you can walk away from Street 509.

S: What?

M: An online genius would like to buy Street 509 for $10 million and keep you on as creative for three years at 150k.

S: Are you joking?

M: I never joke.

S: I am coming over.

In the short time that she was walking over, I talked myself out of the deal. We were going to make a deal under desperate conditions. She was almost there with the cash flow. She had worked so hard just to give it away. Yes, give it away. Ten million seems like a lot, but it's not. Half would go to taxes, and ten percent would go to me. Four million for all the blood, sweat, and tears (and that's not just a figure of speech!) was a bad deal.

She sat down and was literally bouncing up and down in the chair like a little child about to blow out their birthday cake, but waiting for the last picture to be taken.

"Street, I don't think this is a good deal."

"What? Are you crazy? Do you know how hard it's been? Look at me. I have lost so much weight." In fact, she had and looked anorexic. "This is God sending me a lifeline; do not tell me it's a bad deal; no one else has made an offer, you have been talking to investors for months."

She was right, but wrong. The first guy never had any intentions of investing, and I should have felt that out.

"Street, this is only the second guy. There will be more. Sorry the music guy didn't work out, and I wasted everyone's time on him. But trust me, if you are being offered ten million, and you are just under a million in sales, and I do understand ten million is a game changer, but if we wait a year—" That struck panic in her. I repeated, "If we just hang on one more year, you will be over the million-dollar mark, and we can ask for a hundred million for the company. That is not a game changer, that's a life changer."

She dropped her face in her hands. "I can't. I can't make it another day. I am going to die on the factory floor. Please, God, help me." She fainted.

She was so tiny and fragile, it seemed like the arms of the chair caught her. "Street," I went around my desk. But Ninja was already there with water and whiskey. (Not sure what she was planning to do with the whiskey.)

"I'll call 911." Her pulse was weak, and she was losing color in her face. Oh my God, please don't let Street die, I prayed; she is so close to living her dream. The EMTs quickly arrived. They strapped an IV and oxygen mask on her, and as they carried her away, they asked if any one of us was family.

I emailed her fiancé and told him to meet us at the hospital. Can you believe I didn't have his phone number? All of us at the office were in the waiting room when fiancé walked in.

"What happened?" he said in a calm voice. "She left the factory beaming, saying she was coming back with good news."

I explained what the good news was, but how I thought we should wait it out when she started to cry, saying she was going to die.

"Why would she say that? We are back on track, we have enough cash flow for production, we have two fashion students interning for us that have been amazing, and we hired that crazy guy that rides around Tenth Avenue with his daisy bike and his pink tutu to help us pack. He is an amazingly hard worker." Huh? Street had a completely different story going on.

The nurse walked in and asked, "Who is family of Street 509?" I elbowed the fiancé.

"I am her husband."

"Come with me, you can see her."

It turned out Street was severely dehydrated and malnourished. Demons from her childhood had come back to torment her. She needed some time and space to recover. Like they say on Broadway, the show must go on. The fashion interns did their part in designing a monthly collection. I didn't dare give them the task of developing the future collection for wholesale—that could wait. We had to stay focused on the moment now. The production factory stepped up its game, making us the first samples. The business was running like a well-oiled machine. This crisis worked out for the best. The company had to set up independent procedures without Street doing all the work. During her recovery, she agreed that the brass ring was so close and a hundred million dollars was a life changer. We kept South Africa on the line, bamboozling him with rhetoric to buy more time.

Whose Dream Is It Anyway?

The investor sent me an email weeks after this happened. "I would like to have another sit-down with you about our investment on Street 509." I wrote back "game over," and that she was offered a hundred million for the company (wishful thinking).

I got the longest email back from him. It started with how he always missed excellent opportunities because of procrastination. Skip, skip, skip. He had learned not to count on friends to start a business, skip skip, skip . . . and he'd always wanted to start his own fashion line. Huh? Go back. Start over.

It seemed that his younger self had dabbled in starting a fashion collection. He still had the leather T-shirt—don't ask—and he wanted to base the collection around it. He was asking if he could come in and speak to me about it.

I sent him the link to our feasibility consultation. He signed up, made the payment, and was in my office the next day with samples to show me.

"Not much of anything going on," I said. "It looks like you went into your wife's closet and pulled out some of her favorite things."

"Actually, they are all her favorite things," he said.

"That's not really how it works—there needs to be a common denominator. Something that looks like a brand. You have leather leggings and a pirate blouse that I think Seinfeld once wore. You have a pair of bell-bottom jeans with embroidery and a leather T-shirt that only a person with a teeny, tiny head can get into. You have a rocker hippy living in the '80s look going on. Don't think that's a good target market."

"Fair enough. How do I start to design a line?"

"You don't; you don't have anything here to work with. A woman came to my office once with a leaf, and we were able to turn that into an elegant, comfortable collection! With you, I have nothing to work with."

"Could I hire a designer?"

"Why would you want to do that?"

"Because I have so many ideas," he said, pointing to the leather T-shirt. I shook my head. He put it on the floor and continued without missing a beat. "Ideas that I haven't been able to realize." I was still shaking my head. "Well, I spoke to a startup in Brooklyn that is doing all kinds of things with emerging designers, and they seem very happy to work with me."

Ethical dilemma time: Should I have just said no, knowing that he was going to do it anyway and get ripped off? Or should I have said yes with a stop clause, like if he didn't get one appointment his first season, we'd stop? That's a low standard—I hoped he got what I was saying, which was an appointment; I wasn't even going for an order— and if we didn't reach it, then we'd have to call it quits.

"Oh, my wife knows all the managers at all of the boutiques in New York City, and they're all looking forward to the line," he reassured me. Store managers are not buyers.

We hired a ghost designer. One of the best. I had used him before when designers needed a little pick-me-up or had a mental block. He would work it out with them. He had a talent for extracting the imagination of a person and making it 3-D. The designer and the investor would meet at my office after hours, because they both had day jobs. They'd work together on mood boards, and I would help with what would be sellable. "No 18-inch-wide bell sleeves! Who are you, Prince?"

Son of a gun! The collection was gorgeous. Well balanced, well priced, and drum roll: it had a signature touch of pleating that could be translated into the next collection. Every single step of the way one of us had to be there with the investor, because he wasn't known for making the right decisions. He was buying leather and wanted it trimmed with velvet for a summer short with a twist. We hired a professional photographer who had a full package deal, model, hair, makeup, catering, studio, and photo retouch. He didn't have a stylist, but after going over the "moods" as a group, even with the ghost designer included in the meeting, we felt that the investor could be trusted to do the shoot. I came back from a business trip to find a giant, hot mesh: that mesh being chicken wire, a giant leather travel bag (something he made a long time ago), and accessories that were so massive they dominated the photos from the shoot. They were, of course, his wife's favorite. If you don't make it, don't shoot it. I took a discount from the photographer; the cha-cha queen insisted that he let his clients express themselves creatively. Bullshit, this wasn't playtime in kindergarten, and I was paying him to be the adult. I made him reshoot the lookbook.

The investor's friends who had said they would do sales for him because they had a showroom never came to collect the samples. The store managers couldn't get the buyers to come. It's a thing, with managers and the buyers in these uppity stores. The girl in his office who was going to do the social media posted once—a very cute photo of his daughter.

Stop clause in effect. It was game over.

The Wolf in Gold

I wondered how Street was doing. I had been following her on Instagram, and we texted every other day, but it was weird that I hadn't seen a sales report in three months. No news is not good news.

M: Hi. Did you see my email about the numbers? I think it might be time to reach out to South Africa and see if he is willing to relook at our numbers. Which I need.

S: Hey! I just spoke to Ratish (my business partner), and we really want to have a conversation with you first before going back to South Africa. Can we meet in person next week at your office?

M: You have a new business partner? Isn't that something we should have spoken about before you made that decision?

S: That's why we want to meet with you in person.

M: When?

No one knew Street's business better than I did. Not even Street, because she had long and dire tunnel vision. I wanted to have a dash of hope that he would be the one to take her to the next level, but that dash was outweighed by my doubts. She wasn't in an emotional condition to make any decisions. That was the reason why I hadn't been part of the new investor conversation.

They came in for a meeting, Street trailing behind as the Indian Mr. T walked in like he owned the place. He was wearing enough gold chains to keep King Kong tied down. Before we even introduced ourselves, he asked for a cup of tea.

I thought to myself, OK, I know this type. It's easy, they know everything, so let him tell me the plans.

We sat in my office, Mr. T on the sofa and Street sitting just a bit too far away on a chair by the door, giving me the impression this was no longer her idea. I sat as closely as I could without having to sit on his lap. Body language is important when establishing power and dominace. I have learned this the hard way. When I have found myself in a situation where I am negotiating a deal, if the person (man) steps in to give me the price and I step back, I lose. When I step in, even if it means being cheek to cheek, if they take a step back, I win.

Tea was served, and I leaned back in my chair and started by asking what the overall plans were. He didn't answer, but instead went into a half-hour historical review of his life's accomplishments. My one takeaway was that twenty years ago he was the top vendor for JC Penney's denim, and that he was ready to come out of retirement to invest in a new business, since he felt he was too old to start something new himself.

I'll translate all of this: Twenty years ago JC Penney went directly to factory to source their denim, and since he had lost a crucial account, he'd sold his assets and had been either living off his savings or had spent twenty years trying to reenter the market without success. He was looking for a schmuck whose business he could easily steal.

"Sir, that's all very impressive," I said, leaning in, "but that was twenty years ago. I am interested only in what your plans with Street are today." I leaned back into my chair in my thinking pose. Hand to face, with one arm crossed under the other.

"She says you have a lot of plans for the brand, but not the financial resources. Tell me more about those plans."

"That's not what we are here for; we are here because you are now her investor and you must have reasons for this investment. I would like to know what those reasons are, and the plans to execute them." This whole time he had been sitting with one leg crossed on top of the other and his arms spread across the top of the sofa—the "I own this bitch" pose. Now, he put both feet on the floor and leaned in with his hands on top of his knees.

"Well, you know she has a lot of untapped opportunities."

"Yes, indeed I do."

"So, let's do this; why don't you tell me what your first step in growing the brand was."

"My first step is to make sure an opportunistic, parasitic vulture doesn't swallow Street up." I laughed at the end of that comment and smiled at him. He grinned back, but he wasn't sure if I was joking or not. I never joke. He knew I was on to him. He started to talk about department store business.

"Fantastic, how will you put the supply chain in place and who will sell to the department stores?" I asked him.

"I still own a factory in India that we can contract to do the production, and my original company still has a vendor code with JC Penney, so we can use that."

"Street, do you understand what this all means?"

"Yes, it means I don't have to worry about production or sales, and I can just spend my time designing."

"Or it means that not only have you given him a percentage of your company, but now you are one hundred percent dependent on him.

You haven't even told me how much he owns or how much you charged him. He owns your production, which means that he is making money off that which he is not going to share with you."

I glared at him, hoping he would jump in and contradict me. He didn't. He owned the vendor code, and I was sure he would be charging the company a percentage for the use.

"And he will never have to show a profit to share with you, since the cost of operations that he is benefiting from will be too high to cover the cost. So even if you wanted to sell your percentage of the business, no one would be interested, because it wouldn't show a profit. He'll most likely end up offering you something terrible and make you feel like he's doing you a favor."

"What you left out, Mercedes," he said, "is that peace of mind has a cost. Street is now stress free in her business, a trade she was willing to make. It was something I could offer her right now, and nothing you could even come close to offering."

He got up and reached over to shake my hand. I didn't offer it.

"I don't shake hands with the devil."

He laughed and told Street to come along.

"Street," I cried out, trying to offer a lifeline.

"It's too late," she said, walking behind him out the door.

WHEN ELEPHANTS FIGHT

We have many international clients, so understanding broken English has become an art form in our office. Oreo Ninja even has her own interpretation dictionary. For example, when PrinceZion74@aol.com called with his thick accent and said, "I wanna make some stuff . . . I wanna be with Mercedes," she knew he called for a consultation and not for a date.

I have made the mistake of judging people by their lack of fluent English. I was in Peru for a cotton conference when I was introduced to a group of "farmers." I took a look at them. They were native Peruvians and looked like some of the indigenous people I had worked with in the past. A conference leader asked if I would spend a few minutes explaining how the retail supply chain worked in the United States, before I started my seminar. It's a complicated conversation, so I did my best to dummy it down so that the farmers would understand and have a better insight into what my workshop was about. In simple Spanish, I went on about consumer perceptions of cotton and how I felt it should be a luxury fiber. They seemed lost in the conversation, so after just a few minutes I wrapped up by thanking them for their time. They were all very complimentary about my comments and they each gave me their business cards. It wasn't until I got to the hotel that I read their titles: PhD in agricultural farming, MD-PhD in chemical engineering, professor of microbiology PhD. It seemed I was the only dummy in the group.

Prince was one of the most interesting people I had ever met. I didn't expect such a composed gentleman. After all, he was wearing multizippered acid-washed jeans topped with a red Michael Jackson "Thriller" jacket. He was a walking fashion contradiction. Ninja wasn't paying attention to his clothing, but to his gorgeous, shiny-smooth, midnight-black skin, which she still talks about to this day. Unlike posers who talk big money, he was humble with a polite and reserved demeanor. In person, he was a little easier to understand.

"Miss Gonzalez, of all the money I've made, I've foolishly spent it on a mansion in New Jersey, fast cars, and even $8,000 on one single window treatment. You know what I'm saying?" Not a lot of people admit that up front. We weren't turned off by his bragging, unlike some other experiences we'd had.

Take the basketball player who wanted to design jeans for tall people over 6′1″. He went on and on (and on) about how fabulous his jeans did at Saks 5th Avenue, how he had a men's store where all of his basketball buddies would come and hang out, how it wouldn't be a problem for some of the top basketball stars of the moment to become the brand spokesperson, how he personally designed a fourteen-piece collection, and how retailers were calling him every day to see when his collection would finally launch. Of course, between the business bragging there was also the personal bragging: how he hated to fly commercial, how the upkeep on his multiple homes was a small fortune every month, and how much money he spent on custom clothing every year. After eight very patient hours of what felt like an interrogation, we got down to the truth. He admitted he didn't sell Saks. He had, in fact, spent a large amount of money making jeans at a tailor to do an event with them, where nothing was sold. His friends did hang out at the store, but those were the key words—hang out. In reality, no one was going to be a spokesperson for his brand, because they all had exclusive sponsorship agreements. It also came to light that he was maxed out from living his lavish lifestyle. He was in fact looking for an investor to fund the collection.

He was the total opposite of the gentleman now sitting in front of us.

Prince said that he wanted to get into the fashion business because he needed an investment, something he had learned from going to the school of hard knocks . . . literally!

It seemed that Prince was a diamond dealer. How he got into that business, we're not sure, but over the course of many months he did give us some insight into his heartbreaking upbringing.

He had been kidnapped from his village in West Africa at the age of eleven. The village was burned to the ground, and all the boys were taken to be trained as soldiers. He had witnessed some of the boys being murdered in cold blood as an example of what would happen if you didn't follow the rules. He and another boy decided to make a run for it. They escaped into the jungle, where they lived for months until they were finally found by missionaries. His friend had died from a fever, and his body was never found—something you could tell was excruciating for him to talk about. An American missionary adopted him and they relocated to China. So it turned out that he was fluent in Mandarin and German, although I never got the German part of his story. He told us how he got his MBA while serving some time in jail for tax evasion. He had been sent to a white-collar federal penitentiary filled with Ivy League grads. They schooled him on finance and told him that his biggest mistake was just spending money and not investing it. So now he wanted to do things right and create his own legitimate business: a denim line.

During that first meeting he warmed up to us and pulled out his phone to show us a photo of someone he had met at a Hamptons party. It seemed everyone knew who she was, and it bothered him not to know. He swiped past famous athletes, movie stars, and music moguls— all of whom enjoyed a considerable amount of bling—until he got to the photo of the woman that was in question.

"That's only the queen of fashion," I said, "Anna Wintour!" There he was, looking all official next to one of the most important people in fashion. The one person that could make or break a brand with a simple twitch of her nose.

"I have her cell number since I was working on a piece for her daughter," he threw into the conversation casually. Are you putting all of this together? He is funded, had a real celebrity following, and was BFFs with Anna. All we needed now was a designer to put the collection together.

Sustainability Is a Point of View

I asked him what he was envisioning the collection to look like and if he had already come up with a brand name. He mentioned he was working with a designer, and the concept was going to be based on sustainable, organic cotton jeans made in ethical factories in Africa. Industry buzz words such as sustainable, organic, fair trade, ethical, and fair wages are words that are thrown around while most people don't understand what they truly mean. I don't think it's done with malice; there is just a lack of understanding and education with some hidden political agendas thrown in for good measure. Do you feel good when you donate your used clothing to give to some poor African country? By doing so, you are killing jobs in manufacturing, apparel, and footwear.

You might argue that they are so poor the children don't have any shoes. They will stay poor and dependent on your charity if they don't have jobs. I recently met a woman who told me that for years she'd run a shoe drive for children in Guatemala. She boasted how they weren't used shoes, but new shoes. I gave her the suggestion to pay a local factory to make the shoes and sell them at a deeply discounted price. This is the way you build economic development and not dependence. The factory will have cash flow to invest in training and new equipment. They will be able to export to different countries where a premium is paid for handcrafted footwear. Some countries like India have stopped all imported donations of used clothing. This has significantly increased their employment. I have a friend who runs a charity in Calcutta, and one of the things he does is run a store. Donations of saris are collected four times a year at private schools. The saris are then cleaned (a paid job), reworked into bags or accessories for export sales (another paid job), or sold to the local people. The shop workers are also paid. If a local cannot afford to buy one of the garments, they can trade their time for it. They can help someone go to a doctor's appointment, sweep up the local streets, work in the shop, or teach a child a skill. There are many ways to trade. That's the key, trade and not aid.

Some brands are now asking for certifications, which are given by very reputable established companies. But these certifications come at a high cost, which many factories, especially the family-owned ones, cannot afford. Family owned means the whole family is working, including children. Depending on the country and who is doing the ethical certifications, this means no one under the age of thirteen should be working. They should be attending school. But if there is no money for school and the children cannot work, they become a burden to their family. This is when you read about children being sold as domestic workers (slaves) or into the sex trade market. I'd rather a child be working alongside his mother and grandmother than in one of these horrific options. Fun fact: Do you know why in the United States we have summer vacation and not winter vacation when in some parts of the country children are waiting in below-freezing temperatures in the dark to get to school? It's because children had to work on the family farm in the summertime. There were no Disney summer vacations when the United States was developing as an agricultural nation.

Nothing is genuinely sustainable, and for sure, nothing can be one hundred percent organic. You might be able to grow something organically, but once it's processed, dyed, and transported, it's impossible for it to maintain its organic legitimacy. One example is organic cotton from India. All goods need to be fumigated for woodworms and other insects, thus rendering any "organic" qualities nonorganic and full of chemicals. As far as "sustainable" goes, bamboo was once considered the poster child of sustainability. The chemicals they use to make bamboo soft enough for fabric —sodium hydroxide and carbon disulfide—are extremely toxic to the drinking water of these communities. Some websites would suggest otherwise, noting that there are no harmful effects if the chemicals are disposed of "properly." Yeah, good luck with that.

Fair wages are another trendy topic of conversation. A living wage is a salary with which a person can provide a home and feed and educate their children, and is a better conversation that no one initiates. The Rana Plaza collapse had nothing to do with sustainable manufacturing practices, but everything to do with corruption and politics. They could have been canning tuna fish in that eight-story building instead of manufacturing clothing for companies like Walmart. How about the diversion of clean drinking water? Have you ever seen those late-night TV ads where they ask for donations to build a well for a small village that doesn't have access to clean water? As a tribal leader, what do you think are the two priorities when looking for a place to inhabit? Clean water and fertile soil. The reason why these villages don't have water is that it has been diverted for hydroelectric power, which has been proven to be too expensive for the local people it was built for to begin with. The water is also diverted to grow millions of acres of cotton.

I had the opportunity to sit in on a roundtable discussion in Kenya about using GMO cotton plants that used only a third of the water other cotton needs to grow. This is an incredible scientific breakthrough, considering that cities like Cape Town, South Africa, are running out of water. The person representing the European Union at this roundtable opposed the concept relentlessly, without even hearing the science behind the genetic engineer's argument. I will just note that this was a black woman with a PhD in genetic engineering, and she was published in just about every scientific journal. Her research is considered unprecedented by her peers. Yet the European government official could note only what the regulations said and how it couldn't be set forward and applied. I guess in some parts of Europe people eat their clothing.

Helping a Brother Out

The designer—whom Prince had met at a laundromat—had supposedly worked for big names like Calvin Klein, Tommy Hilfiger, and Ralph Lauren. We tried to look him up while Prince was still in the office, but nothing came up. No Facebook, no Instagram, no Twitter, and nothing remotely close to the companies he said he worked for on LinkedIn. I asked Prince if he had a business card or even a reference from him, and he just shrugged his shoulders. I gave the designer the benefit of the doubt, since many ghost designers do use a pseudonym when designing outside a contract they might have had with a more prominent brand.

"It's OK," I said. "I'll ask him more details when he comes in. How much are you paying him?"

"$5,000 a month," he said proudly. I am not sure why he said it with such satisfaction. Was he proud that he was employing someone? Did he think that was a good deal?

"Ok," I said, shaking off my hesitation. "How long has he been working for you?"

"About three months." Now he was questioning himself, like everything he was saying out loud was not adding up. Anticipating my next question, he said, "I should have the mood boards this week."

"This week?"

"Yes, that's right. The designer said it takes at least eight to twelve weeks to develop a concept for the mood board."

"Did you give him any direction?"

"Yes, I gave him samples of Diesel and D&G jeans that I own and pages from magazines to show him everything I like."

Adding things up in my head, this guy had $15,000 and a couple thousand dollars in denim with no searchable name or business card with an address. I didn't want to go into hyper-defense mode, but it was time to call him in for a meeting.

I should mention that designers should not be paid a monthly retainer. They are notorious for not having a sense of urgency. Instead, they should be paid a flat fee for the project. "Bring him to us," I said in my best *Scarface* voice, figuring I had to channel someone gangster at that moment.

The first thing I noticed was that he didn't look like your typical industry creative. He was no Giorgio Armani, with his white tee tucked into his mom jeans that rode up somewhere around his navel. "Does he actually work at the laundromat?" Ninja whispered.

"He does smell so Downy fresh," I tried to sympathize.

As for what he had been doing for the last three months, he kept giving excuses. "Oh, I'm still doing more research, getting my looks together for his target market—you know, the usual stuff. You caught me off guard with this emergency meeting, but I will have it all together by next week." Even though we were doubtful, he was saying all the right things. We played along, hoping he was going to give us an extraordinarily cool concept, considering the amount of time he was given.

A week went by. I had asked him to feel free to contact me directly if he had any questions, but not one text, email, or phone call. The day of truth was upon us. Prince had come a little early with some personal samples to ask about the different washes in the jeans. We had come up with a factory in Mauritius that met all of his requirements and had the added bonus of reusing ninety-nine percent of the water used for production. We had met the owner of the factory during a trade show in Madagascar, where the factory owner asked me, "Where do you think the other one percent goes?" He didn't wait for me to answer. "It gets evaporated!" he said with cheer in his voice.

Judgment Day

The designer walked in sheepishly and late. "If you are on time, you are five minutes late" said Prince. His attitude toward the designer was different today. The designer had been late to the first meeting, and it hadn't seemed to bother Prince at that time.

I honestly had high expectations for his presentation, but when he started to take paint chips from the local hardware store and a stack of magazine clippings out of his duffle bag, we just stood there in disappointed shock. Prince looked at Ninja and me, looking for affirmation of what we were all thinking.

"Are you fucking kidding me?" I exclaimed. "After $15,000, this is the shit you bring us? It's been three months, you fucking leetol caca-roach."

I was channeling *Scarface* again—not sure to this day why I thought that would be appropriate. I broke it down for him. No more leaving it up to him: he had to give us twenty looks, including CADS, colorways, and fabrications, by the end of the month. He had three weeks. He started to give some excuses and I completely shut them down. He was taking advantage of Prince and I wasn't going to have any of that. Reluctantly, he agreed, mumbling that the timeline was too tight.

Designer then wouldn't answer my emails, only Prince's. It became a merry-go-round of communication: designer emailing Prince, Prince calling Ninja, Ninja updating me, me delegating to Prince, and so on. Still, Designer didn't email with any substantial progress. Time was up.

For this meeting, Prince showed up with a friend. Let's call him the Enforcer. According to Ninja, he was even more handsome—like-a-god handsome—than Prince. He sat in Ninja's office while we caught up on Prince's situation. He told me about how hard it was becoming to get his parole officer to sign off on his crossing of state lines. He was still living in New Jersey, and our office is in New York. He mentioned how backed up the system was, and how some of the ex-cons sitting and waiting with him for their appointment with the parole officer were surprised to find out that Prince had gone to a white-collar prison and not to the state penitentiary. They referred to it as the country club. He told them he was in for tax evasion, which was why he went to a white-collar prison. "That don't matter when you're black," one of them had informed him.

In the middle of that conversation, Designer walked in, blowing past everyone and coming into my office completely frazzled. The tension in my office thickened immediately. I felt like the office was on fire, the heat steadily increasing. That was when I saw Ninja actually was physically turning up the heat. It was so hot that the Enforcer had to take off his vest and roll up his sleeves, which was her intention the whole time. Ogling over him while we continued to discuss our business—priorities, people!

"Ninja, come in here. I need you for this meeting." Prince wasn't the only one who would have an enforcer.

The only thing Designer had to give us was a bunch of excuses. It was insulting and infuriating. "The printer ran out of ink and I didn't have any money to print it elsewhere."

"Why didn't you email it to me?"

"My internet was out, because I didn't have money to pay the bill."

Ninja jumped in. "Business slow at the laundromat?"

"Why didn't you bring your computer? We would have printed it here."

"It's too heavy for me to carry since I have a bad back."

"It's called 'take a cab.'"

"I had bad shrimp that gave me food poisoning for a week."

I completely lost my patience. "Okay, you know what, I've had enough of this bullshit. It's obvious that you're completely unqualified to get this job done. You are a fake and a fraud."

Prince interrupted, "You try to give a brother a break—this is why brothas can't raise each other up. I believed you man, but now I want my money back."

Designer skirted the issue. "Let me go home and get my computer; could you give me some money for a taxi so I don't have to carry it on the subway? I'll come back in an hour or two and we can print out the collection."

"N***a, have you no brains?" I think he meant to say "have you lost your mind," but it was equally as effective. Prince started slapping the back of his hand on his open palm, emphasizing each word that he was now shouting at Designer. "I don't think so. We need to go downstairs right now with your ATM card so you can give me back my money. I just want the last payment. You need to go to the ATM!" He continued slapping his hand in frustration.

"I don't have your money. I had to pay my mortgage and my mother is in the hospital with cancer." As the conversation grew louder, the Enforcer got the clue that he needed to stand in the doorway blocking any quick escape Designer might have in mind.

Prince continued, "If you're going to leave to get your computer, I need you to leave me your ID!"

"I'm not going to give you my ID!"

"Where is your ID, man? Give me your ID!"

"I don't have any IDs on me!" He cowered like a frightened dog with his tail between his legs.

"Didn't you need ID to get into the building, N***a? Don't be lying more to me."

I stepped in. "Someone's going to get hurt. You had to have some ID, even a library card to get into the building. Give me something, because if you leave here with them, it's not going to end well."

Prince had had it. "N***a, I need to know where you lay your head down at night." Hand slaps and all.

It was intense. I knew it was time to move the conversation forward. "We have to drop this guy and move onto a new designer."

"Not before we take care of this business." Prince shot a look at the Enforcer, who then planted a firm hand on Designer's back like he was dancing the tango, leading him out of the office. He had definitely done this before. Prince followed them out.

Moments later, we heard sirens. After forty-five minutes, they reappeared, Starbucks cups in hand, wanting to know what the next steps were. Ninja asked what happened, and Prince replied, "When two elephants battle, no one thinks of the grass getting hurt."

A few weeks later, I picked up a call (must have been fate since I never pick up the phone) and immediately recognized that it was Prince. "Miss Mercedes, you're the only phone call I'm allowed, but I'll be back in touch as soon as the new grass grows."

ZOOLANDER IS A DOCUMENTARY

$\mathscr{T}$he label guy that we worked with said he had a client that was desperate to get his spring samples ready for New York Men's Fashion Week. "You know that's six weeks from now, right?"

"I know, that's why I'm calling you. Aren't you the guys that get shit done? To quote you."

"Well, I have been known to say that. Can you give me a little bit more detail about the project?" He said the collection was in its fourth season, which meant to me that they must have had some kind of experience. I wouldn't be working with a novice. I asked where they had manufactured before. He said that everything had been done in New York City. That's not going to happen this time, I thought to myself. There are no capacities in the Garment District this late in the game. It would have to go overseas, most likely South America.

"Okay," I said to Label Guy. "Put me in touch with him. He'll have to come in today." About two seconds later, and I'm not even exaggerating, Dilapidated Dandy (to be referred to as Dandy) skated in. Yes, he skated in and kicked up his board, landing inches from me.

He greeted me with a "Yo, dude! When do we get started?" I looked around the office with a *what the fuck is going on here?* look on my face. Was I supposed to know this guy?

"Do I know you? Or better yet, do I want to know you?"

"Yeah, yeah, yeah. Yo, yo, yo, I was just recommended to you by Label Guy."

"Yeah? I just hung up with him." Did he teleport here, or was he already on his way before the phone call was made?

"Yeah dude, so sick. That's why I'm here, yo. I heard you was dope and shit. And you gon' make my shit happennnn."

I turned to Ninja. "Can you please translate for me?"

Luckily, she spoke urban dictionary. "I think he's happy you took him on as a client."

I turned to Dandy, squinting a little, trying to figure him out. Did he have a language problem? Was he mentally challenged? Had pizza-eating turtles raised him in the subways of New York? "Show me what you got." I thought I would keep my language as simple as possible.

"Ah yeah, man, peep this." He whipped out his phone and brought up a bunch of sketches, rapidly flipping through them. "My dope-ass friend did these. So talented, right?" That would be a matter of opinion, I thought.

"Where's the pocket? Is there a zipper here? Why doesn't he have a neck? What fabric is this made out of? Strips of paper? Because from this, it's hard to tell." He smirked, brushing it off.

"Yeah man, anyway, my collection this year is pretty gnar."

I glanced over at Ninja; "Is . . . gnar a good thing? Because it sounds like an STD." He let out a whiny, sarcastic, weak, condescending snicker, which I assumed was his laugh. "I can't work with any of this crap." I was trying to find a cooler word than crap to speak his language, but crap is crap. "I can't use any of this. These are all artistic sketches. Where are all of your tech packs, your color stories, your CADs?" His face dropped and he looked like he was about to cry. His lip started trembling. Then he looked up at me with puppy eyes.

"Yeah, yeah, yeah, dope. I know, I don't know jack shit about all that wack technical science junk." His hands were super animated, throwing random gangsta signs at us. Was he mad, was he sad? At this point, I didn't give a shit. I knew he had some serious sponsors: a footwear company, a men's skincare line, and a vodka company. It wasn't his first collection, and he wasn't reinventing the wheel with his brand. It was just a matter of cut-and-paste product development with a mix of his "signature" polka dots. Adidas has stripes, Nike has a swoosh, Lacoste has an alligator, and Dilapidated Dandy had dots.

I physically had to grab him by the shoulders to sit him down. Staring him right in the face, I told him, "I need you, Dandy, for just one second, to settle down, focus, and talk to me in clear English. What do you have done and what don't you have done for this collection? I need to know so I can start from where you left off."

He was doing his best to be calm and collected when giving me the details. I understood this took great effort on his part. Weren't there medications for this? We talked about his past collections. He told me all the drama he had with some of the New York City factories. Some of the factories had shorted him on fabrics or just outright "lost" the fabric. Patterns were misplaced, production never finished, and the samples couldn't fit humans. All of this is very real in our industry. Not just factories in New York, but globally. You can't ask a factory to make you samples. You have to tell them to make you a sample by a certain date and time, and you have to check on them twice a day in the most incredibly pleasant way until you become such a pain that the samples magically appear on time. Another strategy could be that if, after feeling out the factory, you note that you're not being taken seriously because you're too sweet, you take the opposite approach. The approach of an insane, irrational person. You know the one—it's the one that shows up at the factory at random times, yelling at workers who don't understand a word you're saying. Maybe flipping a table or two, until your samples magically appear.

I joke about not having to need a production manager in New York, but instead an enforcer who is like the muscle for a loan shark and makes sure that your samples magically appear. So many designers insist on manufacturing in New York for sustainable and ethical reasons. I can assure you that New York City has its share of sweatshops and illegal immigrant workers. It's a necessity in an industry that is growing and dying at the same time. I don't endorse these situations, but they're a fact of the industry.

I needed to get more direction on the brand integrity, so I reached out to Label Guy after our meeting. The labels were straightforward. As a matter of fact, they were on the low-budget side. They can make or break a brand's image. The Label Guy never makes it any easier. He literally has thousands of label samples to show, and he shows them all. He can spend five hours, nonstop, showing an emerging designer all the different types of labels: the different fabrics, woven vs. nonwoven, synthetics vs. organics, printed vs. embroidered, plastic-over-leather, plastic-over metallic, and, introducing his new collection . . . wood. Let's not even talk about the hang tags that should complement the labels, or skipping the label altogether and going with a screen-printed "label." And of course, once the designer makes up his mind, he starts all over again by whipping out his hi-tech prototype case. One example is a GPS label that can track your kids' underwear while they're away at camp. There are even hang tags that are made of seeded paper and that when planted, wildflowers will grow. These blow everybody's minds, and we spend another five hours on them, but they're not feasibly priced.

I wasn't getting the DNA or the signature of the brand, besides the stupid polka dots. Slapping a logo on a garment doesn't make it a brand. For one thing, you need product differentiation. You partly get there with styling, quality of fabrication, emotional connection to a tribe, or a specific substance that isn't physically tangible but connects to the subconscious, meeting one's desire to belong.

Before we started the project, we had to come to an agreement to cover our cost of developing a collection from concept to runway execution within six weeks—and most importantly, during the time I take my summer vacation (which I now had to give up). I wanted half of our fees for a deposit, but he said he hadn't received all of his sponsorship money yet. So we settled on enough to cover the cost of the samples, but barely. I felt like—well, he made me feel like—so many industry people had taken advantage of him in the past, and I wanted to prove to him that there were still people with integrity in this industry. While he considered himself a fashion designer, he was merely an editorial stylist with a few friends in convenient corporate positions.

Week one:

We started putting together mood boards with color story and analyzed the trends to put together a production style-out. Then, we contacted factories, reviewed their history closets, and pulled in-stock fashion blanks in order to customize with Dandy's "signature dots." We also needed to put together a timetable in order for the more elevated styles, fabrics, and patterns to make it just under the wire for the runway show. To fully develop a collection correctly, it can take six months or longer; since we had connections and factories that owed us favors, we were able to beg, barter, and harass our way to an expedited sampling process.

Week two:

One of Dandy's sponsors was a local sandwich shop that did the catering for his fashion shoots. Somehow, he had finagled a bountiful lunch at our office. I casually mentioned, "I can't pay the rent with a hoagie. Have you spoken to your sponsors about the check?" He just turned and introduced me to his "team" (which was made up of two people) to check on the progress. He introduced us to a guy first, his "Business Coach," and a girl, his "Social Media Guru." Both of them together couldn't have been twenty years old.

Over the process of the following six weeks, we realized that the business coach was a glorified hype man whose job was to keep Dandy happy and feeling secure. He accomplished this with hugs and saying "it's all right, man" way too many times, often for no reason at all. The girl was his true emotional caretaker and acted as a buffer. If tempers ever flared, she would baby him so much that we were practically a minute away from her whipping out her tit for him to suck on. Now don't get me wrong, I appreciated them being around because it limited his street slang and animated poser antics, and there was only so much I could take.

The real business at hand was that we heard back from some of the factories, and they didn't have many blanks in stock. They were too busy with fall production to make us any quick samples. We would have to wait until mid-August, and considering that the show was in July, that wasn't an option. We would have to go with Plan B and find a ghost designer to develop a few more elevated fashion pieces so that the collection wouldn't look so stale and ordinary. We would have to find a women's designer who might have some time for us, since women's market came later on the calendar. We found the perfect candidate: a graduate from Central Saint Martins in London who had worked for the house of Alexander McQueen. He was in the United States and was temporarily between jobs. He moonlighted doing drag shows in some underground NYC clubs where cash prizes were at stake. He had an extraordinary talent, since he could design, pattern, and cut and sew his own samples. He also wasn't cheap, and we had to make sure that he would get the project done on time. So we enlisted our mutual friend Tito to "take one for the team" and make sure that the only "drag" the designer would be doing would be from home.

Week three:
We picked a day to go to the Garment District to pick up the fabrics and trims for the color-block shorts that our designer was making. Of course, picking a day to go to the Garment District wasn't an easy feat, since Dandy was all caught up in the rhetoric and hype of producing a fashion show. His people would condescendingly tell me that he was a very busy man. He was busy with things like negotiating a cover story in *GQ Magazine* (I was wondering whom he was sleeping with to get that), having lunch at Fred's with a Barney's buyer, a go-see with supermodel Tyson Beckford, getting swag bags together for the show, and meeting with producers of Men's NYFW to secure a free

venue. Sometimes people don't understand what the priorities are. Without product, all you have is possibly a nice idea. I couldn't make him understand that there would be no fashion show without samples.

Being in the market with him was beyond frustrating, because he didn't know his fabrics. He said he wanted "something soft and blue," but what he really wanted was chambray. He also claimed to know all these "dope-ass people," but in reality it was a list of all the people he wished he was "super chill with." Walking around the market was an extra treat, because he was wide eyed and mentally putting his label on everything he saw. Instead of focusing on the samples, he was concentrating on his image. His job wasn't a hard one. He had to make one choice. I wanted to grab him by his pocket square and tell him to pick a fucking fabric already. Instead, he was too busy checking what his Instagram followers thought of his selfie in front of the Sewer Statue on 7th Avenue. When he finally graced me with a decision, I made him think it was all his.

When it came down to paying for the fabrics, he turned to me and said, "Can you just put this on my invoice?"

As I was pulling out my credit card, I asked him, "What's going on with your sponsors? We're two weeks away from the fashion show."

He let out that whiny, sarcastic, weak, condescending snicker of his, which got under my skin. "Yeah, yeah, yeah, yo, yo, yo, don't lose sleep over dis. You know I'm good for this shit. I got family connections, know what I'm sayin'? It's all good in the hood. I gotchoo gurrlll." It was pointless to even have this conversation on the street, so I just nodded and handed over my card to the store clerk.

Week four:

We quickly realized that the only way to get Dandy to come into the office on time was to give him an earlier time. If we asked him to show up at noon, he'd show up at two (which is what we wanted). He rolled in as usual one day, which was when I noticed his "signature" dots were all over the bottom of his board. Ugh. We were excited to show him how terrifically the first samples came out, when all of the sudden he froze, walked to the corner, and crouched, making a constipated meowing sound. Where was his Social Media wet nurse when you needed her? We gave him a minute, a technique that Business Coach had shown us, and approached him.

Suddenly, he stood up, whirled around, and got right in my face. "This color is going to ruin me! I wanted robin's-egg and this is blue! Incredible! This is such a stupid mistake! I might as well kill myself!

My career as a designer is ruined!" What was shocking to me was not that he was freaking out, but that his language suddenly went from party boi to Ivy League scholar.

I shook my head. "Umm, you jackass—you wanted robin's-egg. Robin's-egg is blue. So . . . you didn't want it to be blue?"

"No, I wanted blue, but I wanted sky blue!"

"Well, why didn't you say sky blue?"

"Oh, it was really more of a periwinkle mixed with cobalt and a dash of azure!"

The blue conversation went on for way too long, which was pointless, because he was going to eat the samples whether he liked it or not. He kept going on and on about it being so desperately wrong, so I did what anyone in my position would do: I rolled up a WWD issue (it was newspaper back then) and smacked him on the nose. I knew it wasn't going to hurt, but at least it shook him out of the fucking blue conversation, and now we needed to move on.

I started to hear "Bitch Better Have My Money" in my head. "Bitch, where's my money?" I demanded. I was channeling my inner Rihanna (we all have an inner Rihanna, by the way). Dandy gave me a double shoulder shrug, like all of a sudden he didn't understand English. This pushed me over the edge. OK, playtime was over.

I held him by the shoulders close and whispered in his ear, like the Godfather's kiss of death, "I want to be perfectly clear with you. You will not get your samples if I don't get paid. I am not running a not-for-profit or a daycare here, and do not mistake me for your friend."

He slapped down his skateboard, looked over at Ninja, and said, "That is one cold-hearted bitch!"

Ninja replied, "You know she never jokes. You better have a solution to your cash flow situation."

Rolling away down the hallway of our building, he yelled back, "It's not always about the money! It's about having some integrity and some purpose in your life!" The elevator dinged, and he was gone.

I looked at Ninja. "We're not gonna get paid."

"Oh, we'll get paid. I'm going to his party."

Week five:

Dandy threw a party at his new "office" in SoHo. I wasn't invited, and neither was Ninja, but you know she made an appearance. The party was the usual scene: the skaters, the stoners, the hipsters, the pseudo influencers with a hundred followers. Dandy's mother was going around trying to ignore the cloud of pot smoke while she played Betty Crocker in her little apron and cookie tray. Ninja took it all in, including Dandy's garmento father standing in the corner, who Ninja found out was quite the sweater executive, having had contracts with Walmart and Kohl's before selling his business. Then came Dandy's TV-reality-star brother, who ended up being the only person Dandy's father talked to during the party. Ninja got the feeling that Dandy was living in the shadow of his father and brother, and his mother was overcompensating for their lack of emotional connection.

Mingling with the crowd, Ninja bumped into a few of his sponsors. "Oh no, we don't actually give him money. We're giving him samples of our newest aftershave that we're launching during Men's Fashion Week for his goodie bag."

This was the sponsor that was supposed to be our paycheck. Aftershave, my fellow humans. Aftershave is not a cryptocurrency. Ninja snatched up as much sponsored booze as she could fit in her backpack, coat pockets, and pants. On her way out, she grabbed a tray of cookies as insurance for the inevitable munchies that would come with a contact high.

"I can't pay the rent in aftershave," I told Ninja after she broke the news to me back at the office. Here I was, sewing on the labels—and let me remind you, I am a person who cannot sew a button, and I was frustrated to no end. What were we going to do? If he didn't put on the show, it wasn't going to be him that looked like a jerk, it would be us. He was going to manipulate and glamorize the situation as an unfortunate victim who had, yet again, been bamboozled by the industry. Oh hell no, I wasn't going to let that happen. We would give him his samples one by one and make him sweat it out until the very last moment before the show. He would find the money.

Week six:

It was show time, and we were ready. The person who wasn't prepared was . . . Dandy. After he called each of us (thank you, caller ID) and no one answered, all of our cell phones blew up. Even our poor receptionist was getting hate texts from him. He begged Ninja to have pity on him, and offered empathy for her having to work with such a "miserable, hateful bitch." We all giggled, reading the text messages out loud to each other. Didn't he know we were all sitting in the same room? Then, there was a weak knock on the door. Our office door is one of those old-fashioned doors with a wood frame around a glass that's wedged between chicken wire. You can't see clearly inside, but you could most definitely make out the silhouettes. Ninja jumped up; we were expecting this visit. The door was double locked. He texted us.

Dandy: Can you let me in? 🙏

ON: Nope can't do that. 🥷

He could clearly see Ninja's silhouette standing on the other side of the door.

Dandy: Are my samples there?!

ON: Yeah they're beautiful. 😍

Dandy: 😩

ON: You have our $$? 👹

Dandy: I'll have a check waiting for you at the show. I'll sign it right over to you.

Ninja looked over at me and showed me her phone. "That's not gonna work. He needed to make a bank check out to us," I said loud enough for him to hear. He texted back to Ninja.

Dandy: Can I have three samples for the fitting?

Ninja showed me the phone again. I nodded my head. Ninja squeezed three of the T-shirts through the mail slot. We heard an audible "YESSSSS" from the other side of the door.

Dandy: Could I have one of the jackets? 🙏

Ninja looked at me and showed me the phone again. I shook my head no. "We would have to open the door."

"Oh yeah, right," she agreed

ON: 👹 Ur pushing ur luck. 🍭

"Yeah, yeah, yeah," we heard from the other side. "Bring it to the show two hours before. I'll have the check by then."

"BANK CHECK," I yelled back at him.

I could only imagine what a mental breakdown this guy was having, considering that a color ruined his day. I kinda felt bad, but I kinda didn't feel bad. He knew he set us up, and he didn't have the money. He might have been lucky in the past, but he wasn't going to have that luck with us.

Two hours until showtime, and we all had a drink from Dandy's sponsored booze. "A toast to us, getting shit done," I said as I put my high-heels on. I painted my lips red. I most definitely didn't want to look like part of his entourage, a groupie, or a wannabe dressed in yoga clothing and $1,200 sneakers. We announced ourselves to the bouncer with the clipboard and said that we had his samples. We told the bouncer to say not to bother to come out if he didn't have my bank check. We would jump in a cab and go back home. The bouncer didn't communicate that at all. Instead, he just called over the radio that Mercedes was here. Fuck, that killed all my drama.

He came out nervously pacing with his Social Media Guru / Babysitter acting as his buffer. He wanted to talk to us through her. "Are you fucking kidding me, Dandy? I'm not here to play games. Do you have my check, yes or no?" He could see that Ninja and the team were holding all the garment bags. "Do you?" I asked again.

He asked SMG/BS for his checkbook, then handed it back to her, asking if she could write the check since his hands were so shaky. Cue my eye roll. He started babbling about how we should be nicer people and a little more generous with our time. He said that not everyone has our abilities, and we had put too much pressure on him. He was trying his best and we had expected too much from him. He suffered from acceptance anxiety, and we should learn to handle everyone as an individual. "I need to be surrounded by people that are uplifting," he explained. What the fuck, I thought. Was he talking to himself or me?

I was just trying to get this girl to spell the name of the company correctly. She had already asked me three times whom to make it out to, and then how to spell it. "G-L-O-B-A-L P-U-R-C-H-A-S-I-N-G C-O-M-P-A-N-I-E-S," I said, rolling my eyes again. We are not a nursery school for narcissists with privileged backgrounds. Get over yourself. She handed me over the check with the rubber I could almost physically feel. But I kept my word and handed over the samples. It took five people to carry the three bags of samples. I wasn't even going to question it.

As we walked away, he yelled out, "I hope this makes you happy." I thought, I hope what makes me happy is that I don't have to see your fucking face again.

The show went off with much fanfare and success, with ex-NBA players whom he worked as a stylist for in tow. As you might have guessed, we weren't invited to the show. I was almost sure there were photos of all of us at the door with the warning, "Don't let these bitches in."

He did manage to triple his Instagram followers overnight without a single valid post from an editor or buyer; those are the only people that truly count in the industry. And as you might have guessed, the check bounced. When I mentioned this to the Label Guy, he told us that he still had all 5,000 labels for production in his office because he hadn't paid. I said, "He had some labels, because I sewed them into his samples."

"Yeah, he came crying to us a week before the show saying you were going to kill him if he didn't get you some of the labels."

"You know I never said that."

"It doesn't matter; who can take his whining?" I wanted to tell Label Guy about the drama with the samples and the text messages, but I didn't want my reputation to be in question for any reason. You will have difficult moments, you will have lack of cash flow, you will make mistakes, but at the end of the day, all you have is your reputation.

After several phone calls to Dandy's office and being told he was unavailable, we finally broke his office assistant (more like an unpaid intern). "Yeah, yeah . . . he's on vacation in Tulum," she finally revealed. I couldn't believe it. The balls he had to not only go on vacation with me holding a returned check for lack of funds, but he was missing Men's Market, the trade show week when the designers are supposed to be selling their collections.

I guess it was never his intention to sell. When we had asked him about doing line sheets for the buyers, his answer was "I don't need to do that because people already love me." He has burned a lot of bridges in this industry. I can't understand how he continues to do fashion shows, grow his followers, and get new sponsors. Although, the quality of the sponsors has gone down quite a bit. He is down to a dog poop bag company that offers the bags in the fashion colors of the season, an adhesive tape company that makes their tape in prints, and a razor burn prevention cream whose pictures of before and after would make you lose your lunch.

You can have a considerable following (which I now wonder if he pays for), and you can have a supportive mother, a garmento father, and a famous brother, but if you don't have product, you have nothing.

Unless, of course, your plan all along is not to have a successful collection, but for you to become the "brand" so you can get paid styling and fashion magazine gigs. Maybe with the free fashion show venue and the paid sponsor he might have made money on his shows. I have a friend that is an adjunct professor for film, and every few years he puts out a movie (no comment on how good they are) so he can claim to be relevant in the industry. Maybe relevance is his goal. Maybe he will start a fashion show production company. Maybe I am giving him too much of my energy. I am.

This industry is full of privileged con artists. Some of them dress very well.

ALWAYS A RETAILER

$\mathscr{A}$ retailer, by definition, buys items at wholesale and resells them. I have been doing just that since the age of seven.

I started selling snap caps to the kids on the block. Snap caps were the necessary and fun part of owning a cap gun, an aluminum toy gun that I am sure was painted with lead paint. Snap caps were hard to come by, since the corner bodega didn't carry them, but a discount department store in New Jersey, where some of my aunts lived, did. We would go to Two Guys (that was the name of the store) to buy household products, and I would buy my industrial-size bag of snap caps for $1. I don't remember how many it had, but it was like a bottomless pit. I would go home and sell them outside my stoop, two for twenty-five cents. I had a fast-growing business, and it was wildly profitable. I always had my duro frío money, and my favorite flavor was coconut.

Then Ivelisse accused me of price gouging. Of course, she didn't call it price gouging at the time; it was more like "Hey, you're fucking ripping me off." Yes, we were seven. She was a grade behind me and a year older, but we shared the same homeroom. Ivelisse and the only white girl I went to school with, Stacy, both gave me and my brother a hard time. No, a hard time would have been fine. They tortured us by calling us church boy and church girl. Every once in a while my mother would dress us in our Catholic school uniforms, because as my mother would say, they were perfectly fine garments that we hadn't outgrown. Those were the days we would fight. It was never much of a fight, though. It was more like a stare down with a shove. Whoever shoved first walked away, and since I wasn't allowed to fight, Ivelisse always shoved first and "won." This irritated me to no end and terrified my poor brother. Until that day, the day I was accused of ripping off the neighborhood (it was just one block). They challenged me on my way home to a schoolyard fight the next day.

It was on, and like Rocky prepping for a fight I spent the night shadow boxing and doing sit-ups, to the amusement of my grandfather. I have no idea how that was supposed to help, because all it did was wake me up with a sore middle. Not the best position to be in for the fight! That morning, I made a clear decision: I had to be the one to shove first. It would be hard to shove first when it was two against one. I had to make some type of plan to ambush them, and it had to be done in a way that my mother wouldn't find out I was fighting in school.

The coat closet! New York City public schools at the time had a wall in the back of the room with hooks and a cubby to put your things in. I made sure I was the first one to get to class, took off my dress as to not rip it in the fight, and waited for them in my slip to come in and hang up their coats. I knew luck was on my side and that they wouldn't get to class at the same time. Stacy's mother was an alcoholic that never woke her up on time.

Some of my other classmates came in and asked me if I was ready for the fight. I answered, "There's not going to be a fight," and no one even asked why I was in a karate pose in my slip standing in the coat closet. Apparently, I had been known to do stranger things.

Ivelisse was first. Pop to the head—she never saw me coming. She was on the floor. I grabbed her by one of her pigtails and pulled hard, with the intention of ripping it off. She just yelped a little. That surprised me. I thought it would have hurt more. I could see that she was crying. I didn't care.

"That one was for my brother, and if you ever mess with us again . . . " I was thinking of what to say . . . "Next time, I am ripping both of them off."

She covered her face. "I'm sorry," she said. "Stacy is the one that hates you." What? I didn't have time for this. I had to get back in position.

"OK, OK, OK." I said. "Go sit down like nothing happened . . . or else."

I wasn't sure what the "or else" was about, but it felt like the thing to say. And she did.

Stacy got a kick right to the knees that almost flipped her around. I straddled her, using my legs to pin her arms down, and covered her mouth with my hand, because the teacher was now in the front of the class writing the day's lessons on the chalkboard. "You don't know me, and you don't ever want to know me. Ivelisse and I are now friends, and we hate you. You better never mess with me or my brother again, or else." Or else . . . once again, I wasn't sure what that meant, but since it worked with Ivelisse, why not use it again? She picked herself up and walked out, limping a bit, and sat down. I put my dress back on with a victorious smile and sat at my desk. All the kids knew what was going on.

The teacher had turned around to start her lesson when she noticed Ivelisse's messed up pigtails. Then she noticed Stacy trembling in her chair like a shitting dog. That's my nod to Wes Anderson's *Grand Budapest Hotel*—it described her perfectly. Bullies are dog shit alone, something even with business I learned. The teacher asked her what was wrong. They both looked at me, and I gave them the hardest look. Then the teacher looked at me.

I said, "Stacy must be cold from her walk to school; maybe I could take her to the coat room and give her my sweater." I sneered at Stacy, which the teacher took for a smile.

"I'm fine," Stacy yelled out.

Ivelisse's mother came that night to tell my mother about the fight. My mother defended me to the end, mentioning that if it was such an extreme fight that I ripped hair out of her child's head (not true), why wasn't my dress even dirty? While the moms were arguing and then agreeing about raising girls in the kitchen, I made Ivelisse a deal. I had a lovely profit margin in my snap cap business, and since I wasn't allowed to cross the street or go to the housing project she lived in, I would pay her ten cents for every two caps she sold. I grew my business, helped a fellow entrepreneur, and made a lifelong friend.

I have sold bras, mostly store returns from Victoria's Secret, at NYC street fairs with the company name "Victoria's Sister: Our only secret is our price." I have owned retail stores, one of my favorites being "Confetti: Where every day is a reason to celebrate." I currently own a discount boutique called "Just Shop: Just shop and be happy." But my all-time favorites are the pop-up "sample sales."

I have run some incredible sales, and it all starts with a math game. When you are buying lots, everything becomes a commodity. It doesn't matter if it's Gucci or $5 puffy coats. In one of the sales I ran, I bought 1,500 puffy coats for $1, so $5 was a great return. They were perfectly nice, poly-filled and with a hood. At the same time, I had a lot of designer goods from a website that went bankrupt and whose goods I bought at auction. I love those auctions; most people don't know the brands when they read them on the manifest. Usually, they were looking for electronics or hard goods. I got to snap up some great deals without a lot of people trying to outbid me. Well, that was then, but today there are so many people in the game that you have to be craftier to get goods. Those designer goods are the ones that people fight over. Literally.

My sales are cash only, no try on, no returns. And if you try to bargain with me at the checkout, I take the goods away from you and throw them in the "put back box." If you still want them, you have to stand at the back of the line, because you wasted everyone's time. I have signs all over the place that say "I have no friends" and "I have the final say on prices." These are two of my most vital signs. Do you know how many people try to change the prices of the goods? Or tell me they are a friend of a friend and wonder if they could have the friend's discount? We use a colored-sticker system that is easy to peel off and stick on something else. But what people don't know is that I can remember the price of every single item in the store. I'm like the idiot savant of pricing. I have been crunching numbers and playing the math game since before I owned it. I unpacked it, I priced it, and I hung it (of course I had help). I buy it cheap, and I sell it cheap. I hate packing up after a sale, so on the very last day, the very last hour, I do a bag sale. You buy a shopping bag for x number of dollars, and everything you can fit in it without breaking the bag and still being able to hold it by the handles is yours.

You can't believe what people will try to get away with. One person couldn't fit an extra pair of $300 jeans in the bag without it spilling over, and was pissed at me for not making an exception. I was like, "Lady, just buy another bag for $25, it's still a bargain." Her answer was no, because she didn't want anything else. There was a woman who spent an hour walking around the sale in her underwear, asking people if they had seen her pants while continuing to shop. They turned up at the register. I told the woman trying to buy them that they were not part of the sale, and she casually mentioned that she thought it was odd they were still warm when she picked them up off the floor. There was the West Side hooker who would bring her tricks in to buy her things while she flashed her boobs at Tito, who has worked with me in every single pop-up that we have done.

The shoplifters (which I have a budget for) get more and more bold. We had a shoplifter put on a shearling coat and walk right out of the store past security when we had all told each other to watch her. She had been looking around and picking things up and putting them down in different places. A typical shoplifter MO. It was a summer sale, too. At the last sale, we noticed that the music suddenly had stopped, and caught a guy walking out the door with our wireless speaker. Which brings me back to the puffy coats that weren't selling. We run our sales in SoHo, and once word hit in Chinatown just a few blocks from our sale, we were overrun by Chinese ladies grabbing as many of the coats as they could fit in their hands. At the time, I had an assistant who was Korean, and she felt the need to tell me that "they were not her people." They sold out in less than a half hour.

Sample sales and discount stores have become a joke. Samples sales are no longer the sale of showroom samples like they once were. In fact, I haven't found a bargain in years! Discounters, well, there just aren't enough goods in the market to keep a fully stocked, multinational department store. What they do is make cheap products under brand names to sell them cheap. We haven't even started to see the disaster this market is. Stores closing hasn't hit peak yet. This is all good news for the consumer, emerging designers, and independent retailers. The junk food of fashion will be gone. It's toxic to all of us. To make my sales stand out, so the consumer knows that we offer a different experience, we have had everything from a tin band playing outside to Godzilla walking the streets of SoHo announcing the Monster Sale. I try to channel my inner Crazy Eddie—the man who pioneered the Christmas in July sale. Brilliant. This is part of what is going on in retail today. The consumer has grown savvy, finicky, and stingy. We were selling high-end Italian panties three for $12, and people were asking me to help them find their size. Are you kidding me?

This is the result of decades of department store training. Yes, training, as in wait for the one-day sale. Thank you, Macy's. Wait for our anniversary sale. Thank you, Nordstrom. Shop our everyday low prices. Thank you, Walmart. Get the max for the minimum. Thank you, T.J. Maxx. With all of that discounting it has become a race to the bottom on pricing, and who can get it in the consumer's hands, by any means possible, cheaper and faster than anyone else. Even if it means you are losing money. Thank you, Nasty Gal. No one wins this race. The whole idea of Black Friday has been completely bastardized by opening on Thanksgiving. No one made more money by being on sale an extra day. If the consumer had $500 to spend during Black Friday, all they did was spend the same amount of money over two days. The retailers that have chosen to go down this path have alienated their employees, ruined an American tradition, and sacrificed margins. You're actually a loser if you're a winner. Karl Lagerfeld metaphorically explained that losing weight is the only contest that you win by losing. That applies here, except no one is going to look fabulous afterward.

Small Business Saturday, typically done after the madhouse of Black Friday, is sponsored by American Express. This scheme, for lack of a better word in the industry today, is a scam. American Express fancies itself an advocate of the small retailers, the mom and pop, Main Street, USA. They support the indie retailer with hashtags like #shoplocal and #shopsmall, and they even made merchandise like shopping bags, doormats, window signs, and a bunch of other "shop small" branded goods for you to buy for this special shopping day. They have several videos on their website dedicated to "helping" small retailers on how to market your store and bring in traffic. The advice consists mostly of discounting and giving stuff away. Here is my favorite part: What does the retailer get if the consumer uses their American Express card on Small Business Saturday? Absolutely nothing! They don't even waive their fees on that one day. And speaking of one day: I am sick and tired of promoting the one day when it should be every day, but I am even more tired of retailers crying chicken when they don't do anything to help themselves.

Jack & Diane

I sit on the board of two universities, one in Nebraska and the other in Arkansas. You might wonder why a city girl would be on the board of these two schools. The simple answer is that they asked me. Sitting on these boards has afforded me an interesting point of view that is lost when visiting only big cities. For example, it was common knowledge to say that fashion comes last to Small Town, USA. That is far from the truth. Thanks to social media, your cousin in Los Angeles, her best friend in Bisbee, Arizona (the one who moved there because of a new boyfriend), and your college roommate who now lives in Mexico City are all on social media reviewing and posting their fashion trends. Everyone and their sister is a stylist. It also keeps me in check with pricing! Did you know that fewer than three percent of the US population would pay more than $100 for a pair of jeans? Well, now you do. You're welcome.

Open Your Own Door

The most critical aspect of sitting on these boards is the opportunity to network and get to know some of the most significant retailers in the United States. Dillard's and Walmart joined me in Arkansas, and Cabela's and the Buckle in Nebraska!

You have to be active in the industry to be successful. They say it's about showing up, but it's really about showing up at the right event. I used to go to industry meet-ups, and all I found were people looking for a job. I loved when this guy walked up to me and said, "I would like to work on a project with you."

I was like, "Sure, what type of project is it?"

"Oh," he said. "I was hoping you had a project for me."

Sometimes you have to reach out to people and tell them what you can do for them. It's always helpful if you can get someone to introduce you, but don't wait too long for that to happen. For years, I stalked American Apparel. I just knew I was going to run into Dov, the owner of American Apparel at the time, and I was going to tell him exactly what needed to be done to fix his retail business. To prepare, I would walk into every American Apparel store I saw, announce that I was from corporate, and have the manager read off to me all of their numbers. Seriously, I got so obsessive that my husband wouldn't walk into an American Apparel store with me because he was sure my photo was behind the counter with a note saying "beware of fake employee." I knew so many people who knew him, but I waited too long for the introduction. I should have just shown up at his offices before he was asked to leave his own company. I will wait until he is onto the next project. An exercise I encourage my clients to do is think about a person who, if they met him or her, they could change the trajectory of their business. Who would that person be and what would you ask or tell them? Personally, I have dozens of these scenarios worked out in my head. And one of them came to fruition.

The Walmart Main Street Initiative. I pitched this plan to a board member who was part of the Walmart marketing team. Walmart doesn't have the best image in the industry. They have a reputation for being abusive managers, environmentally toxic, and notorious for putting people out of business. They are not viewed as a good guy. There have been dozens of books written about the evil empire, and documentaries on their destructive nature of crushing everyone in their way. I am just going to call it as I see it: most of that is bullshit. I don't understand why Walmart doesn't do more to polish its reputation, but I guess when you can rank yourself as the twenty-fifth largest GDP (that is, if Walmart was a country), then who cares.

My pitch was a program where Walmart would educate and give resources to Main Street businesses to help keep them in business when a new Walmart opens nearby. No one, not even Walmart, benefits from a total shutdown of Main Street. It would be a very positive driver: increase the local economy and create traffic that won't suffer from the standard sameness that is happening in every mall. "Shop locally so that a little girl can get her dancing shoes." It's one of those pathetic posts that I see on social media during the holidays. You shouldn't have to guilt people into shopping in your store.

Before my BIG pitch, I wanted to study Walmart from the inside. That meant I had to get a job at Walmart. I went to my local Walmart in Kingston, New York, and applied for a job. I said that I had been a shop owner but that I recently had to close my store because of the rent. The interview process was mechanical, and the focus was mostly on if I had any felonies. A quick background check was done on me, no resume was needed, and I found myself sitting in front of a TV watching a video on their procedures: how I needed to clock in and out and what the basic store policies were, etc., etc. The next day, the area manager showed me my daily tasks. I was going to stock and price goods in the pet area.

Nothing too exciting happened all day until it was break or lunchtime. The employee area was a stage for a Mexican soap opera. If you don't know what I am talking about, I'll tell you that Mexican soap operas are the epitome of drama. A typical episode might involve a woman with brain trauma from a car accident that almost killed her, who can't remember her brother, whom she is trying to seduce. A gardener, who is the father in disguise, tries to see how his family would handle his kidnapping. A maid is not sure whose baby she is carrying. And let's not forget the backyard goat, which is actually the grandmother whom a witch had cast a spell upon.

The same stories were happening in the employee area. Who stole someone's boyfriend? Who gave whom a dirty look? Who disrespected whom? It was such stupid, petty stuff, but when you have nothing better to do, it's easy to fall into the gossip trap. I thought about the mouse that fell into the well. He tried to climb out but eventually stopped trying and died. I wished there could be a type of empowerment class Walmart could offer, or maybe just some home economics classes. If we depend on government to educate and empower people, it's a lost cause. Don't say it's not in Walmart's best interest, because it is. They could keep employees longer. The cost of employee turnover would cover the cost of these life development skills. I made a mental note to do some numbers on this.

I was two weeks into my hands-on experience and ready to quit when my area manager called me over because she wanted to talk to me. Damn, I thought, yesterday I should have just walked away and not said anything when one of the girls accused me of thinking I was better than her. She had pointed out the salad I'd brought from home, and I'd told her, "Yes, I do make my lunch," and added, "because the thing is, I have all my teeth."

She wasn't expecting that, since the whole time I was there I kept to myself. This wasn't a social experiment I was doing, but I wasn't going to back down from a bully. She was picking on the quiet person. She mistook quiet for weakness. I packed up and walked out before she had a comeback.

Or maybe the area manager had noticed how I remerchandised the pet area. I put all the heavy dog food bags on the bottom shelf. Why hadn't that already been a thing? I put all the small toys together because I know that small dogs like cat toys, too. I did a little color story just for visual interest. You could tell I was bored. The next challenge I had given myself was to merchandise by price point.

My manager happily announced that I was getting a promotion to cashier and a small raise. "Just after two weeks?" I asked.

"Yes."

"Why?" I said, hoping she would mention my merchandising.

"Because you showed up on time every day and didn't miss any work." Such low standards. I had all the information I needed.

The Walmart Main Street Initiative started with a weeklong Retail 101 class. It was followed by a feasibility study on each of the businesses that took the weeklong course. It wasn't surprising to me that they were poor retailers. They didn't have a clear understanding of budgeting, and most didn't have a computerized register POS to track sales and profitability. Just about all of them were owner operated, with maybe one staff person. When I asked them why they felt their business was doing so badly, they all complained about the economy, the president, and the weather, and best of all, they blamed Walmart. And Walmart hadn't opened yet. It wasn't that business was terrible, they were just running a bad business. They weren't even buying correctly. They were buying online, or from a traveling salesman, or maybe one year they went to a trade show and took home some catalogs. I said it before: buying is a full-time job. You have to make up your mind. Are you running a business or a hobby?

The first group of stores we worked with was a small-town Main Street in Kansas. They already had a nearby Walmart, and another was going to open even closer. Fun fact: ninety percent of Americans live twenty minutes away from a Walmart. They took the course without asking an overwhelming amount of questions. This surprised me, since the average retailer had been in business for at least ten years. The group seemed to have a handle on what needed to be done.

We decided that we were going to give a test at the end of the weeklong workshop. The people who passed the test and conceptually understood what being a merchant entailed would then get to do a feasibility study. The results of that study would allow them to apply for grants. This considerably narrowed down the number of stores that qualified for the grants.

For example, there was a fine-jewelry store in town. Walmart sells seventy percent of all the diamond engagement rings in the country. I know, I know, kind of sad, right? During the review of this jewelry store business, we came up with an action plan of not going head to head with Walmart on price. They were not going to win that. The plan was to offer something that they couldn't, like emotion. Let's face it: a ring from Walmart doesn't say I love you like a box from the local jewelry store, even if the diamond ring is smaller. We had to update all of their packaging, including the tissue paper, the boxes, and the bag that enclosed it all, in order to give it an air of sophistication. Think about when you see that little blue Tiffany bag with its white ribbon. You know, that emotional connection you feel before you even open the gift. Well, at least that was the idea.

The jewelry store was given $20,000 to develop and stock its new marketing packaging. Instead, they went to an online retail packaging company and bought the standard animal print that didn't give it the high-end look I had recommended. That cost only about $1,500, so they pocketed the balance and went on a long-dreamed-about family vacation. They had to close the store during their vacation because they had no employees outside of family members. I found this out only when I checked on them a few months after the grant was given to them. I realized that it is one thing to take a class, and another thing to execute the advice.

One store received a grant to refixture the store and buy new mannequins. They ended up painting the old fixtures and buying dress forms, which were considerably cheaper and did not show off fashion clothing as well. Another store—like the John Mellencamp song—took the money and ran, thus closing the store. My whole project was trashed.

Yes, it is easy to compete with the giants: children's boutiques that carry special-occasion dresses and not just knits like Walmart, a women's boutique with career clothing, a gardening store with predesigned gardens that can be laid out depending on space and budget. The consumer is not necessarily money poor. They are time poor. People don't have the time or energy to search for a product in these gigantic stores. Everyone thought bigger was better and that bigger meant convenience. Convenience means everything under the sky, and that's why the sky is falling, Chicken Little.

EPILOGUE

Exit through the Gift Shop: Pick
Up What Works for You

My dad taught my siblings and me to question everything. Over breakfast, he'd have us read the headlines of the Sunday paper and ask us, "Is that a fact or opinion?" One headline read "Eighty percent of the US working class hates their job" (or something like that). I told my dad that it had to be an opinion, because it sounded so unbelievable. He asked me to read the full story. It turned out to be a very detailed study, and eighty percent of the study really did hate their jobs and wanted to quit. I still couldn't believe that it was a fact.

I asked my mother, "Do you like your job?"

"No," she said. The kids were impossible to deal with and she would rather be at home.

I asked my dad if he liked his job.

"No, standing all day cutting hair is no fun."

I made a conscious decision then that I would never be part of that 80 percent.

When I was still in school, it was all about getting good grades and keeping "bad" stuff off your permanent record. By the way, who keeps track of those permanent records? The government? Amazon? God? When I graduated from school, the contest changed to who could make the most money. Some played the baby game, but that wasn't for me.

Some final advice:

They say that as a leader you should follow the rule of People, Planet, Profit. That's a lie. If you don't put profit first and run a business to make money, you can't pay people, and no one will care about the environment. It's always about the money.

The best education comes from experience, and it doesn't have to be your own. I love talking to the old garmentos. Even though I've known some of them since grade school, they still always have one more story to share with me that I learn from.

It's about being a boss. School is not where you learn to be a boss! You become a boss from experience and balls. Yes, balls. I'm not sure why we use that word, since balls by nature are actually very delicate. But its meaning, to be strong and fearless, is universally understood.

It's about destroying the bullshit lies told to us, like "do what you love and the money will follow," or "follow your passion." It should be outlawed to even say that!

In reality, it's about making money doing the things you love.

Now, turning fifty years old and looking back at my career, I most definitely am a part of the twenty percent, and I am beginning a new career—one of sharing stories.

THE GARMENTOS

If you're hooked on Mercedes Gonzalez's no-holds-barred, tell-it-like-it-is approach to the businesses of fashion and retail, her next book is for you. For *The Garmentos* Gonzalez collected stories from the people that ran the garment industry in New York City from the '60s to the late '80s—a time when the apparel industry was in its heyday and then its ultimate demise. Sweatshops, sex, money laundering, and even murder were all intricately woven into the fibers of the industry. Told in Gonzalez's signature style, the writing mixes a matter-of-fact tone with gritty dark humor.

Follow recurring characters as they embark on epic journeys into the industry. There is also insight into their personal life, from the American dream to the cocaine drug parties of the hedonistic '80s. This subculture didn't play by any rules. The tribe was more important. The book is a mix of Mad Men meets the Sopranos but even more ruthless and better dressed.

Introduction

I should start by giving you the definition of what a Garmento is. For anyone outside a very small district in New York City, the Garment District, the definition you will find is someone that works in the garment industry. Simple enough, but not the true definition. For some, the definition could have a derogatory meaning, like the label "mobster" or the adjective "ball buster," which are just part of the full definition of what a Garmento is. Being a Garmento is also geographically specific. One can only be a New York Garmento; there is no such thing as a California, Miami, or Chicago Garmento. Some might argue that, but they are wrong. They were men, self-made men that got their formal education on the street. They shared a kindred brotherhood more secretive and exclusive than that of the Free Masons. The laws of business outweighed morality but were justified. Loyalty was rewarded. Betrayal punished. They drank, gambled, womanized, cursed, lied; I would say cheat but to them it's called "outsmarting the system." They owned "pieces" of the industry and monopolized them. They were members of the Friars and the Playboy Club. They worked in cash and the bankers were their drinking buddies who, with every throwback of whiskey, offered insider information on businesses that were failing. They lived in the city and had summer homes at the Jersey shore or on Long Island. Growing up in their shadows, working in Uncle Manolo's factory, I was just a little girl wearing dresses and playing in factory boxes. I wanted to be like them.

There are few true Garmentos left in this world. They are becoming extinct and being forgotten in history. Like 8-track tapes and fine Corinthian leather seats, I don't want their legacy to be long forgotten. It would parallel the tragedy of socks with flip flops if their fearless balls-to-the-wall attitude, their vision, and their wisdom in this cut-and-paste world were left untold.

A proud native New Yorker, Mercedes grew up in fashion, grinding away at her uncle's apparel-manufacturing company in the heart of the NYC garment district. After earning an economics degree from New York University, she went back to work full-time with her uncle, where she restructured the company and ensured a stronger bottom line. Soon after, Mercedes joined the fashion industry as a buyer. In 1998, Mercedes proceeded to establish her own buying office, Global Purchasing Companies. Today GPC is hired to consult and optimize domestic and international businesses in the fashion and retail industries. Her experience and continued effort to stay up to date in the industry have led to her expertise in the retail and design facets of fashion.